The Wire and America's Dark Corners

The Wire and America's Dark Corners

Critical Essays

Edited by ARIN KEEBLE
and IVAN STACY

McFarland & Company, Inc., Publishers
Jefferson, North Carolina

ALSO OF INTEREST AND BY ARIN KEEBLE

The 9/11 Novel: Trauma, Politics and Identity (McFarland, 2014)

LIBRARY OF CONGRESS CATALOGUING-IN-PUBLICATION DATA

The wire and America's Dark Corners : critical essays / edited by Arin Keeble and Ivan Stacy.
    p.   cm.
Includes bibliographical references and index.

ISBN 978-0-7864-7918-4 (softcover : acid free paper) ∞
ISBN 978-1-4766-1960-6 (ebook)

1. Wire (Television program)   2. United States—On television.   I. Keeble, Arin, 1977– editor. II. Stacy, Ivan, editor.

PN1992.77.W53W526 2015
791.45'72—dc23   2014046592

BRITISH LIBRARY CATALOGUING DATA ARE AVAILABLE

© 2015 Arin Keeble and Ivan Stacy. All rights reserved

No part of this book may be reproduced or transmitted in any form or by any means, electronic or mechanical, including photocopying or recording, or by any information storage and retrieval system, without permission in writing from the publisher.

On the cover: homes in Baltimore (Thinkstock/Media Bakery)

Printed in the United States of America

McFarland & Company, Inc., Publishers
  Box 611, Jefferson, North Carolina 28640
  www.mcfarlandpub.com

Acknowledgments

We would like to acknowledge our families, friends, and colleagues for their support—particularly those who have endured interminable discussions of *The Wire* for many years.

We would like to thank the host of scholars who have supported and inspired us: Dr. James Annesley, Dr. Anne Whitehead, Professor John Batchelor, Professor John Beck, Dr. Laura Leonardo, Professor Robin Humphrey, and Dr. Simon Tate.

We would also like to thank all of the contributors to this book who have been patient, diligent and, in our opinion, brilliant. Finally we would like to thank Newcastle University for its institutional support.

Arin: In particular I'd like to thank my dear friend, the poet Toby Martinez de las Rivas, my mentor Dr. James Annesley, Professor Simon James, Dr. Sam Thomas, Professor John Batchelor, Professor John Beck, Dr. Ellen Turner, Dr. Pablo Mukherjee, Dr. Rebecca Gill, Dr. Laura Leonardo, Dr. Jon Begley, Professor Robin Humphrey, Dr. Neelam Srivastava, Heather Pope and Victoria Bryan. I would be remiss not to add a final personal thanks to Ivan for being so patient, insightful and hard-working. Finally, a big thanks to my wife, Holli, with whom I first enjoyed *The Wire*.

Ivan: I'd like to pay particular thanks to Anne Whitehead and John Beck for their superb supervision during my Ph.D. studies: the skills that I acquired during that period were overwhelmingly a result of their guidance and rigor. Thanks also to Robin Humphrey, Simon Tate and Laura Leonardo for their efforts in running the Doctoral Training Programme at Newcastle University, which helped to give me the flexibility to strike out from the safe ground of "proper" literature to the murkier terrain of television, and the breadth of knowledge to be able to edit a theoretically diverse volume such as this with confidence. As always, I'm grateful to my parents for their love, support and enthusiasm for my undertakings. Thanks to Adele Black for lending me Season One in 2008 (I think): it started me on quite a journey! Finally, thanks to Arin for innumerable academic conversations over a pint, and of course for initiating what has been a thoroughly rewarding project.

Table of Contents

Acknowledgments — v
Preface — 1
Introduction — 3

Part One. Bad Dreams: American Identity Post–9/11

History, Freedom and Bureaucracy
    ANDREW MOORE — 13

Mythological Fictions and the Game Paradigm
    NIALL HEFFERNAN — 31

The American Dream: Capital, Codes and Consensus in the Early 21st Century
    MICHAEL GOW — 49

"It's all in the game": Citizenship as the "Missing Middle"
    MICHAEL LISTER — 67

Part Two. The Target: The War on Drugs and Its Cost

The Corners of Crime
    ROBERT ANDERSSON, JØRGEN BRUHN and ANNE GJELSVIK — 81

The Paper Bag Compromise: Hiding the Problem of Drug Dependency in Hamsterdam
    J.D. TAYLOR — 95

Insurgency, Accidental Guerrillas and Gang Culture
    TIFFANY POTTER and TOBIAS SIRZYK — 114

The War on Drugs and the War on Terror
    Arin Keeble   133

Part Three. The Detail: Domestic Policy in Bush-era America

Rethinking Space
    Anca M. Pusca   153

Watching, Policing: Surveillance and Complicity
    Ivan Stacy   170

A Dystopian Fable About America's Urban Poor
    Peter Dreier and John Atlas   192

Post–9/11 Educational Reform and the Epistemology of Ignorance: A Critique of No Child Left Behind
    Laura Bolf-Beliveau and Ralph Beliveau   208

About the Contributors   221
Index   225

Preface

This book's beginning can be traced back to enthusiastic discussions over coffee and occasionally ale. We completed our doctoral degrees in 2012 (Arin) and 2013 (Ivan), and taught together for many years at Newcastle University. Like many scholars working in the humanities (and beyond), we found discussion of *The Wire* hard to avoid during that time. Such was the popularity of the program in academia—perpetuated by its rapturous reception in *The Guardian* and other influential publications—that those who hadn't watched it were sometimes thought behind the times. While we recognized the irony in the academization of *The Wire*, we felt that in many ways it lived up to the hype and warranted the attention.

Our research areas are contemporary literature and culture, in different but intersecting subjects. Arin works on the representation of disaster and terror in the contemporary novel, with a particular focus on 9/11 and Hurricane Katrina, and Ivan works on the representation of trauma and complicity, with a particular focus on the work of Kazuo Ishiguro and W.G. Sebald. Our casual interest in *The Wire* began to lurch toward the scholarly when, inevitably, we began considering it in light of our own intellectual interests and began drawing connections and sharing ideas. The quite substantial body of published criticism on *The Wire* includes some excellent work, but we felt that there were areas that had not yet been addressed in depth. For instance, in the area where our own interests in the program met—the wider historical and political background of the program—*The Wire* has been underserved by scholars to the extent that we felt obliged to begin work on this book. Our aim, then (as we set out in detail below), was to assemble a volume of essays which discusses *The Wire* in terms of the historical period of its production (2002–2008), a period which more or less coincided with the Bush presidency.

As we received and reviewed contributions for this volume, one particular thread—explicitly addressed by some of the authors and implied by others—began to emerge: the events of global import in which America was involved tended to conceal or divert attention from matters of pressing concern within the U.S. itself. It is these matters, the "dark corners" of America, that *The Wire* chronicles in detail; it is *The Wire*'s representation of these aspects of American life, and their relationship with U.S. policy at this time, that our volume examines.

—Arin Keeble and Ivan Stacy

Introduction

In an uncharacteristic moment of sincerity, Sergeant Jay Landsman (Delaney Williams) refers to Baltimore as "a dark corner of the American experiment" (3.03). The underlying argument of this volume is that *The Wire* examines the realities hidden in the dark corners of Baltimore and the United States.

The Wire ran from 2002 to 2008, a period almost exactly contemporaneous with the Bush presidency, years which may be associated in the popular imagination with images of 9/11, the wars in Afghanistan and Iraq, and Hurricane Katrina. However, the effects of this period of American history, as it changed the courses of individual lives, sometimes in small ways and sometimes calamitously, were and are still being played out across the U.S. It is these effects that *The Wire* depicts. These are, in a sense, the forgotten consequences of the Bush years: while the glare of national and international attention turned elsewhere, Baltimore continued to slide into violence fueled by deprivation and a rampant drug trade barely held in check by an underfunded police force and a preoccupied FBI. The purpose of this collection of essays is therefore to examine the way in which *The Wire* represents these hidden realities. It does so in the context of the historical moment at which the show was first aired, with particular attention paid to its impact on this period in terms of American identity, the relationship between U.S. foreign policy and domestic policy, and the lives of individuals living and working outside the gaze of national and international media.

The Wire is not always entirely complimentary about academic endeavor. Particularly damning is Howard "Bunny" Colvin's (Robert Wisdom) ill-fated foray into the academic world during Season Four. After a disastrous meeting which condemns his research project (it was trying to explore alternative pedagogical approaches for "corner kids") and results in the termination of its funding, despite encouraging initial results, the project leader David Parenti (Dan DeLuca) attempts to console Colvin by reassuring him that it "still makes for great research," and that their findings will at least receive attention from other academics. An exasperated Colvin replies: "What, they gonna study your study?!" (5.13). The implication here, of course, is that like the other institutions or sectors of the neoliberal city that the program examines, academia fails to engage with the hidden America of *The Wire* in any meaningful way.

Yet here we are, not only casting a retrospective eye over *The Wire* but studying the studies that have emerged in the years since its conclusion in 2008. But if *The Wire* shows us anything, it is that the ways in which information, data, and representations are circulated, used and abused, can significantly impact policy and social realities. We can only hope that as we continue to view, read and critically assess *The Wire*, the conversations we have about it can be significant to the failing systems and structures of the post-industrial West that the show represents.

—⚎—

In the final movement of Season Three, when Slim Charles (Anwan Glover) is trying to rally a beleaguered Avon Barksdale (Wood Harris), he makes an obvious allusion to the War in Iraq, which was in full swing when the episode was broadcast and had already been subject to widespread national and international protests:

> Fact is, we went to war, and now there ain't no going back. I mean, shit, it's what war is, you know? Once you in it, you in it. If it's a lie, then we fight on that lie. But we gotta fight [3.12].

It would be difficult to find a more crystalized and damning reference to the War in Iraq in American television, and particularly in television broadcast during this period. But what does it mean to evoke the Bush Administration's war room in the battlefields of a Baltimore ghetto? Can we make productive connections or comparisons? What does *The Wire* have to say about the distance between Slim Charles and Donald Rumsfeld or Colin Powell in this moment? This is a program that both engages with the larger themes of the War on Terror, and dialectically dramatizes the hidden realities that were forgotten as the world's gaze fixated on terror, torture and war in foreign battlefields.

This dialogue between Slim Charles and Avon Barksdale is one of many moments when *The Wire* invites its audience to both compare and contrast the War on Terror and the War on Drugs. But *The Wire*'s allusions or reference to this fraught period of American history are not always this obvious; they appear through a variety of representational strategies, and approach many different aspects of Bush America, often subtly or circuitously, but always critically. It is our argument that while on the surface *The Wire* is a complex police procedural, determined to blur the distinctions between good and evil, it is deeply instructive when examined in its wider context. The dust has not yet settled on Bush America, as demonstrated by the recent revelations about mass surveillance conducted by the National Security Agency (NSA), the scope and implications of which are still unfolding at the time of writing. What is certain, however, is that these were seismic years in the United States both in terms of the country's international engagements and domestic policy. Most obviously, the terrorist attacks of 11 September 2001 (henceforth referred to as "9/11" in this volume) delivered a blow to American confidence and security, and ushered in a period of aggressive foreign policy: under Bush, the U.S. led invasions of Iraq and Afghanistan as part of a broader "War on Terror." Foreign policy had a domino effect on the domestic front, notably in the form of the Patriot Act's security measures, which included an easing of restrictions on domestic surveillance and anti–money laundering policies. Moreover, the War on Terror resulted in a change in priority for federal resources towards counter-terrorism and national security, and away from fighting the narcotics trade.

The 2002 September National Security Strategy was the official policy document of this shift, and the backbone of what has come to be called the "Bush Doctrine" (Holloway 2008, 4). In addition to aggressive and preemptive foreign policy and domestic securitization, Bush's second term also saw Hurricane Katrina devastate the coastal areas of Louisiana and Mississippi, and the post–Katrina flooding of New Orleans brutally highlighted persistent racial inequality in America. The federal response to this disaster provided by FEMA (Federal Emergency Management Agency) was criticized for its slowness and inefficiency, bringing into question the efficacy and justness of American systems of support for its most vulnerable citizens. As Wai Chee Dimock points out, "the nation-state seems unbundled by the hurricane in ways both large and small—not only as a system of defence but also as psychological insurance, political membership, and academic field" (2008, 36) Katrina was seen by *The Wire*'s creators as vindication for the didactic element of the program in the way it brought the "hidden America" that it explores to the attention of the world: as the show's creator David Simon states, "we knew we had a good argument, we just didn't know how good" (2009). While it is hard to disagree that *The Wire*'s "argument," about the plight of America's underclass, was reinforced by the tragedy of Katrina, this rhetoric is typical of Simon's desire to locate *The Wire* strictly in the realms of documentary realism and resistance to discussions of the program that look beyond its surface-level paradigms.

This is perhaps surprising given that Simon, famously, has been eager to situate *The Wire* in opposition to mainstream American television, a mainstream which has largely struggled to provide meaningful engagement with the national and international politics of the Bush Doctrine. American television responded in various ways to 9/11 and the War on Terror and by many accounts, it has either produced problematic representations of torture, otherness and Islam, or engaged with the major themes of the day through allusion or oblique allegory. Another facet of our argument is that despite being, on the surface, a localized police procedural, when examined in context *The Wire* is a more illuminating representation of the Bush era than any other mainstream American television show of this time, even including the politically charged programs that attempted to engage with its key issues.

NBC's *The West Wing* (1999–2007) was the first major network drama to respond to 9/11, rushing a special episode, "Isaac and Ishmael," into production for airing on October 3, 2001. In many ways this "one-off" episode echoed the conflicted message emanating from the White House, a message which wanted to simultaneously recognize a new world order, while also groping for historical reference points or precedents, and harnessing nostalgia for past military prowess. A prologue to "Isaac and Ishmael" sees Bradley Whitford, who played Deputy Chief of Staff Josh Lyman, describe it as a "storytelling aberration," and everything in its form and structure indicates rupture and change. Nevertheless, the premise of the episode, which sees the White House staffers lecturing a group of curious high school students as the building is in lockdown, ultimately situates 9/11 on a historical continuum of global terrorism and religious fundamentalism. This fundamental tension is very revealing, but "Isaac and Ishmael" was mostly notable for its gross conflation of Islam and Islamism, for which it has been widely criticized; Lynn Spigel describes the way it relies on the "fundamental precepts of contemporary Orientalism" (Spigel 2004, 244). Problematic representations of Arab or Islamic "others" were particularly prevalent in this period, often appearing in mainstream television in what Amina Yaqin and Peter Morey describe as "the restricted, limited ways that Muslims are stereotyped and 'framed' within the political, cultural and media discourses of the West" (2011, 2). Torture was another topical theme that television of this era engaged with—most notably in Fox's *24* (2001–2010), a program which came to embody the military aggression and exceptionalism of Bush America. *24* was and is incredibly popular (it has recently been revived following the original series' conclusion in 2010), though it has been widely criticized for including torture in its "whatever it takes" rhetoric. An alarming article by Jane Mayer in the *New Yorker* revealed the way *24*, which has been particularly popular in the military, and with students at the United States Military Academy at West Point, has filtered into the beliefs and actions of American soldiers (2007, n.p.). In *The Wire*, nowhere is the tension between wanting to directly confront the definitive political issues of the era, and wanting to examine the hidden and buried realities, more prevalent than in its depiction of torture and "otherness." A key turning point in the narrative of Season One is the torture of Brandon (John Bailey), whose body was mutilated and displayed prominently in "the pit." Any instance of the representation of torture, in this era, evoked its controversial use in the War on Terror, and the fact that Brandon's homosexuality made him a conspicuous "other" in his world makes this more prominent. Yet we are also struck by the fact that a man's body could be mutilated and displayed openly in a major American city and still escape the wider attention and interest of its citizens, remaining out of focus.

While *The West Wing* or *24* were well-placed to address 9/11, the War on Terror and the Bush Doctrine, a program that is oddly closer to *The Wire* in the way it approaches these subjects is ABC's supernatural drama *Lost* (2004–2010). In Season One, *Lost* repeatedly explores themes of otherness and torture in its story about a group of individuals trapped on a mysterious tropical island. *Lost* uses what Holloway describes as "allegory lite" to "at least allow audiences to begin exploring contemporary debates by objectifying them in other circumstances and scenarios" (2008, 80). However, where *Lost* is circuitous or oblique, displacing key themes so that they can be worked through without bias, *The Wire* is dialectical. 9/11, terror, torture, otherness, the War in Iraq, and the Patriot Act are all clearly evoked in *The Wire*, but what the program really engages with is the machinations of the urban centers of capitalism on which American military ventures depend.

This brief survey of how popular television responded to 9/11 indicates that some of the choices made with regard to aesthetics and content were either problematic or inadequate. *The Wire* has garnered a sizable body of scholarly attention in the few years since the series concluded in 2008, much of which describes the show's narrative and aesthetics in more positive terms. Tiffany Potter and C.W. Marshall's edited collection, *The Wire: American*

Television and Urban Decay (2009), Stephen Shapiro and Liam Kennedy's *The Wire: Race, Class and Genre* (2012), special issues of both *Darkmatter* (2009) and *Criticism* (2010), and Slavoj Žižek's recent podcasted lecture, "The Wire or the Clash of Civilizations in One Country" (2013), are significant examples. It has also been built into university curricula all over the world, including, famously, at Harvard (Wilson 2010, n.p.). However, while we believe that the works mentioned above are generally outstanding, they have, with some notable exceptions, focused on the subject of Shapiro and Kennedy's subtitle: race, class and genre. We seek to build on this body of work by looking specifically at the way *The Wire* explores these themes and others within a larger national and international context, and crucially, to consider the way it speaks to the unique historical moment in which it first appeared. Specifically, we address the ways in which *The Wire* represents America responding to the Bush Administration's attempts to redefine the nation's global role following 9/11 (including, of course, the effects that this redefinition had on national identity and the domestic climate); the relationship between the War on Terror and the primary subject matter of *The Wire*, namely the War on Drugs; and the way in which the show represents in detail the underside of American life.

The essays in this book explore the theme of hidden realities and the ways in which *The Wire* casts light on them. Part One of this volume, "Bad Dreams," examines *The Wire*'s representation of America's self-image following 9/11 and the Bush presidency's aggressive foreign policy. We begin with a piece which encapsulates the argument posited in this volume, with Andrew Moore's contention that a national grand narrative serves to divert attention from a sickening domestic situation. He examines the presence of providential accounts of American history, themselves influenced by the likes of G.W.F. Hegel, Alexis de Tocqueville, and Francis Fukuyama, on American policy under George W. Bush post–9/11. He argues that *The Wire* takes an oppositional stance to such conceptions of history and, influenced by the thinking of Hannah Arendt, critiques the idea of history as inevitable progress towards democracy. In particular, Moore examines the way in which providential accounts of history tend to efface agency, and argues that much of the hopelessness present in *The Wire* stems from a kind of bureaucratic paralysis rather than the upward mobility that democracy and free market economics seem to promise. Niall Heffernan then traces American meta-narratives of apocalypse and purification from their puritan origins, through their Cold War manifestation in Game Theory and into the use of metaphors of war to justify both foreign military interventions and a deleterious drug policy at home. As such, he argues that the neglect shown towards the disenfranchised areas of Baltimore stems from the way that these narratives justify identifying sections of the population as "other," and hence as an enemy. Heffernan makes the case that the notion of American exceptionalism rests on a number of myths, and that *The Wire* takes these fictions to task, particularly in Season Five's examination of the media and narrative.

Further exploring the notion of a national narrative, Michael Gow discusses the presence of the American Dream in *The Wire*. He begins with David Simon's comments that America is now a tragically and "utterly divided" society. However, drawing on Bourdieu's theories of fields and forms of capital, he argues that, although the show seems to present Baltimore as a fragmented indictment of American values, vestiges of a common identity provide some ideological common ground for the protagonists in the varied spheres of activity in the city. Next, Michael Lister focuses on the domestic representation of America in *The Wire*, arguing that the show omits to represent in any depth those outside the "games" of the drug trade or politicking within the institutions represented across the five seasons. These normal working people, generally referred to as "citizens," are therefore the "missing middle" of *The Wire*'s representation of Baltimore. Lister argues that this omission is part of *The Wire*'s critique of a privatist view of citizenship which, fueled by greed and self-interest, has withdrawn from concepts such as the public good and civic responsibility. These failings, he suggests, are responsible for the fragmented society portrayed; however, in showing them, *The Wire* acts as a call to more active and engaged forms of citizenship.

Part Two, "The Target," examines in detail the relationship between foreign and domestic policy in terms of the War on Terror and the War on Drugs. Robert Andersson, Jørgen Bruhn and Anne Gjelsvik discuss Season Three of *The Wire*, and specifically Major Howard Colvin's "free-zone" experiment, in the context of U.S. drug policy. They combine a discussion of the failings of zero-tolerance and mass-imprisonment with a reading of the episodes which depict the area which comes to be known as "Hamsterdam," wherein the drug trade is effectively decriminalized. They argue that, by presenting the free-zone through a number of "witnesses," the show achieves a polyphonic and novelistic form of representation which relies upon ambiguity for its power rather than any didactic conclusion. J. D. Taylor also focuses on Hamsterdam and argues that, with reference to Spinoza's concept of the social contract, Colvin's renegade initiative is an attempt to arrive at a new kind of contract as a reaction to the failure of the aggressive policies of the War on Drugs. Moreover, this examination of Hamsterdam indicates that a degree of compromise may prove to be more effective than current policies, but that any such effective compromise will not be reached easily, and will necessarily involve a delicate balance of forces.

Tiffany Potter and Tobias Sirzyk identify the reasons for many of the protagonists' involvement in the drug trade, drawing parallels between the War on Drugs as conducted on Baltimore street corners and in military strategy. They identify how the shifting loyalties of those involved in the drug trade are similar to the process by which potential insurgents become "accidental guerrillas." They argue that poverty and lack of opportunity force the "corner boys," often grudgingly or unwillingly, into positions of loyalty with the drug organizations rather than with legitimate institutions. That the attempted interventions on the part of the legal, educational and social security systems fail is thus a damning indictment of the current state of the American social and political structure. In the next essay, Arin Keeble reads the program's series-long dramatization of the War on Drugs as an "intradiagetic allegory" of the War on Terror. Keeble focuses on the implications of *The Wire*'s much discussed imperative to "blur distinctions between good and evil," as well as the narrative of the rise and decline of the Barksdale empire, and subsequent rise of the Marlo Stanfield organization, an example of the unknowable, cyclical, and constantly renewing "enemies" in the War on Terror.

Part Three, "The Detail," focuses on aspects of domestic policy between 2002 and 2008. Anca M. Pusca examines the relationship between space, representation, and vision, drawing on the thinking of Walter Benjamin. She argues that *The Wire* shows the Baltimore elite's attempt to divide the city into "hardened," as opposed to "fluid" or "dynamic," spaces. Moreover, this hardening of space results in violence being done, in the name of law and justice, to the occupants of those areas designated as "troubled." Pusca thus notes that a rhetoric of "urban renewal" hides what is, in fact, a continuation of a segregationist logic which seeks to identify, separate, and break up "troubled" areas of the city. This "hardening" relies on pervasive surveillance which is carried out not just by the police, but by all inhabitants of the city. However, she argues that, where communities are able to retain their space as "fluid," these areas function as sites of resistance against the increasing encroachment of a destructive bureaucracy. In her discussion of surveillance, Pusca notes that "the more we see and hear, the less we seem to know." Ivan Stacy builds on this observation, addressing the apparent paradox of how, within a culture in which surveillance is pervasive and inescapable, some parts of the city seem to inhabit blind spots beyond the reach of the forms of vision represented in *The Wire*. Stacy argues that these blind spots are the result of statistical approaches to government, within which self-interest, and specifically the protagonists' desire to hide their own failings, cause statistical representations to produce the opposite of their intended effect. These statistical approaches to government are part of a broader inclination to govern populations as a whole, an approach identified by Michel Foucault as "biopower." The culture of surveillance represented in *The Wire* is not, therefore, solely the product of post-9/11 paranoia, but is the result of the internal workings of power and observation in Baltimore, with all protagonists at once observed and observing, and all complicit in a blindness to the areas of the city which are allowed to wither and die.

Peter Dreier and John Atlas address some of *The Wire*'s omissions with regard to its representation of the domestic situation. They argue that the show brings to light many of the problems facing contemporary America but, with this caveat, they criticize it for representing Baltimore as a "dystopian nightmare" within which the protagonists have little or no agency and from which they therefore have no means of escape. They provide a number of examples of grassroots and community activism in order to challenge the picture of Baltimore as being in hopeless decline and the more general sense that the poor lack agency through which they might better their lot. Laura Bolf-Beliveau and Ralph Beliveau turn their attention to education, providing a detailed analysis of how Season Four of *The Wire* critiques educational policy during Bush's tenure. They identify the ways in which *The Wire* shows standardized testing—one of the key features of the Bush Administration's No Child Left Behind Act—failing to serve the interests of those whose education it is intended to promote and facilitate, and in fact further disenfranchises and oppresses them. Using Charles Mills' theory of the "epistemology of ignorance," they identify the nature of this oppression, and suggest ways of resisting it, although *The Wire* is far from optimistic in this regard.

WORKS CITED

Dimock, Wai Chee. 2008. "World History According to Katrina." *Differences: A Journal of Feminist Cultural Studies* 19.2: 35–53. Print.

Holloway, David. 2008. *9/11 and the War on Terror*. Edinburgh: Edinburgh University Press. Print.

Mayer, John. 2007. "Whatever It Takes." *The New Yorker*. Available online at http://www.newyorker.com/reporting/2007/02/19/070219fa_fact_mayer?currentPage=all.

Morey, Peter, and Amina Yaqin. 2011. *Framing Muslims: Stereotyping and Representation After 9/11*. Cambridge: Harvard University Press.

Simon, David. 2009. "Introduction" in Alvarez, Raphael, *The Wire: Truth Be Told*. London: Canongate. Print.

Spigel, Lynn. 2004. "Entertainment Wars: Television Culture After 9/11," *American Quarterly* 56.2: 235–270. Print.

Wilson, William Julius, and Anmol Chaddha. 2010. "Why We're Teaching *The Wire* at Harvard." *The Washington Post*. Available online at http://www.washingtonpost.com/wp-dyn/content/article/2010/09/10/AR2010091002676.html.

—Arin Keeble and Ivan Stacy

PART ONE

Bad Dreams: American Identity Post–9/11

History, Freedom and Bureaucracy

Andrew Moore

We Are Not This Story's Author

On 14 September 2001, President George W. Bush addressed the American people during a prayer service at the National Cathedral in Washington, D.C. In the immediate aftermath of the 9/11 attacks he spoke about the victims and particularly those who died while trying to help others. He spoke with admiration for the generosity and bravery of average citizens, and at one point spoke decisively about America's coming military response to the attacks. "This conflict," he said, "was begun on the timing and terms of others; it will end in a way and at an hour of our choosing" ("Prayer" 59–60). Reading this line more than a decade later, the president's hubris is almost too much to bear. The assertion that conflicts would unfold and conclude according to the will of the American people indicates a stunning confidence in America's ability to make manifest its will in history. Granted, one must be careful not to conflate rhetoric with policy; the demands of the moment no doubt placed unusual pressures on the president to instill confidence in a wounded and frightened American public. But this line, delivered at an emotionally charged moment in a sacred space, actually did become public policy when it was quoted as an epithet in Section III of the 2002 National Security Strategy of the United States of America just under the heading "Strengthen Alliances to Defeat Global Terrorism and Work to Prevent Attacks Against Us and Our Friends" (White House 5). Significantly, President Bush's conflation of world history with American will was neither unprecedented nor without grounding in philosophy and political theory. The claim evidences a view of world history derived, in some fashion, from the works of G.W.F. Hegel, Alexis de Tocqueville, and, more recently, Francis Fukuyama. Each of these thinkers share a view of world history as purposeful or directional, and all three contend that the "end" of history is human freedom.

One of the reasons that it is so interesting to consider *The Wire* alongside this particular political moment is because the show is focused on the question of human freedom, and how historical and political imperatives inhibit rather than support the spread and development of that freedom. Here I will suggest that the representation of politics we see in *The Wire* is designed specifically to interrogate and disrupt this providential conception of history, which both featured prominently in President Bush's public speeches and shaped the administration's foreign policy. There *is* a sense of inevitability in *The Wire*, but the idea of historical progress—particularly the advance of freedom—is cast in doubt; at times it is openly mocked. As just one example, consider the montages that conclude every season. In each season we see criminals arrested, police officers promoted, civilians and corner boys killed. However, despite the achievements, or even the deaths of individual agents, the field of human action remains unchanged. As each season ends, we see drugs changing hands, kids standing on street corners, and police arresting dope fiends. These montages suggest not so subtly that Baltimore does not change despite the best efforts of individual political actors.

For David Simon, *The Wire*'s principle architect, the inability to change American politics has to do with the intractable problem of post-modern institutions. The show investigates what it means to "be beholden, as we all are in some way, to the institutions that form a city" (1.01 audio commentary). In contrast to Bush's insistence that the "spread of democratic values ... encourage[s] the peaceful pursuit of a better life" ("Freedom Agenda" 170), *The Wire* exposes the oppressive underbelly of American democracy. In this way *The Wire* finds a philosophical bedfellow in Hannah Arendt. Arendt is best known for her thorough and incisive examination of the implications of totalitarianism, but she also spent much of her career exploring the problems of bureaucracy, which she termed "rule by nobody" or "a form of government in which nobody takes responsibility" ("From Hegel to Marx" 77). The influence of Arendt's thinking upon Simon is suggested by the stock story that he tells whenever he is asked about the first time he met his collaborator Ed Burns at a library checkout desk and in which he recalls that the latter had with him, among other things "a collection of essays by Hannah Arendt" (Simon "Introduction" 13).[1]

In addition to her criticisms of bureaucracy, Arendt was also highly skeptical towards providential accounts of history. For Arendt, the horrors of World War II crippled the argument that history was somehow on the side of human freedom. Arendt was also not a believer in the inevitability of historical progress (or doom). According to Elisabeth Young-Bruehl, like "prophets of many sorts" Arendt "wanted to raise an alarm, but her alarm was not about the future, which she did not think knowable"; rather her concern was with "things as they are," the "experience of things pressing upon us" in the here and now (19–20). As prophets of the present is also a useful way of thinking about the creators of *The Wire*. In his introduction to *Truth Be Told*, Simon himself claimed that the Bush Administration made prophets out of the show's creators:

> We could not have imagined Katrina and the hollow response to that tragedy. We could not have fathomed the empty lies and self-delusions that brought about the senseless misadventure in Iraq. We had a good argument, as far as we knew; but in the beginning we didn't know how good [5].

The show's Arendtian "argument" illuminates a modern disconnection between the operations of power and traditional human ends. It depicts a political order that has lost sight of (or abdicated) its responsibility to advance the common good; what we see instead is a system that is designed to sustain itself, irrespective of the human cost. One of the particular aims of the series was to challenge the national rhetoric about a paradisal, global, liberal democratic capitalist future and redirect the gaze of the nation, turning it away from the fantastic vision of a democratic Middle East and towards the oppressive reality of an impoverished and sick American city. In so doing, the series deliberately calls into question the wisdom of exporting American democracy when the promises of freedom and economic opportunity being offered to citizens of Iraq have still not been delivered to Baltimore, Maryland. *The Wire* thus interrogates the Bush Administration's freedom agenda, and specifically America's suitability to advance that agenda.

To be clear, this essay is not meant as a critique of Hegel's philosophy, Tocqueville's social history, or Fukuyama's political theory. Rather, it is an analysis of the political mobilization of those thinkers by the Bush Administration. More precisely, it is an examination of how *The Wire*, with its Arendtian outlook, troubles and criticizes that mobilization.

It was perhaps Virgil who first demonstrated how useful it could be for particular administrations to position themselves at the teleological end of a grand historical narrative. Such a maneuver establishes the present order as both necessary and good—the glorious outcome of a divinely ordered universe, and thing towards which all human activity has been directed. Most importantly, for those in power such narratives can represent the present order as something *that could not have been otherwise*. Both Arendt and Simon are similarly skeptical about narratives that do not sufficiently account for human particularity, individual agency, and the possibility of political change. Using different means they suggest ways we might think ourselves out of sweeping providential histories and reconceive ourselves as actors in a malleable present.

In his 2001 Inaugural address, President Bush claimed, "We are not this story's author, who fills time and eternity with his purpose" ("First Inaugural" 5). *The Wire* tries to reclaim the story for the individuals who find themselves caught in the grand historical narrative of liberal democratic "progress." The show contends that the narrative of American freedom spreading throughout the globe does not correspond to factual reality. Even the empirical data that suggests democracy is actually spreading is incomplete, too general, and does not take adequately into consideration the particular costs exacted upon the underclass by the uneven delivery of America's promise (Fukuyama "Reflections" 31).[2]

The Long Flow of Time

After 9/11, if not before, the Bush Administration clearly understood itself as participating in a grand historical narrative. The administration consistently represented history as a story of human progress and America as an important (perhaps even the most important) actor in the advancement of that story. President Bush concluded his 2003 State of the Union Address, delivered just months before the start of the Iraq War with the statement: "We Americans have faith in ourselves, but not in ourselves alone. We do not know—we do not claim to know all the ways of Providence, yet we can trust in them, placing our confidence in the loving God behind all of life, and all of history" ("108th" 164).[3] Crucially, this view did not originate with the Bush Administration; it is not even an American idea. It has rather deep philosophical roots, stretching back to nineteenth-century thinkers, such as Hegel and Tocqueville. Hegel understood world history to be a long march towards freedom under the direction of providence: "It is this final goal—freedom— toward which all the world's history has been working. It is this goal to which all the sacrifices have been brought upon the broad altar of the earth in the long flow of time" (22). Moreover, Hegel believed that freedom was advanced, in part, by "world historical individuals" who often find themselves in direct conflict with the received wisdom and *mores* of their particular historical moment:

> The great men in history are those whose own particular aims contain substantial will that is the will of the World Spirit. They can be called heroes, because they have drawn their aim and their vocation not merely from the calm and orderly system that is the sanctified course of things, but rather from a source whose content is hidden and has not yet matured into present existence [32–3].[4]

Hegel's heroes are agents of providence, assisting in the spread and advance of human freedom. In this context, it is perhaps significant how frequently in his speeches President Bush references "the call of history."[5] It is clear that the Bush Administration understood itself as occupying a crossroads in world history. The United States, and by extension the leadership of the United States, had a special responsibility to advance the cause of freedom—even in the face of concerted opposition.

Coming to the United States of America from France in 1830, Tocqueville similarly concluded that democracy was the product of God's will. He wrote in his monumental study of American politics, *Democracy in America*, that the spread of freedom across the globe was the inevitable result of a history guided by providence:

> Everywhere the various incidents in the lives of peoples are seen to turn to the profit of democracy; all men have aided it by their efforts: those who had in view cooperating for its success and those who did not dream of serving it; those who fought for it and even those who declared themselves its enemies; all have been driven pell-mell on the same track, and all have worked in common, some despite themselves, others without knowing it, as blind instruments in the hands of God [6].

Significantly, Tocqueville believed that some measure of economic equality, which he called "equality of conditions" (6), was a necessary precondition of democratic politics. For example, Tocqueville notes that democracy took root in America in part because the vast territory available to American colonists made the importation of European-style aristocracy impossible. Colonists could not police the boundary between a property-owning upper class and a plebeian underclass when there was a surplus of property available to colonists on the American continent (29–30).[6] According to Tocqueville, equality of economic opportunity will lead inevitably to political equality. This is a part of the philosophical foundation that motivates the Bush Administration's interest in exporting capitalism in order to assist the spread of democracy. The former president's version of this argument appears in an address to the United States Chamber of Commerce on 6 November 2003: "Historians will note that in many nations, the advance of markets and free enterprise helped to create a middle class that was confident enough to demand their own rights." He echoes this sentiment later in the same speech: "Eventually, men and women who are allowed to control their own wealth will insist on controlling their own lives and their own country" ("Freedom Agenda" 179–80).

Both Hegel and Tocqueville (though especially Hegel) found a modern, secular advocate in Francis Fukuyama whose 1989 essay "The End of History?" published in *The National Interest* used empirical evidence and a normative account of human nature to argue that liberal democracy, while imperfect, was the most satisfying form of government that human beings were ever likely to invent (Fukuyama "Reflections" 28).[7] In his book-length study, *The End of History and the Last Man*, Fukuyama declares:

From Latin America to Eastern Europe, from the Soviet Union to the Middle East and Asia, strong governments have been falling over the last two decades. And while they have not given way in all cases to stable liberal democracies, liberal democracy remains the only coherent political aspiration that spans different regions and cultures around the globe [xiii].

Again in his 2003 address to the Chamber of Commerce, President Bush paraphrases Fukuyama's argument almost exactly. Bush offers up a very brief history of the global spread of democracy, starting in the "early 1970s" ("Freedom Agenda" 178). He then lists democratic movements in Spain, Greece, Latin America, Korea, Taiwan, and South Africa in almost exactly the order Fukuyama discusses them in the second chapter of *The End of History* (13–15). Both Bush and Fukuyama conclude their short histories with an account of Nelson Mandela's release from prison and subsequent electoral victory in South Africa.[8]

Interestingly, Fukuyama's own relationship to the Bush Administration's foreign policy has been conflicted. He initially supported the invasion of Iraq, but later recanted. Writing in the midst of the Iraq War, Fukuyama seemed aware of the ways his own work might have been used to justify an invasion he no longer supported. He stressed in an article in the *New York Times* that it was the failure to find WMDs and the inability to prove a tangible connection between Saddam Hussein and al Qaeda that forced President Bush retroactively to justify the war "exclusively in neoconservative terms: that is, as part of an idealistic policy of political transformation of the broader Middle East."[9] He ended his piece by asserting, "There was nothing inevitable" about the Iraq War ("Invasion"). In a *Los Angeles Times* editorial written about eight months later, Fukuyama bristled at the notion that he had "blood on his hands" and claimed that he had come to acknowledge that "unilateralism and coercive regime change cannot be the basis for an effective American foreign policy. I changed my mind as part of a necessary adjustment to reality" ("Why").

To understand the Bush Administration we must understand this conception of a providential or natural history that moves inevitably, if not always steadily, towards freedom. At points, President Bush did try to qualify his administration's providential outlook, but his qualifications are arguably incoherent. In his second inaugural address he claims to have "complete confidence in the eventual triumph of freedom.... Not because history runs on the wheels of inevitability," but rather because history "has a visible direction, set by liberty and the Author of Liberty" (278). Bush tries to distinguish himself from Hegelian thought by asserting that "the success of freedom is not determined by some dialectic of history," in order to emphasize that freedom is the result of "the choices and the courage of free peoples" ("Freedom Agenda" 179). In moments like these, it seems as though the president is wrestling with the longstanding philosophical problem of reconciling human free will to providence. In short, why is it important for the United States to invade Iraq, if freedom's success is already assured by God's will?

This is precisely the criticism that Arendt mounts against providential accounts of history: such arguments reduce the scope of ethics in problematic ways. Hegel believed that history moved forward through a dialectical negotiation of thesis and antithesis, leading to synthesis. Therefore, according to Arendt, his theory depends "entirely on the ability to harmonize and see something good in every evil" ("Concern" 444). Not insignificantly, this is what allows the Bush Administration to officially refer to 9/11 and its aftermath as a "moment of opportunity" in the *NSS*, a year after the tragedy ("Preamble"). But when faced with the "reality of extermination camps" and "slave labor," Arendt argues, it is no longer possible—and no longer ethical—to refer to all human actions as providential ("Concern" 444).[10] In a lecture delivered to the American Political Science Association in 1954, Arendt criticizes Hegel's conception of history, arguing that "nothing appears more questionable than that the course of history in and by itself is directed toward the realization of more and more freedom ("Concern" 444). Arendt's argument is of course shaped by the horrors of the Second World War, particularly the Nazi concentration camps.[11] Interestingly, Fukuyama agrees that the horrors of the Second World War make it hard to think of history as progressive, but he claims this is a problem of proximity; as instances of totalitarianism retreat into the past, the Second World War seems more like an aberration or a short interruption in a much longer story of democratic advancement (*End* 3–12).

The Wire offers up a rebuttal to Fukuyamic optimism. The series looks, as Arendt did, at the dark corners of modern politics. On the streets of Baltimore, the creators of *The Wire* find new modes of oppression and new forms of human slavery. Simon has referred to the War on Drugs as "a holocaust in slow motion" (Vulliamy). Perhaps more than anything else, this statement illustrates Simon's Arendtian leanings, his skepticism about the advancement of freedom and the ability of capitalism to liberate.

Mission Accomplished

The Wire employs numerous strategies to interrogate the Bush Administration's freedom agenda. One of the most potent appears in the opening scene of Season Three.[12] As the season begins, Mayor Clarence Royce (Glynn Turman) delivers a rousing speech, greeting an exciting new chapter for the city of Baltimore which is signaled by the orchestrated implosion of two towers. Royce stands atop a platform; behind him is a banner that reads "Building for the Future." The moment is a clear reference to President Bush's speech delivered on the flight deck of the USS Abraham Lincoln on 1 May 2003. On that day, the president stood under a large banner which read "Mission Accomplished" and declared that "major combat operations in Iraq have ended" ("Warship"). Since that day, over 4,000 U.S. service members have died in Iraq. This scene with Royce is used to criticize presidential hubris and the idea that military force can be used to solve systemic problems.

In his speech, Royce talks about the problems of drug trafficking and drug abuse in the city: "A few moments from now the Franklin Terrace Towers behind me, which sadly came to represent some of this city's most entrenched problems, will be gone." The implosion is revealed as part of a public relations strategy, not a governing strategy: the towers are *symbols* of a societal problem, and by eliminating them it will be *as if* the problem has been eliminated. Royce further argues that while "mistakes have been made," his administration is committed to "reform." As the towers collapse, they produce an ominous cloud of dust that spreads through the streets, reminiscent of the dust that spread through the streets of New York in the immediate aftermath of the 9/11 attacks. The moment deeply undercuts the optimistic tone of Royce's message and foreshadows the spread of drug trafficking from the towers outward onto the streets (3.01).

The scene is a palimpsest, a deeply overdetermined allusion to the early years of the Bush presidency. It targets the confused causality and premature celebration of the Bush Administration's first term. The declaration of victory aboard the Abraham Lincoln occurred before Saddam Hussein was captured and eight years before the United States formally withdrew military personnel from Iraq. The spread of freedom was far from certain. *The Wire* exaggerates the confusion: here, the declaration of victory occurs even before the towers have fallen. Further, the implosion is an obviously deficient solution to the city's drug problem. One cannot eliminate drug crime by simply blowing up the place where crime happens. *The Wire* thus challenges the notion that bombing can create a clean slate upon which idealistic fantasies of progress can be written. In sum, progress is revealed more as a story than a reality.[13]

Royce's implosion photo-op happens alongside the reintroduction of some mid-level members of Barksdale's gang, Preston "Bodie" Broadus (J. D. Williams) and Malik "Poot" Carr (Tray Chaney). Poot laments the fall of the towers, and waxes nostalgic because it was there that he lost his virginity. Bodie jokes that it is also the place where Poot repeatedly caught sexually transmitted infections. In the accompanying audio commentary, Simon notes that this image of Poot repeatedly engaging in risky sexual behavior and repeatedly going to the clinic for treatment is a comment on "our own political logic, the fact that we just keep voting for the same stupid shit," while executive producer Nina K. Noble adds, "the same mistakes." However, the story of Poot's sexual activity also has another connotation, and the allusion to contagion implicitly condemns the naïve belief that American values can be spread easily across the globe. The Fukuyamic vision of democracy's advance is replaced by a grotesque and comedic image of liberal democracy as the clap. Further, the image of Poot's sexual infections, along with the ominous cloud of debris, also symbolize the potential unintended consequences of the Iraq War: instead of the spread of democracy, might we not instead see the spread of extremism? This one scene alone gives us a clear sense of Simon's skepticism of the Bush freedom agenda. *The Wire* justifiably questions, given the inability of the United States government to make manifest the American dream in West Baltimore, whether or not the Bush Administration can institute a well-functioning democracy in the Middle East.

Freedom's Triumph

The National Security Strategy of the United States of America (NSS) outlines the Bush Administration's foreign policy agenda, but it is only partly a policy document. It is also a philosophical manifesto that outlines the relationship between the United States and world history.[14] The document's preamble begins by channeling Hegel, Tocqueville, and Fukuyama: "The great struggles of the twentieth century between liberty and totalitarianism ended with a decisive victory for the forces of freedom—and a single sustainable model for national success: freedom, democracy, and free enterprise." The preamble ends with a call to humanity to live up to its responsibility to history and "further freedom's triumph" (Preamble). The United States must embrace the "lessons from our past" and use "the opportunity we have today" to "look outward for possibilities to expand liberty" (3). The advancement of capitalism and free trade is understood as one of the chief means to that end: "The lessons of history are clear: market economies, not command-and-control economies are the best way to promote prosperity and reduce poverty" (17). Free trade is a "moral principle" and the ability to buy and sell goods freely "is real freedom" (18). The NSS likewise insists matter-of-factly that it is only a matter of time before all nations accept the self-evident correctness of liberal democracy and free trade. For example, "in time, China will find that social and political freedom is the only source of [national] greatness" (27). Now again, the connection between democracy and free trade is not wholly arbitrary, nor is this argument entirely self-serving. Tocqueville argues persuasively that material equality is a necessary prerequisite of political equality.

However, this is precisely the argument which *The Wire* throws back in the face of the Bush Administration. If equality of condition, as both Tocqueville and the Bush Administration agree, is essential to the "unleashing" of human potential, what must the status of American democracy be when equality of condition is utterly unattainable to a large plurality of citizens? One of the most painful and memorable images of the gap between the haves and have-nots in American society comes in Season Four when Howard "Bunny" Colvin (Robert Wisdom) rewards a group of at-risk youths for their work in school by taking them to a upscale steak house. Initially the teenagers are excited: eating steak at a restaurant with real waiters and menus is a rare treat. But upon arriving at the restaurant, the students, unfamiliar with the standard protocols, quickly become anxious. Unsure how to respond when hostesses offer to take their coats or pull out their chairs, Colvin's students are overwhelmed by feelings of inadequacy. The fun night out is a failure. Instead of making the world of restaurants and polite society accessible to his students, Colvin succeeds only in making them feel utterly alienated (4.09).[15]

The ultimately fruitless attempt by Russell "Stringer" Bell (Idris Elba) to legitimize his drug profits and thereby legitimize himself is another illustration of the gap between the two Americas. It is not insignificant that one of the fronts for Stringer's underworld business dealings specializes in *making copies*;

Stringer too copies the strategies of modern capitalism, routinely applying the principles he learns in his college business classes to drug trafficking. When his lieutenants question how the loss of the Franklin Terrace Towers (their prized drug-dealing territory) will affect their business, Stringer refers to the auto industry and the lessons of globalization. He cites specifically the difficulties that American car companies have when "you got niggers ridin' around in Japanese and German cars in America all day" and concludes that "territory ain't shit" (3.01). However, Stringer's long-term ambition to infiltrate the upper echelons of Baltimore society end dramatically when he is ambushed and killed by Omar Little (Michael K. Williams) and Brother Mouzone (Michael Potts) inside a downtown property he is trying to renovate. The symbolism is powerful. Stringer's real estate holdings were supposed to be his path "into a world he craved: legitimate high-rolling capitalism" (Alvarez 264). But as he runs up the stairs of the building—higher and higher—he ultimately finds himself trapped, unable to escape his criminal past (3.11). If someone as skillful and as well connected as Stringer cannot ultimately escape the corners, what chance does a Bodie or a Poot have? In what sense can we describe such characters as free? Their particular struggles, their inability to transcend their circumstances and enjoy the benefits of the progress gives the lie to the Bush Administration's claims about the relationship between liberal democracy, capitalism, and freedom.

The fundamental loss of human dignity is both a consequence and a cause of the permeation of capitalist principles throughout Simon's Baltimore; for in the absence of other forms of more human recognition or respect the only avenue to dignity is money.[16] The pursuit of dignity through materialism permeates all aspects of city life. After Rhonda Pearlman (Deidre Lovejoy) tells Jimmy McNulty (Dominic West) that picking fights with Barksdale's lawyer, Maury Levy (Michael Kostroff), could have negative consequences for her career, McNulty rails against materialism in Baltimore. He claims that the problem is that all the "motherfuckers in the State's Attorney's Office" want to be judges and partners in downtown law firms. So no one is willing to stand up to someone as influential as Maury Levy. "Everybody stays friends, everybody gets paid, and everybody's got a fucking future!" (1.11) McNulty's outburst illustrates why it is that bureaucracies have such a firm grip on American society: because they provide modes of recognition and advancement that are seductive to individuals. Consequently, a huge amount of human labor goes into supporting and upholding bureaucratic systems even if their continued existence comes at great cost to other individuals. This is the key insight that Simon and his co-creators share with Arendt.

The emblem of bureaucratic evil—a banal evil—for Arendt is, of course, Adolf Eichmann, the Nazi war criminal who facilitated the mass transportation of Jews to the concentration camps. Arendt's main point about Eichmann is that he did not seem to her to be an ideologue, an insane person, or a villainous mastermind, but rather, he seemed to be an average bureaucrat. In fact, Eichmann joined the Nazi party not because of commitment to the cause – "he did not even know the Party program, he never read *Mein Kampf*" – rather, he joined because he wanted a career with opportunities for advancement (*Eichmann* 32–3). It is notable that Eichmann in his testimony often claims to forget the events that are most relevant to the courtroom: "His memory proved to be quite unreliable about what had actually happened." However, what Eichmann could remember most vividly were "the turning points of his own career" (53). One could plausibly argue that David Simon and Ed Burns (with his collection of essays by Hannah Arendt) had Eichmann in particular in mind throughout the series. For bureaucrats on *The Wire*, career advancement and job security are always the subjects of the story.

Rule by Nobody

It is difficult not to think about *The Wire*'s police and civic bureaucrats when talking about Arendt's Eichmann, the Eichmann who could speak only in "officialese," and whose "inability to speak was closely connected with an inability to think" (Arendt *Eichmann* 49). This inability to think clearly, or to think outside of the parameters of bureaucratic edicts, typifies Simon's Baltimore, as evidenced in 1.06 when Major William Rawls (John Doman) explains the nature of Baltimore Homicide to McNulty:

> We work murder cases here, Detective. We work 'em as they come in one at a fuckin' time. It's called a rotation. You're up 'til you catch one. When you catch one, you step down. You work it for a while. Someone else steps up. It's a simple but effective way to do business in a town that has 250 to 300 cases a year [1.06].[17]

As Simon says in the audio commentary, Rawls' speech is the result of "someone who ha[s] lived too long in a dysfunctional institution." It is not essential for the case to be solved; it is only important that it be "worked." The speech is indicative of the endlessness—that is, without conclusion or purpose—that typifies modern bureaucratic regimes. Arendt describes bureaucracy as "rule by nobody" or "a form of government in which nobody takes responsibility," even though many people within the bureaucratic structures "may demand an account" ("From Hegel to Marx" 77–8).[18] In *On Violence* Arendt writes:

> In a fully developed bureaucracy there is nobody left with whom one can argue, to whom one can present grievances, on whom the pressures of power can be exerted. Bureaucracy is the form of government in which everybody is deprived of political freedom, of the power to act [81].

That this account resonates with the depictions in *The Wire* should be clear. Perhaps above all else, bureaucracy is *The Wire*'s primary target; it explores human action within the context of "institutional and systemic corruptions" (Simon "Introduction" 5), or, as Anmol Chaddha and William Julius Wilson argue, the show reveals how "institutions work together to limit opportunities for the urban poor" (165). However, *The Wire*'s depiction of systemic oppression intersects with the show's criticism of providential history in important ways, because bureaucracy, Simon suggests, is the one of the main inhibitors of political agency, or freedom.

The suggestion that bureaucracies are hostile to freedom is another way the series criticizes Bush's freedom agenda, since Bush's administration was powerfully attracted to bureaucratic solutions to political problems. The clearest indication of this is, no doubt, the administration's decision to respond to the 9/11 attacks with the creation of the Department of Homeland Security. According to the president,

> The changing nature of the threats facing America requires a new government structure.... America needs a single, unified homeland security structure that will improve protection against today's threats and be flexible enough to help meet the unknown threats of the future.

The creation of the DHS marks "the most significant transformation of the U.S. government in over a half-century" (Bush *Department* 1). The notion that the solution to the extremism in the Middle East was the exportation of American institutions—both economic and political—is of course, a further indication of the Bush Administration's bureaucratic zeal.[19]

The Wire consistently expresses suspicion of programmatic change. It is not coincidental that the show's most charismatic figures—the closest thing *The Wire* has to protagonists—are those who either resist or disrupt bureaucratic processes. McNulty is one such figure, who from the series' first episode delights in forcing the police bureaucracy to investigate crimes despite itself. Another is Omar, whose idiosyncratic solitariness, his code of honor, and his open homosexuality locate him somewhere outside the mainstream.[20]

However, while the series does highlight, season by season, the dysfunction of the police department, unions, government, the school system, and the newspaper industry, *The Wire* is not wholly hostile to programmatic change. There do seem to be moments throughout the series in which programmatic approaches to human problems offer the prospect of hope. Dennis "Cutty" Wise (Chad Coleman) opens a gym and does good in the neighborhood. Reginald "Bubbles" Cousins (Andre Royo) works at a soup kitchen. Unions are generally championed as forces for good, which have become corrupt out of necessity. After his retirement from the police force "Bunny" Colvin helps to run an alternative education program for at-risk youth. One gets the sense from watching the Hamsterdam experiment that there is a longing for a programmatic solution to the War on Drugs in *The Wire* – something daring and innovative, but also compassionate. Though in practice the results of Colvin's experiment are horrifying, the notion of a "free-zone" that offers a sanctuary from violence and police harassment is understandably appealing. What one notices perhaps most of all though is that these programmatic initiatives are all developed at the level of the neighborhood, the particular: they are not national imperatives or state initiatives. They are not even citywide programs. They focus on the district, the results of "community policing." The initiatives that are championed in *The Wire* are consistently politics writ small. They are particular solutions developed by individuals to assist their neighbors; they are decisively not the consequences of international liberation strategies, or products of providence, but the fruits of human kindness and initiative. In his introduction to *Truth Be Told*, Simon claims *The Wire* demonstrates "an abiding faith in the capacity of individuals, a careful acknowledgment of our possibilities, our humor and wit, our ability to somehow endure" (31).

Arendt is relentless on the question of ethical freedom. In her final assessment of Eichmann she says, as McNulty might, "in politics obedience and support are the same" (279). Thus the excuse that one was simply carrying out orders is, for her, unacceptable. Neither the difficulty of historical circumstances nor the severity of economic and bureaucratic pressures exempt human beings from the field of ethics. This is apparently one of the features of Arendt's thought which Simon finds particularly attractive. On 9 July 2013 Simon used his blog, The Audacity of Despair, to recommend an essay published in the *New York Times* by Roger Berkowitz, Director of the Hannah Arendt Center for Politics and the Humanities at Bard College. Simon commends Berkowitz for his defense of Arendtian thought and offers up his own celebration of the German political theorist. Simon took issue with those who oversimplify human evil, both "those that see us all as ripe for totalitarian brutality given mere circumstance," and "those that see nothing systemic in the world." Simon goes on to commend Arendt for "finding a more truthful place between fixed, ideological points when it came to Eichmann" (Simon "banality"). *The Wire*, we might say, found a similar "more truthful place." Individuals on the show are victims of powerful institutional pressures, but they retain some degree of agency, or perhaps more precisely, they retain responsibility even if they lack political agency. According to *The Wire*, the lessons of history are clear: reforms that impose willed imaginaries on peoples without attention to their particularity will fail and they will fail spectacularly and harmfully. Reforms that take up and emphasize the particularity of individuals are generally more successful and ultimately more human. In short, we should seek reforms that understand humans not as cogs or tools in grand historical processes, but instead as individuals.

Notes

1. The other two works that Simon consistently remembers being in Burns' possession are John Fowles' *The Magus* and Bob Woodward's *The Veil*.
2. The Washington-based democracy watchdog Freedom House has published an annual report on the global state of democracy since 1972. Their 2013 report identifies 118 electoral democracies in the world, up from 69 in 1989. However, that number is down slightly from a high of 123 electoral democracies in 2005 (29).
3. Patricia Owens argues that the combination of political realism and a traditional account of good and evil, the blending together of "power *and* morality," of "interests *and* values" is the essential marker of neoconservative foreign policy (266).
4. Arendt notes that similar thinking was used to soothe the troubled consciences of members of the S.S. during the Holocaust: "What stuck in the minds of these men who had become murderers was simply the notion of being involved in something historic, grandiose, unique ('a great task that occurs once in two thousand years'), which must therefore be difficult to bear" (*Eichmann* 105).
5. See for example "State of the Union Address to the 108th Congress" (164), and "State of the Union Address to the 109th Congress" (337).
6. Of course the acquisition of this territory necessarily came at the expense of native populations. This is one of the gaps in Toqueville's thinking; though he is surprisingly forward-thinking on the subject of slavery, he is consistently silent on the systematic extermination and expulsion of native peoples.
7. Michael J. Mazarr at least has noticed something of this trend in the Bush Administration's thinking. He notes that former Secretary of State Condoleeza Rice "waxed positively Fukuyamic" when discussing how "powerful secular trends are moving the world toward economic openness and—more unevenly—democracy and individual liberty" (512).
8. In an address to West Point, President Bush also gives a succinct synopsis of Fukuyama's central argument: "The 20th century ended with a single surviving model of human progress, based on non-negotiable demands of human dignity, the rule of law, limits on the power of the state, respect for women and private property and free speech and equal justice and religious tolerance" (131).
9. Robert Kagan makes a similar argument, claiming that members of the Bush Administration began as realists and were forced by the 9/11 attacks to adopt a "more expansive and

28   Part One. Bad Dreams

aggressive global strategy" (30). Mazarr frames the question somewhat differently, arguing that the discrepancy is not so much between pre–9/11 and post–9/11 approaches to foreign policy as it is between what Bush Administration officials said governed their policies and what *actually* governed their policies (502–504). It is possible that 9/11 altered Bush's sense of his role in history; however, the president's commitment to providence can be traced back to his first inaugural address in 2001, months before the 9/11 attacks. There he refers to God, or some divine spirit, as an angel riding in the whirlwind of historical events ("First Inaugural" 5).

   10. Opposition to grand historical narratives was also the reason for Arendt's criticism of Israel's prosecution of Eichmann: "Justice insists on the importance of Adolf Eichmann.... On trial are his deeds, not the sufferings of the Jews, not the German people or mankind, not even anti–Semitism and racism" (5).

   11. For Arendt, a new radical evil emerged in the camps that calls into question, not human freedom, but the innately positive nature of human freedom:

> The tragic fallacy of all these prophecies, originating in a world that was still safe, was to suppose that there was such a thing as one human nature established for all time, to identify this human nature with history, and thus to declare that the idea of total domination was not only inhuman but also unrealistic. Meanwhile we have learned that the power of man is so great the he really can be what he wishes to be [*Origins* 456].

   12. In the audio commentary for this episode, Simon notes that the first scene of each season is used to set up the key tensions and themes for that season. He goes on to say that in this scene in particular they intended to take a "glancing blow" at "the post-9/11 world," and specifically the invasion of Iraq.

   13. Dona J. Stewart describes one of the other ways that rhetoric did not map on to reality in the build up and execution of the wars in Afghanistan and Iraq. According to Stewart, the Bush Administration's conceptions of the Middle East ignored "geographical reality" and employed an "imagined geography" that whitewashed the historical, political, and cultural heterogeneity of Middle Eastern, African, and Asian countries (401).

   14. The first page of the NSS declares that the United States is an unprecedented world power "sustained by faith in the principles of liberty, and the value of a free society, this position comes with unparalleled responsibilities, obligations, and opportunity" (1). Other sections of the document are less grandiose and more practical: "Building on the free trade agreement with Jordan enacted in 2001, the Administration will work this year to complete free trade agreements with Chile and Singapore" (18). Sanjay Gupta argues that the NSS "heralds a marked departure from the policies of deterrence and containment that has generally characterized American foreign policy since the Cold War" (182).

   15. Significantly, Tocqueville cites the American education system as one of the pillars of American democracy. By establishing "provisions that create schools in all townships and oblige the inhabitants, under penalty of heavy fines, to tax themselves to support them" Americans ensure equality of opportunity (41–2). Season Four echoes Tocqueville's argument and demonstrates America's spectacular failure to make good on its founding promises.

   16. In an interview with blogger David Mills, Simon describes the substitution of material worth for human dignity:

> The creation of wealth and the diminution of labor. The corner boys are more and more expendable; the cops who know their business are more and more expendable; the longshoremen are more and more expendable; the East European and Russian prostitutes who are coming in boxes—every day, human beings are worth less.

   17. Rawls gives the same speech to Lester Freamon at the end of the Season One when he is posted to homicide (1.13).

   18. In the audio commentary Simon says:

> This show is really about the American city and about how we live together and it's about how institutions have an effect on individuals. And how regardless of what you're committed to whether you're a cop, a longshoreman, a drug dealer, or a politician, a judge, a lawyer

you are ultimately compromised and must contend with whatever institution you've committed to [1.06].

19. Another disturbing connection marks the similarity between modern liberal democracies and twentieth-century totalitarian regimes. In *Eichmann in Jerusalem*, Arendt discusses the Nazi use of language rules. For example, the Nazis rarely referred to the Holocaust with words like "extermination," "liquidation," or "killing": "The prescribed code names for killing were 'final solution,' 'evacuation' (*Aussiedlung*), and 'special treatment' (*Sonder-behandlung*)" (*Eichmann* 85). Code words like these made it possible for Nazi officials to carry on their work while maintaining "order and sanity" (85). They were not designed "to keep these people ignorant of what they were doing, but to prevent them from equating it with their old, 'normal' knowledge of murder and lies." The Bush Administration's use of similar code words to "package" or market their policies is well documented. The War on Terror is of course the most obvious example. No one opposes a War on Terror any more than one opposes a "final solution." Other examples include "axis of evil" ("107th" 106) and "rogue states" (NSS 14).

20. Christopher Hanson notes that Omar and Bubbles seem to be the only two characters on the show who "avoid profanity, the show's lingua franca" (66). We might consider this another marker of Omar's essential difference.

Works Cited

Alvarez, Raphael. *The Wire: Truth Be Told*. New York: Grove Press, 2009.
Arendt, Hannah. "Concern with Politics in Recent European Philosophical Thought." *Essays in Understanding 1930–1954: Formation, Exile, and Totalitarianism*. Ed. Jerome Kohn. New York: Schocken Books, 1994. 428–47.
_____. *Eichmann in Jerusalem*. New York: Penguin, 2006.
_____. "From Hegel to Marx." *The Promise of Politics*. Ed. Jerome Kohn. New York: Schocken Books, 2005. 70–80.
_____. *On Violence*. New York: Harcourt, 1970.
_____. *The Origins of Totalitarianism*. Orlando: Harvest Books, 1976.
Bush, George W. "Bush makes historic speech aboard warship." Transcript of speech. CNN.com. 1 May 2003. Web. 14 Sept. 2013.
_____. "First Inaugural Address." *Selected Speeches of President George W. Bush, 2001–2008*. The Bush Record. The White House. Web. 15 Sept. 2013. 1–5.
_____. "National Day of Prayer and Remembrance Service." *Selected Speeches of President George W. Bush, 2001–2008*. The Bush Record. The White House. Web. 15 Sept. 2013. 59–61.
_____. "Remarks on the Freedom Agenda." *Selected Speeches of President George W. Bush, 2001–2008*. The Bush Record. The White House. Web. 15 Sept. 2013. 177–87.
_____. "Second Inaugural Address." *Selected Speeches of President George W. Bush, 2001–2008*. The Bush Record. The White House. Web. 15 Sept. 2013. 273–8.
_____. "State of the Union Address to the 107th Congress." *Selected Speeches of President George W. Bush, 2001–2008*. The Bush Record. The White House. Web. 15 Sept. 2013. 103–113.
_____. "State of the Union Address to the 108th Congress." *Selected Speeches of President George W. Bush, 2001–2008*. The Bush Record. The White House. Web. 15 Sept. 2013. 149–64.
_____. "State of the Union Address to the 109th Congress." *Selected Speeches of President George W. Bush, 2001–2008*. The Bush Record. The White House. Web. 15 Sept. 2013. 279–93.
_____. "West Point Commencement." *Selected Speeches of President George W. Bush, 2001–2008*. The Bush Record. The White House. Web. 15 Sept. 2013. 125–32.

Cech, Scott J. "Burning Man." *Teacher Magazine* 18.1 (2006): 34–9.
Chaddha, Anmol, and William Julius Wilson. "'Way Down in the Hole': Systemic Urban Inequality and *The Wire*." *Critical Inquiry* 38.1 (2011): 164–88).
Freedom House. *Freedom in the World 2013: Democratic Breakthroughs in the Balance*. Washington, D.C.: Freedom House, 2013. Web. 19 Dec. 2013.
Fukuyama, Francis. *The End of History and the Last Man*. New York: Perennial, 1992.
_____. "Invasion of the Isolationists." *New York Times* 31 Aug. 2005. Web. 19 Sept. 2013.
_____. "Reflections on the End of History, Five Years Later." *History and Theory* 34.2 (1995): 27–43.
_____. "Why shouldn't I change my mind?" *Los Angeles Times* 29 Apr. 2006. Web. 13 Sept. 2013.
Gupta, Sanjay. "The Doctrine of Pre-Emptive Strike: Application and Implications during the Administration of President George W. Bush." *International Political Science Review* 29.2 (2008): 181–96.
Hanson, Christopher. "Some Last Words on *The Wire*." *Film Quarterly* 62.2 (2008): 66–7.
Hegel, G. W. F. *Introduction to The Philosophy of History*. Trans. Leo Rauch. Indianapolis: Hackett, 1988.
Kagan, Robert. "The September 12 Paradigm: America, the World, and George W. Bush." *Foreign Affairs* 87.5 (2008): 25–39.
Owens, Patricia. "Beyond Strauss, Lies, and the War in Iraq: Hannah Arendt's Critique of Neoconservatism." *Review of International Studies* 33.2 (2007): 265–83.
Simon, David. "The banality of ideology." *The Audacity of Despair*. davidsimon.com. 9 July 2013. Web. 15 Sept. 2013.
_____. Interview with David Mills. *Undercover Black Man*. Blogger. 22 Jan. 2007. Web. 13 Sept. 2013.
_____. Interview with Marc Steiner. *The Official Blog of Marc Steiner*. Wordpress. 4 Mar. 2008. Web. 13 Sept. 2013
_____. "Introduction." *The Wire: Truth Be Told*. New York: Grove Press, 2009. 1–31.
Stewart, Dona J. "The Greater Middle East and Reform in the Bush Administration's Ideological Imagination." *Geographical Review* 95.3 (2005): 400–424.
Tocqueville, Alexis de. *Democracy in America*. Trans. and ed. Harvey C. Mansfield and Delba Winthrop. Chicago: University of Chicago Press, 2000.
United States of America. The President of the United States. *The Department of Homeland Security*. By George W. Bush. Jun. 2002. Web. 14 Sept. 2013.
_____. White House. *The National Security Strategy of the United States*. Sept. 2002. Web. 10 Sept. 2013.
Vulliamy, Ed. "The Wire creator David Simon eviscerates the dystopia creating war on drugs." rawstory.com. 25 May 2013. Web. 13 Sept. 2013.
Young-Bruehl, Elisabeth. "The Art of Alarm." *The Good Society* 16.2 (2007): 19–24.

Mythological Fictions and the Game Paradigm

Niall Heffernan

Formative Mythological Fictions and the Prism of History

What is seen in *The Wire* is the disparity between the fictions of a functioning society that the neoliberal free-market requires to sustain the myths of equal opportunity and justice, and the reality of life for a growing underclass in America. This essay argues that *The Wire* details a Game paradigm institutionalism that is based upon market-required fictions of a just and equitable society, which in reality has a destructive and dehumanizing effect on individuals and society. This is most immediately evident in its criticism of the War on Drugs, a so-called war that follows the same logic as all of America's foreign and domestic wars, stemming from its formative apocalyptic mythology, whereby barriers to progress and utopia can be reset-to-zero through a purifying violence.[1] The drug problem, and the "others" who constitute it, present a barrier on the path to the promised utopia. The problem must be "fought," therefore, using the means of commerce and science, and the drug-addled or pedaling "other" (effectively the poor) must give way to commercial progress in the way the natives gave way to profit and expansion in the formative years. The numerals of the unfettered neoliberal market are the scientific and commercial means by which America's wars are fought, and *The Wire*'s depiction of the War on Drugs details the Game-Theoretical underpinnings of Baltimore's police system. In this depiction can be seen the contradictory heart of formative American mythology; the liberal utopia, or the dawning of heaven on earth that the pilgrims imagined could only be brought about through an apocalyptic upheaval and through the bearing of scientific and commercial enlightenment. This, the underlying logic of the War on Drugs, is revealed whereby "war" has been waged on a social and public health problem, and the fighting is carried out via the numbers systems of Game Theory, a radically capitalist American ideology. Just as the formative exceptionalist American myths of liberty and justice for all were predicated on the destruction of the natives, so too is the current methodology fraught with terrible contradictions. *The Wire*'s depiction of an empire in decline is based upon the disparity between a numbers game which conceals terrible social injustice for the sake of the all-pervasive free-market, and the reality of life's struggle for a growing number of Americans who are disenfranchised by a system which no longer requires their labor.

The "game" is used throughout *The Wire* to refer to the street drugs trade, most often in the street dictum "it's all in the game." The "game" in the macro sense, however, refers to the circular and autotelic logic of the interlocking drug and police institutions. The monetary by-product of this game, as is clearly detailed in *The Wire*, flows by a kind of osmosis towards the higher echelons of the economy, while the human by-product is poverty, injustice and suffering. The unencumbered free market, now largely disconnected from the means of "legitimate" production for its growth has no investment in those who generate its growth, and this happens to an increasing degree in the wake of the "death of work" via the "illegitimate" means of the narcotics market. The logic of the "War on Drugs" has created a sort of merry-go-round between the nominally opposed institutions of the drug trade, police and justice system; a "game" that is played to the benefit of few. The human tragedy and injustice caused by drugs and the so-called war against them has no bearing on the unfettered financial market because it has no investment in those who are surplus to its labor requirements—since the death of industrial labor and its collectivist power—in the means of the generation of its profits.

The game, on the nominally illegitimate side of the marketplace, means playing for profit and climbing the hierarchy while trying to avoid assassination or arrest. The game on the legitimate side means abiding by the numbers and maintaining the fiction of institutional efficacy, even above and beyond the institution's nominal function. The municipal institutions of *The Wire*'s Baltimore are run according to the numbers of Game-Theoretical foundations, which are prescribed ultimately by the market, and thus must adhere fundamentally to efficiency and profitability. The numbers dictate that in order for those who populate the police force, for example, to maintain their positions or to advance their careers they must adhere to the prescribed numerical targets. Survival, adaptation or rapaciousness leads to the manipulation of the statistics by individuals at varying levels of power within the institutions, which is referred to as "juking the stats" throughout *The Wire*. What is required by the dictates of the market is a statistical picture, a fiction, of police effectiveness. Those within the police, for the most part, are self-preserving and will therefore abide by the requirements of the institution to maintain itself in the marketplace. The Game paradigm that *The Wire* depicts, therefore, is one of neoliberal economic virtualism. The myths of American exceptionalism, such as equal opportunity, a good life as a reward for hard work, individual autonomy, justice, and so forth are statistical simulacra; fictions weaved by the numbers of the Game paradigm.[2]

American exceptionalism is filtered through the prism of its formative mythology, in particular its Millenarian and Puritan sense of the duality of apocalypticism/utopia.[3] Heathen and uncivilized sinfulness was embodied and represented to a large extent by the "naked savages" who inhabited the bounty that was given by God to the settlers. The "Puritan errand" to hew paradise from the wilderness was not simply religious; the mission was also a commercial, scientific and ideological one (*The Rites of Ascent* 30).[4] Science and commerce were the means of civilization, of God's guiding light, and the native "other" was the embodiment of non-civilization. The sinfulness that the natives embodied was the sinfulness that would bring about Armageddon, only after which heaven would finally dawn. The formative American apocalypse is, therefore, embodied to some extent by the "cleansing" and "purification" of the natives; their removal by force or coercion from the land of justice and liberty for all. This reality of America's formation, therefore, reveals its myths of justice and equality as contradictory and fictitious from its inception. The formative myth that remains so potent in American life, therefore, is one whereby only after a barrier is removed, usually through a violent "purification," can justice and equality be truly established.

Game Theory was formulated, and came to be integral to the United States' nuclear strategy, during the Cold War; a "virtual" war which was seen through the prism of these formative apocalyptic terms.[5] It was apocalyptic not only because of the existence of the Bomb, but because of the perceived clash of ideologies, the fear of the "red menace" mirroring Puritan fears of miscegenation, and the "Godlessness" of the Russian other. Game Theory was formulated by John von Neumann, who was avowedly anti–Russian, and the theory, as a result of its developers and the ideologically charged atmosphere of its formulation, is predicated on radically individualistic assumptions.[6] When the Soviet Union collapsed, the means of radical neoliberal capitalism, including Game Theory were "proved" in the binary of the opposed ideologies to be apodictically "correct." At Fukuyama's "End of History" there was no other economic ideology and so in the intervening years neoliberal capitalism and its institutional adjunct, systems analytical Game Theory have not only become yet more radicalized, but are now *de facto* economic and institutional systems across the developed world.

The War on Drugs is symptomatic of America's responses to "barriers" to utopia and it is "fought" via the means of the apodictically correct ideology. Commerce and science have been the light of civilization since America's inception, which was "proved" again in the Cold War's battle against the heathen other, and with the certitude of numbers and science it would surely neutralize these new problems. The strategy method that "won" the Cold War, however, is used to "fight" a public health and social issue, and as *The Wire* depicts, any results, outside of the generation of profit, are fictional. Effectively the War on Drugs creates institutional factions, a splintering of society, whereby those pushed by circumstances or pulled by the logic of capitalism into the drugs trade are marked as the "other."

This essay gives a brief explication of the formulation of systems analytical Game Theory, as is seen in detail in *The Wire*'s depiction of the police force. It will go on to draw comparisons between the use of these statistical models in the Vietnam War and the terrible effects this methodology has on *The Wire*'s disenfranchised West Baltimore as a way to discuss *The Wire*'s take on two different policing philosophies. The policing required by the Game paradigm is illusory and dehumanizing, creating institutional factions and the othering of a poor underclass, while empathy and communication are shown to be consistently effective. The essay will go on to discuss the effects of all-pervasive free-market institutionalism on society, as depicted in *The Wire* and how its treatment of virtualization and illusion go to the heart of the contradiction between austerity and myths of equality and justice.

Cold War Games

The Wire's institutions are run according to statistical quantifications of efficacy, specifically Game-Theoretical models which are derived from Cold War American technocracy. The anxieties over the potential for a nuclear holocaust if inherent human fallibility was allowed to permeate the governance of strategy saw the development and implementation of supposedly rational and objective quantification models, which are based upon the assumption of fundamental human self-interest.[7] In this way, the concept of rationality became bound up in assumptions of self-interest, which in turn, became synonymous with rationality. Fred Kaplan's *The Wizards of Armageddon* (1983) details the development of these supposedly rational technocratic models and the political power they commanded in their adherence to capitalist "rationality" and their claim to objectivity. Adam Curtis's documentary series, *The Trap*, features interviews with some of the Cold War technocrats whose Game models have become the *de facto* frameworks for institutions across the post-industrial West, including James Buchanan, the economist who devised Public Choice Theory, and Alain Enthoven, who devised Systems Analysis.[8] Enthoven's Performance Target model purports to "liberate" the individual to achieve their nominal target in creative ways; thus they are supposedly motivated by a fundamental self-interest instead of perceived nonsensical abstractions such as "common good." The result, it is hoped, is greater institutional efficiency.[9]

The first practical application of the Performance Target model was in the Vietnam War, when the then American Secretary of Defense, Robert McNamara, attempted to "rationalize" the war according to mathematical objectivity. He had Alain Enthoven, his deputy assistant secretary of defense, devise a "Body Count" Performance Target system that set quantitative goals for the number of enemies killed. This "rational" method, however, saw soldiers lie about their own numbers or, much worse, shoot innocent civilians and count them as the enemy.[10] The Body Count system was a nightmare manifestation of the "juking of stats" that foreshadows *The Wire*'s portrayal of institutional corruption across Baltimore's police, education and political systems. Despite the disastrous outcome of Enthoven's application during the Vietnam War, statistical models based upon Performance Targets have nevertheless become the all-pervasive institutional mechanism.

In sustaining or advancing their positions within the institutions, the more ruthless and political individuals in *The Wire* will "juke the stats" to their own end. The police management, in particular Rawls and Burrell, respond to political pressure from the mayor by sustaining the fiction of police effectiveness. Similarly in the fourth season, the school system is shown to sustain the fiction of its efficacy by bolstering its own statistics, while the reality of George W. Bush's "No Child Left Behind" policy is tragically different.[11]

The War on Drugs: A Framework for the Illusion of Policing

In the tearing down of Major Colvin's (Robert Wisdom) free-zone experiment can be seen the socially destructive and fallacious aspects of the War on Drugs and its foundation in statistical targets. What is also revealed is an intertextual reference to the Vietnam War. The escalation of that particular conflict to a bloody stalemate was facilitated, to a significant degree, by a lack of communication, empathy, and understanding between the opposed sides.[12] The War on Drugs appears to have a similar effect in *The Wire*'s depiction of entrenched disconnection and enmity between the nominal foes. The statement of waging war on "drugs" is a non-sequitur, of course, the war, in reality, is against those who consume and sell narcotics, and the effect is an entrenched "othering" of urban poor.

Colvin is a major, months away from retirement, who is disillusioned with the futility of the War on Drugs and so sets up a designated "free-zone" for the sale of narcotics away from residential areas, contingent on a non-violent patronage, which becomes known among street touts as "Hamsterdam." Colvin undertakes this policing strategy as a response to the continued pressure from the mayor's office, which filters down through police management onto the rank and file, to reduce crime statistics in Baltimore's beleaguered Western District. Colvin's experiment is crushed by the political and police apparatuses, however, despite the signs of its positive effects on addicts and the wider communities, because it bears no political currency. Decriminalization would, in fact, undermine the police system and political system as they are currently structured and so it is those who bear power in these institutions have a vested interest in keeping the status quo. The top of the police hierarchy in *The Wire*, especially Ervin Burrell (Frankie Faison) and Bill Rawls (John Doman), are the most enraged by the revelation of Colvin's experiment and Rawls later takes an ugly glee in tearing down the Hamsterdam experiment. 3.12 sees Rawls, dressed in navy blues, blow his whistle and shout "over the top gentlemen" at the officers charged with breaking up Hamsterdam as Wagner's *Ride of the Valkyries* blares from his car's bull horn. The episode is sardonically titled "Mission Accomplished" and the ironic use of this piece of music intertextually references the famous helicopter scene from *Apocalypse Now*. In Coppola's film the triumphalism of the music as the Viet Cong in the village are crushed by the huge military might of the 9th Airborne acts as a counterpoint to the absolute futility and slaughter of the Vietnam conflict. The use of *Ride of the Valkyries* in this scene of *The Wire* emphasizes the point that the War on Drugs, like the Vietnam War, is futile and destructive, as are all American attempts to reset-to-zero through regenerative violence.

In the Vietnam War, the "rationalization" of the conflict with the statistics of Performance Targets illuminates the alienation and misunderstanding that proved disastrous for the Americans and their foe. Indiscriminate killing undertaken by American soldiers convinced more and more Vietnamese to join the Viet Cong in fighting off the "invaders," while the vast and incredible technological arsenal at the disposal of the United States did not obliterate the will of the enemy but instead strengthened it. In *The Fog of War*, McNamara recalls attending meetings intended to appraise the Vietnam War, in which past leaders of the United States and the Viet Cong discussed matters such as why the conflict escalated around 1960.[13] In these "Critical Oral History" meetings, McNamara was shocked at the level of profound misunderstanding and misreading of the enemy, miscalculations that would have disastrous effects. McNamara lamented the lack of communication between the enemies and speculated that with greater communication between them, empathy may have developed and the conflict may not have become as bloody and prolonged as it did.

The War on Drugs as is depicted in *The Wire* reveals the same misunderstanding, predicated on the same quantified rationalizations of the "war" and the same narrow assumptions of the so-called foe's motivations. There can be no empathy and no understanding to bridge the gap between the instrument of the state and the ever-expanding underclass who participate in the American Dream, either through their own unsanctioned capitalist Game model or through the transcendence and escapism of a drug high. In a scene from 3.10, "Reformation," Colvin berates Sergeant Ellis Carver (Seth Gilliam) for not having any informants, for not policing the community with humanity, and laments the implied internecine enmity of the term "war" in what is a futile police directive:

> This drug thing, it ain't police work. I mean I can send any fool with a badge and a gun up on them corners and jack a crew and grab vials. But policing? I mean, you call something a war and pretty soon everyone gonna be running around acting like warriors. They're gonna be running around on a damn crusade, storming corners, slappin on cuffs, *racking up body counts* [3.10].

Colvin goes on to emphasize the value of communication and community solidarity in the role of a police officer, an aspect he ruefully laments has been squeezed out of policing to the detriment of the job itself and the larger community. The act of statistics-generation facilitates the lie of effective policing, which damages the institution itself as well as the society.

In "The Political Technology of the Individual," (1988) Foucault discusses the historical relationship of the individual to the state and how a certain concept of policing has arisen in the postindustrial world. "Political arithmetic was the knowledge implied by political competence," he writes, "and you know very well that the other name of this political arithmetic was statistics, a statistics related not at all to probability but to the knowledge of state" (Foucault, 408). The use of technology and statistical technocracy in *The Wire*, in its depiction of the War on Drugs, has a disjointing and alienating effect on society. The police and drug institutions are entrenched in enmity, and the distance between individuals in opposed institutions is both bridged and facilitated by technocratic quantification and spying technology. The police try to infiltrate and gain information about their nominal enemies via spying technology instead of policing methods of interaction and communication, which emphasize understanding. "The wire" to which the wire taps on criminals' phones refers, is also a figurative "wire" that runs through the system, the schemata of postindustrial life connecting us all, but connecting us virtually through the digital and virtual routing of money and through the closed circuit camera that watches.

The enmity between the factions cannot be bridged, mediated or interrogated with either the technology of spying or the strategy of statistical reflexivity. In "The Concept of Enlightenment" (1944), Adorno and Horkheimer write about the general disconnection that comes as the price of "rational" control that humans have pursued since the Enlightenment: "Human beings purchase the increase in their power with estrangement from that over which it is exerted" (7). In *The Wire*'s depiction, the technological distance between the factions prefigures the lack of understanding. The police routinely underestimate or misunderstand their nominal foes and the generation of statistics through meaningless arrests keeps the circular logic of the Game paradigm and the War on Drugs intact. The War on Terror is introduced into *The Wire*'s critical purview from the beginning of Season Three, and it, of course, follows the same patterns of "policing," in that it is virtual, autotelic and carried out via technology, from a distance.[14]

Good policing is generally achieved in *The Wire* by those cops who are swimming against the tide of statistics-generation pursued by *The Wire*'s Baltimore police force. These examples of good policing invariably involve a level of human interaction with both the law abiding and law breaking population, an interaction that is discouraged by the numbers game. In broader thematic terms, *The Wire* concerns itself with the devaluation of people in the postindustrial world and the dehumanizing effects of quantitative models on people within official institutions. There are numerous vignettes within *The Wire*'s overall arc, in which the loss of human interaction and the binding narrative of community are lamented. Most notable for its powerful acting and pathos is a scene in which Detective Bunk Moreland (Wendell Pierce) admonishes Omar (Michael Kenneth Williams) for his part in the destruction of the community spirit they had in their shared neighborhood upbringing. The use of human interaction, communication and reason as police strategies is repeatedly shown to be superior to technological and technocratic means in *The Wire*. Human informants, in the form of Reginald "Bubbles" Cousins (Andre Royo) and Russell "Stringer" Bell (Idris Elba) invariably prove to be more integral to the police operations than the surveillance technology employed. The proliferation of technology means the proliferation of information, the majority of which is inconsequential. In his commentary accompanying 1.01, Simon articulates the program's approach to policing technology, in which he wished to impart "a sense of a world that is increasingly watched, even, watched with a certain indifference." The problem of policing in this world of alienated surveillance, "where there is almost too much information being put in front of the detectives," Simon says, is sifting out what is important or relevant (1.01. Simon commentary).

The Wire shows the difficulty of policing in an information-saturated environment, in which information seems to be endlessly proliferated by technology, to the point where it becomes white noise. The tendency to rely on the safety of statistics and technology breeds a lack of understanding and alienation, further entrenching the polarized factions of the "war."

The policing philosophy that *The Wire* expounds opens out to encompass the broader context of both internal and foreign American political policy. The War on Terror as it has been mythologized by the Bush and Obama administrations—a war against the "uncivilized" and "savage" believers in Islam with the "necessary" invasions of Iraq and Afghanistan—is actually predicated on a lack of understanding of America's antagonists. The technological means of surveillance and destruction have become the primary methods for fighting the War on Terror, while in the media and public political discourse, intractable enmity and binary ideological opposition are the usual response to an anomalous but all-purpose bogeyman, namely al–Qaeda. The lack of understanding engendered by quantification models and surveillance technology is, to some extent, a result of the distances these modes engineer between institutions, between groups, and between individuals. *The Wire*'s criticism of postmodern American politics and culture encompasses both the macro and the micro. The institutional fictions of neoliberal economic modeling permeate the culture and the same fictions that the "cracking of heads" enumerates on a local level are reflected in the macro fictions that underpin American aggression in foreign lands.

The Illusion of Social Functionality Prescribed by the Market

Powerful factors in *The Wire*'s continuing relevance lie in its treatment of the effects of macroeconomic forces on postmodern societies. Here the essay will argue that it is the fiction or illusion of a functioning police force or society that is required by the neoliberal free-market, and not an actually functioning society, as this would result in a reduction of privately owned profit. The fictions attend to aspects of exceptionalist American mythology, such as equal opportunity and free enterprise, which act now, in essence, as propaganda bulwarks that maintain the status quo.

The commercial enterprise of street narcotics, as depicted in *The Wire*, generates enormous profits, which circulate out into the wider economy, either through corruption and criminality or "legitimate" means such as property development. The War on Drugs does not interfere with the generation of these profits, it is simply an oppressive force on the poor, who are interchangeable cogs in the narcotics trade. The entrenchment of neoliberal economics has been ongoing in the developed world since the 1980s, and has been more rapidly advancing since the global downturn. *The Wire*'s treatment of the "death of work" and the fallacy of "doing more with less," in this regard, could hardly be more relevant.

The statistical fictions of institutional efficacy provided by the Game models are inextricably bound to the death of work. The disconnection of capital from its former source, labor, both allows for these fictions and requires them. The labor movement had once been powerful in the United States and elsewhere in the West, precisely because the production of capital was bound up with it. The wholesale dismantling of state industries, the processes of privatization, corporate deregulation, asset stripping and outsourcing, which became a political *modus operandi* in America and Britain in the 1980s, effectively destroyed labor power in those countries and decoupled market profits from the vagaries of collective labor power. As Sheehan and Sweeney have pointed out: "What becomes clear through viewing *The Wire* is that the triumph of capital over labor is accentuated by the triumph of finance over manufacturing capital" (Sheehan, Sweeney, 10).

The free market is a self-sustaining autotelic system, as such amoral, and no longer invested in a society geared towards good quality of life for the majority that sustain it. The fictions that the statistical institutional models attend to are those that contradict the reality of social decline that *The Wire* so vividly depicts. American exceptionalism purports that hard work and honesty can get you more than you need, that equal opportunity abounds, that democracy is just and capitalism is "natural" and fair. These notions are integral to American ideology, yet the reality that *The Wire* depicts is very much contrary to this. *The Wire* depicts a world in which the wealth production that was once dependent on manufacturing and thus subject to some degree to labor power, has been largely replaced by a drugs trade flourishing in Baltimore's disenfranchised urban areas. The solidarity and pride that went with industrial labor have effectively been replaced with the powerlessness and criminality of the narcotics trade, in which many have no choice but to participate. Those Americans who are rendered surplus to the requirements of a postindustrial economy are lured towards the narcotics trade, which mirrors "legitimate" capitalism in every way in *The Wire*'s depiction, bar the brutal consequences of failure for those on the wrong side of the law's divide. This element is expounded most powerfully in the narrative of the business savvy and aspirant narcotics trade reformist, Stringer Bell. Bell's attempt at upward mobility away from the violence and brutality of the street game towards the financialized free market profits of "making like a goddamn bank," by financing the drugs but laundering the profits through legitimate businesses, ends in his violent death (Alvarez, 240). Bell's narrative underscores the subtle race and class issues that *The Wire* explores. Bell, raised in an environment of disenfranchisement and entrenched urban poverty, seeks to partake in the "game," buying into the constantly recapitulated promises of equal opportunity; ultimately, however, his rise is halted by the brutal rules of the "game" into which he was born.

While upward mobility for people at the bottom of the capitalist pyramid is at best extremely difficult, money, on the other hand flows freely from bottom to top. At the apex of the West Baltimore drugs trade in *The Wire* is Avon Barksdale (Wood Harris), followed by his more ruthless successor, Marlo Stanfield (Jamie Hector). In both cases, as with Bell, the profits at the higher end of the illegitimate street trade are enormous. Theses profits are invariably rerouted into general circulation, into property development and other supposedly legitimate channels. The workings of the drugs trade in this regard—the brutality, the disintegration of communities, the suffering caused by drugs and by the "war" on them—are all irrelevant to the overall "growth" of a market that is disconnected from the source of its wealth. The fiction of a functional police system, whereby the so-called war involves police going to drug neighborhoods and making arrests for the purpose of generating stats is part of the circular game logic of police-versus-drug dealers, in which issues of public health and the social aspect of narcotics prohibition are never dealt with in any meaningful way. The War on Drugs is, therefore, a framework for the fiction of policing that does not interfere with the narcotics trade's generation of profits for the overall economy. There is no investment, or need for it, in the communities whose trade and consumption of nominally illicit products creates huge wealth, enriching for the most part those with access to the "legitimate" apex of the market.

The arrests of poor street kids for the most part that the War on Drugs ensures polarization and enmity between different factions of society. In effect, the War on Drugs neutralizes empathy, understanding or collaboration between the two, making meaningful policing of disenfranchised urban communities like West Baltimore practically impossible.

More with Less: The Presiding Fiction of The Wire's *Fifth Season*

The fifth and final season focuses on the newspaper *The Baltimore Sun* (where series creator Simon was once employed as a journalist).[15] *The Wire*'s examination of institutional corruption, under the general aegis of "juking the stats," is hereby extended to the print media. Not only does the media, including broadsheet newspapers, fail to report wide-scale systemic corruption according to *The Wire*'s analysis, but it is, in fact, complicit in endorsing the fiction of a functional society. To this end, the final season introduces the "fake serial killer" plot line and, therein, offers a piercing critique of the fiction of "doing more with less."

The police, as well as those remaining employees of *The Baltimore Sun* who have not been made redundant, are met with the constant and all too familiar everyday austerity mantra: "do more with less."[16] The reality, however, is that the police do less with less resources. Season Five sees the investigation into the Stanfield organization, who the police know are responsible for at least twenty two murders. They have dumped the bodies in abandoned row houses around the city, which Detective Lester Freamon (Clarke Peters) discovers towards the end of the Season Four. The beginning of Season Five, however, sees the investigation into the Stanfield organization hobbled by the diversion of resources away from the investigation, towards areas that hold more political currency for the mayor's office. The outrage precipitated by the murders has dissipated, the national and local media have long since turned their attention elsewhere, the matter no longer has any political currency, and so Mayor Tommy Carcetti (Aiden Gillen) diverts his budget supply away from the investigation, away from the Baltimore Police Department, and towards the political boon that is Baltimore's school system.

In 5.02, "Unconfirmed Reports," one of *The Wire*'s many bar scenes sees Detectives Jimmy McNulty (Dominic West) and Freamon rage to their Homicide Unit colleague and drinking buddy Bunk Moreland over the gutting of the row house investigation. In their interaction they acknowledge the huge racial issue that is mostly implicit in *The Wire*'s analysis. The murders took place in the wrong zip code; they acerbically refer to the murder of young black males as "misdemeanor homicides," pointing out that it if the victims had been white and middle-class the story would be very different.

The injustice of the termination of the row house murder investigation, in terms of McNulty's own vanity as well as those of its scandalous race and class prejudice sees him fabricate a murder investigation into a serial killer of the homeless. Enraged by the thwarting of the investigation for politico-economic reasons, McNulty concocts a fiction about a sexually deviant serial killer who "preys on the weakest among us" in an attempt to get the funding the department needs for him to surreptitiously continue the Stanfield investigation (5.02). "Fuelled by Jamesons and genius," McNulty manipulates the death scene of a homeless man and applies post-mortem injuries to the body in order to make it look like murder (Alvarez, 427). He continues on in this vein, later with Freamon's help, adding little flourishes that will titillate the media. In one blackly humorous scene that could be glibly described as a biting satire of the media, McNulty and Freamon manipulate a corpse with a pair of dentures. They introduce a biting fetish into the "serial killer's" repertoire, a tidbit that McNulty later feeds to the *Sun*'s crime reporter Alma Gutierrez (Michelle Paress) and Scott Templeton (Thomas McCarthy), who has tagged along with her.

In fabricating the serial killer story, McNulty thereby concedes to fiction in order to gain traction within the system. Season Five interrogates the role of fiction, in both reflexive terms and in terms of American institutional life. Marsha Kinder argues in "Re-Wiring Baltimore" that "the plot of the fake serial killer violates the commitment to truth and realism that *The Wire* demands throughout the series" (55–56). In so doing, however, *The Wire* may be making its most pointed criticism of institutional life, and at the same time taking aim specifically at the institution that is most culpable in its acquiescence to fictions. This point is encapsulated, most specifically, in ambitious reporter Templeton's pretense that the so-called serial killer has called him to tell him why he does what he does. Templeton's "City Desk" editor Gus Haynes (Clark Johnson) has extreme reservations about the veracity of Templeton's claims, but the paper's management persists with the supposed scoop regardless, as the story brings them into Pulitzer Prize-winning territory.

Broadsheet newspapers have traditionally been perceived as the watchdogs against corruption and institutional failure in America and beyond. Through the exposing of corruption and injustice, newspapers' nominal job is to prompt public debate and to hold to account those responsible for failures in the system. *The Wire*, however, depicts a newspaper business that has been hollowed out and made acquiescent to the dictates of radical capitalism. The constant refrain of the non-sequitur "more with less," and the persistent cutbacks and redundancies shown in *The Wire*'s fictional version of *The Baltimore Sun*, reveal the all-powerful law of the bottom line to which newspapers and all other American institutions are beholden. As Simon has stated: "*The Wire* is about capital and labor and when capitalism triumphs, labor is diminished. Season Five is the same as what happens to labor and middle management in every other [depicted] institution" (Alvares, 404). The concentrated ownership of newspapers by fewer behemoth corporations is yet another example of the triumph of virtualized capital over labor. Detached from the grounding of its nominal basis in Baltimore, the *Sun*'s interests are unattached to the abstractions of the old (pre–Cold War) world, such as those of journalistic integrity or social responsibility, as it is no longer invested in them. It is invested fundamentally in shareholder profit and every aspect of the paper must be tailored to its profitability, including, of course doing "more with less," meaning in real terms, staff layoffs. The *Baltimore Sun* and newspaper media in general are not simply complicit in the institutional fictions but are a propagator and integral part of sustaining these fictions. The fallacy of "doing more with less" precipitates the fallacy of Templeton's concoction, which in turn reveals a dysfunctional media and institutional system.

In McNulty's serial killer narrative, therefore, there is his tacit concession that the system operates on fictions, and in broader terms that the illusions of functionality that American mythology demands have much more currency than the truth ever can in this system. *The Wire* is taking aim at what it sees as an American unwillingness or inability to look objectively and truthfully at its own reality. McNulty, who is joined in the weaving of the fiction by Freamon (an unlikely participant given his characterization up to this point), is successful in procuring the money and resources he needs. Their fiction, however, over the course of the season's ten episodes, becomes a monstrosity that lurches out of their control, as McNulty receives more manpower and resources than he knows what to do with. McNulty and Freamon engineer a wire tap out of the "serial killer" investigation with which they surreptitiously set up on the players of Stanfield's organization once more. Their efforts lead to the organization eventually being brought down. Stanfield himself, however, is set free on the condition he leaves the Game forever, his pernicious lawyer Maurice Levy (Michael Kostroff) having noticed a discrepancy in the wire tap documents that lead him to be able to procure Stanfield's freedom.

McNulty and Freamon may be inoculated, to a certain extent, from the poisonous morality of their actions, but the same can hardly be said of Templeton. At the early stages of McNulty and Freamon's lie, Templeton weaves his own narrative into what he is unaware is someone else's lie by pretending he has received a telephone call from the killer. This gives the obsequious Templeton an inside track on the story with the paper's managing editor Thomas Klebanow (David Costabile) and executive editor James Whiting (Sam Freed). Templeton's lie becomes a boon for McNulty and Freamon, who see it as a way for them to set up a wire tap. There are a number of instances in which Templeton makes up sources and quotes prior to his taking a "leap" into fully fledged fabrication. Haynes's reservations about the ethical standing of Templeton's reportage is seen in these instances, and in his serial killer claims but Haynes's judgment is overruled by the senior management of the paper, Klebanow and Whiting, for whom the *scandale du jour* and the titillation of a serial killer are too alluring to resist. As a result of its structure and the dictates of shareholder profitability, *The Wire's Baltimore Sun* fails to see the everyday scandal of institutional corruption and thus, in doing less with less, it chases potential Pulitzer Prize-winning fiction instead.

The Game and the Illusion of Apocalyptic Cleansing

The couching of what is essentially a social and public health issue—the social ills that cause and are caused by the illegal drug industry—in the term "war" reminds us again that apocalyticism is perhaps the only truly surviving American metanarrative. The use of *Ride of the Valkyries* reminds the viewer that the apocalypse is now and always will be, so long as America makes its path to Eden, or more specifically, to profit, through violent "purifications." The formative American "purification" of the natives to make way for trade, commerce and "Manifest Destiny" is recapitulated throughout American history and so American wars, both inward and outward, adhere to the apocalyptic myth. Since the end of the Cold War, however, shared and binding narratives have been replaced with the dictates of radically individualistic capitalism. This criticism of postnuclear America runs through *The Wire*, whereby the viewer is presented with a view of the clear erosion of community and collective consciousness in these disenfranchised urban areas. The senses of race and group consciousness embodied by the various civil rights movements of the sixties have been replaced with the dictates of rapacious acquisition and the illusions of equality. The drugs trade, as *The Wire* makes abundantly clear, makes up a considerable portion of the Baltimore economy (as does the illegal drugs trade and black market in general in the overall economy), yet it is those at the bottom of the capitalist hierarchy who suffer the most in the generation of these enormous profits. The War on Drugs and the statistics that prop up the illusion of legal veracity and justice, effectively mask the reality of an inherently unjust system, a lopsided financial capitalism, or as Bodie (J.D. Williams) astutely observes to McNulty shortly before his demise: "the game is rigged" (5.13).

The Game paradigm only seeks the illusion of a functional society, thus the corruption and human tragedy engendered by the numbers system bears no effect on the higher echelons of the capitalist system as it is fully virtualized and freed from any attachment to messy human abstractions. Thus the fictions that the numbers provide are woven into the illusion of a functional society. This illusion is addressed towards pre-existing American exceptionalist myths pertaining to equal opportunity, democracy and the "rugged individualism" of the self-made man. In this way, the Pulitzer Prize that the senior editors of *The Wire*'s *Baltimore Sun* are chasing represents a simulacrum of journalistic integrity. They are chasing the currency of prestige through a fiction (that those individuals within their respective institutions who are seeking agency have fabricated) in a society that is fuelled by fiction.

Thus, *The Wire* engages the fictive aspect of America's recourse to violence, a product of its formative Christian, revolutionary and commercial mythology, in its internal and external politics and in its disastrous domestic and foreign "wars." Its depiction of the social effects of increasing numbers of people who are now surplus to the requirements of a postindustrial economy could hardly be more relevant today, and not just in the United States itself. Its interrogation of the doublespeak dictum "more with less," attends directly to the fallacy of what has become an austerity mantra across the postindustrial globe. The fallacy of the War on Drugs feeds into the fallacy of institutional efficacy and the maintenance of the fabric of American society; all attempt to sustain myths of American exceptionalism. Most pertinently of all, perhaps, *The Wire* critiques an institutional system that is geared towards the maintenance of the system itself above all considerations about how people might live well together. As such, its most potent weapon is its pathos. Its characters are deeply complex in their motivations, in their codes and their beliefs in various narratives, and not simply the self-advancing acquisition-machines that neoclassical economics assumes for all.

Notes

1. This concept is indebted to Richard Slotkin. For more see his texts *Regeneration Through Violence: The Mythology of the American Frontier, 1600–1860* and *Gunfighter Nation: The Myth of the Frontier in Twentieth Century America*.
2. The concepts of virtuality and simulation are indebted to Baudrillard. See *Simulacra and Simulation* for more detail on this, and see *The Gulf War Did Not Take Place* for insight into the virtuality of American foreign and domestic wars.
3. For more on apocalypticism and utopia in formative American mythology see John Gray's *Black Mass: Apocalyptic Religion and the Death of Utopia* as well as Bercovitch's *The Rites of Ascent: Transformations in the Symbolic Destruction of America*.
4. In *The Rites of Ascent* Bercovitch complicates the Puritan influence on America, but nevertheless posits a mixture of commercial, apocalyptic and progressively secular aspects as influences on their "mission," and in turn, the formative American ideology.
5. The American Cold War strategies of the nuclear stand-off, such as MAD (Mutual Assured Destruction) were run according to the means of Game Theory. See the Adam Curtis documentaries *To the Brink of Eternity* and *Fuck You Buddy* for insight into the application of Game Theory to nuclear strategy.
6. Von Nuemann was an advocate of a strike-first policy against the Soviets, setting up the "Von Neumann Committee for Missiles," which proposed this strategy. See Nasar's *A Beautiful Mind* (81). For more insight into the rise of nuclear Game Theory see also Fred Kaplan's *The Wizards of Armageddon*.
7. The attempt to supplant flawed human judgment with the supposedly objective logic of mathematics and machines is the precise focus of *Dr. Strangelove*'s satire.
8. See Michael Hill's *The Public Policy Process* for a clear overview of Public Choice Theory as it is applied to economics, politics and the social sciences. Buchanan received the Nobel Prize in 1986 for Public Choice Theory, as did John Nash in 1994 for his Game Theoretical concept known as "The Nash Equilibrium."
9. According to Curtis's documentary, it was at Margaret Thatcher's request that Enthoven was drafted to overhaul the National Health Service in Britain in the 1980s and to restructure it around the self-interested model of "Performance Targets" instead of the supposedly abstract notion of "common good," upon which it had been based up to this time.
10. See Laing and Blight's *The Fog of War* for insight into "body count" from McNamara's point of view.
11. A policy of aid, backed up by standardized quantifications of educational progress.
12. See Blight and Laing's for McNamara's insight into this aspect of the Vietnam War, in particular the first section: 'Empathize with Your Enemy.'
13. The Errol Morris documentary *The Fog of War: Eleven Lessons from the Life of Robert McNamara* is based upon the initial research of Blight and Laing.
14. Continued drone strikes in The Middle East and Africa exemplify this point.

15. Linda Williams' essay "Ethnographic Imaginary: The Genesis and Genius of *The Wire*" provides insight into Simon's previous role as a journalist, his eventual ignominious parting of ways with the paper and how these factors influenced his writing for *The Wire*.

16. "More with Less" is the title of the first episode of season five.

Works Cited

Alvarez, Rafael. *The Wire: Truth Be Told*. New York: Canongate, 2009
Baudrillard, Jean. *The Gulf War Did Not Take Place*. Sydney: Power Publications, 1995.
_____. *Simulacra and Simulation*. Ann Arbor: University of Michigan Press, 1994.
Bercovitch, Sacvan. *The Puritan Origins of the American Self*. New Haven: Yale University Press, 1975.
_____. *The Rites of Ascent: Transformations in the Symbolic Destruction of America*. New York: Routledge, 1993.
Blight, James G., and Janet M. Lang, eds. *The Fog of War: Lessons from the Life of Robert S. McNamara*. Lanham: Rowman & Littlefield, 2005.
Curtis, Adam. *Pandora's Box: A Fable from the Age of Science*. Episodes 1–6. BBC Two, 1992.
_____. *The Trap: What Happened to Our Dream of Freedom*. Parts 1–3. BBC Two, 11 March–25 March 2007.
The Fog of War: Eleven Lessons from the Life of Robert S. McNamara. Dir. Errol Morris. Sony Pictures, 2003.
Foucault, Michel. *Technologies of the Self: A Seminar with Michel Foucault*. Luther Martin, ed. London: Tavistock, 1988.
Gray, John. *Black Mass: Apocalyptic Religion and the Death of Utopia*. London: Penguin, 2007.
_____. *Straw Dogs: Thoughts on Humans and Other Animals*. New York: Farrar, Straus and Giroux, 2003.
Hill, Michael. *The Public Policy Process*, 4th ed. Essex: Pearson Education, 2005.
Horkheimer, Max, and Theodor Adorno. *Dialectic of Enlightenment: Philosophical Fragments*. Stanford: Stanford University Press, 2002. Web. 16 April 2013.
Kaplan, Fred. *The Wizards of Armageddon*. Stanford: Stanford University Press, 1983.
Nasar, Sylvia. *A Beautiful Mind*. London: Faber and Faber, 1998.
Sheehan, Helena, and Seamus Sweeney. "*The Wire* and the World: Narrative and Metanarrative." *Jump Cut* 51 (Spring 2009). Web. 11 October 2012. http://www.ejumpcut.org/currentissue/index.html
Slotkin, Richard. *Gunfighter Nation: The Myth of the American Frontier in Twentieth–Century America*. New York: Maxwell Macmillan, 1992.
_____. *Regeneration Through Violence: The Mythology of the American Frontier, 1600–1860*. Middletown, CT: Wesleyan University Press, 1973.

The American Dream
Capital, Codes and Consensus in the Early 21st Century

Michael Gow

HBO's *The Wire* hit TV screens in 2002, a point in history at which several powerful external political, social and economic forces were beginning to exert great pressure on the position of the U.S. as the world's only superpower. Barely a year after the events of 9/11, and little more since George W. Bush controversially defeated Al Gore for the presidency, the America we encounter through *The Wire* is one pervaded with a sense of foreboding, rattled to the core by threats to its existence. Such existential threats included al Qaeda and the terrorist attacks on 9/11; the subsequent passing of the Patriot Act which allowed law enforcement almost unrestrained powers to monitor, detain and interrogate suspected terrorists; the Enron and WorldCom scandals which hugely undermined market confidence and underlined apparent serious issues with major companies; the invasions of Iraq and Afghanistan; the search for Osama bin Laden and al Qaeda; and processes such as globalization and the offshoring of America's industries.

Drawing to a close in 2008, just five months before the Lehman Brothers financial crisis brought much of the neoliberal world order to the brink of collapse, *The Wire* depicted an American city already in the grip of a seemingly unstoppable death spiral, if not in its actual death throes. Baltimore's urban problems appear insurmountable: chronic drug abuse and drug-related crime in African American neighborhoods; a police force crippled by bureaucracy and held hostage by the vagaries of city politics; a political system starved of tax revenues and wracked by internecine power struggles; an inner-city school system plagued by too many problems to feasibly identify, the sum of which is far worse than that of its constitutive parts; and a traditional blue-collar sector in terminal decline. As Vest (172) attests, "*The Wire* exposes the challenging, upsetting and negative aspects of 21st century urban American life."

David Simon, the writer and producer of *The Wire*, has become very vocal on what he believes is the increasing segregation of America, "a country now utterly divided when it comes its society, its economy, its politics" (Simon). Simon himself attributes this to the monetarist, free market evangelism inspired by Milton Friedman's economic theories and which took hold in the early 1980s led by the radical governments of Reagan and Thatcher:

> We understand profit. In my country we measure things by profit. We listen to Wall Street analysts ... and the notion that capital is the metric, that profit is the metric by which we're going to measure the health of our society is one of the fundamental mistakes of the last 30 years. I would date it in my country to about 1980 exactly, and it has triumphed [Simon].

Yet for all its grim portrayal of the realities at the sharp end in an American city, *The Wire* manages also to reveal, perhaps unintentionally, the binding strength of an underlying set of values and dispositions that indicate the enduring presence of something which may still be termed the American Dream. While these values are not strictly adhered to at all times, they are recognized as legitimate and true across a broad range of social groups including the addicts, the dealers, the kingpins, the police, the stevedores, the city officials, the judiciary, the teachers and the students. While each of these distinct social groups operates according to the logic of its field of activity, there does exist a common thread of values which serves to bind such seemingly conflicting groups together.

This essay aims to explore, utilizing the concepts of Pierre Bourdieu and Antonio Gramsci, the differences and similarities of those social groups depicted in *The Wire* with the purpose of illustrating not the impending demise of the American Dream, but identifying the durability and strength of ideas central to the contemporary American historical bloc. It first uses Bourdieu's concept of the field, defined as the pursuit of various forms of capital considered desirable in that particular sphere of concern, combined with his notion of different forms of capital, to examine the ways in which the various groups in *The Wire*'s Baltimore continue to pursue their version of the American Dream. Moreover, where *The Wire* has been criticized for overemphasizing the force exerted by structures and hence removing agency from its protagonists (see, for example, Dreier and Atlas in this volume), this essay argues that the protagonists in *The Wire* employ "structured improvisations" as response to otherwise crushing structural forces. It then draws upon Gramsci's notion of hegemony as a means of understanding how and why the actors in Baltimore appear to share a relatively homogenous set of values and dispositions that preserve some traits of the American Dream.

Fields and Forms of Capital in Baltimore

To elaborate this framing of the various social groups depicted in *The Wire*, Bourdieu's concepts of field and forms of capital will be introduced. This is an exercise in highlighting the differences between these disparate communities, often dislocated from one another, yet also constitutive of a wider society in which they all exist.

Bourdieu's concept of the field, according to Webb et al. (21) "can be defined as a series of institutions, rules, rituals, conventions, categories, designations, appointments and titles which constitute an objective hierarchy." Each field will have its own "rules," its own distinct doxa, while agents active in a field will have internalized the "rules of the game." This internalization of the doxic rules, which Bourdieu terms the "habitus," gives rise to a disposition that the forms of capital available in a particular field are indeed worth pursuing and that the "game is worth playing" (Bourdieu & Wacquant 98), a phenomena which Bourdieu terms "illusio" (Bourdieu & Wacquant 98). Webb et al. highlight Bourdieu's recognition of the dynamic properties of a field, noting that a field is not merely equated with the institutions and rules of that field, but extends to the include a consideration of the interactions between institutions, rules and practices.

The first task, then, is to identify the various "fields of activity" depicted in *The Wire*. Broadly, these are the Baltimore Police Department (BPD); the Baltimore drug trade; the addicts; the docks; city hall; the legal system; the schools; and the press. Characters may cross these fields, or occupy positions across multiple fields at any given time, but each character depicted in *The Wire* is generally identifiable with one field as their main sphere of activity.

Each of the fields of activity depicted in *The Wire* has agents engaged in that field and willing to risk their time, and in many cases their well-being, their livelihood and their liberty, in the pursuit of the specific forms of capital peculiar to that field.

The concepts of field and capital are very tightly interconnected (Jenkins; Webb et al.; Bourdieu & Wacquant; Bourdieu). What constitutes capital in a given field is determined by that field and the objective relations particular to it. Bourdieu (241) argues that "it is in fact impossible to account for the structure and functioning of the social world unless one reintroduces capital in all its forms and not solely the one recognized by economic theory," an observation which chimes with Simon's earlier stated contention that reducing measurements of success to financial profit is a lamentable development characteristic of the neoliberal post–80's era which has led to catastrophic social consequences.

Bourdieu identifies three main forms of capital or "three fundamental species": economic, social and cultural, emphasizing that "capital does not exist and function except in relation to a field" (Bourdieu & Wacquant 101). While economic capital is perhaps the most straightforward, referring simply to material possessions, money in the form of remuneration, accumulated financial resources, employment benefits, such as insurance, medical cover, pension contributions and associated perks, it is by no means the central form of capital or the focal point of Bourdieu's theorizing. Economic capital is essentially "that which can be immediately and directly convertible into money and may be institutionalized in the form of property rights" (Bourdieu 243).

The possession of such economic capital may also indicate possession of cultural capital, which is linked to notions of cultural taste, consumption patterns and distinction, inherent to the specific field. Cultural capital can exist in three specific forms, the embodied state, the objectified state and the institutionalized state (Bourdieu).

According to Bourdieu (Bourdieu & Wacquant 119), "social capital is the sum of the resources, actual or virtual, that accrue to an individual or a group by virtue of possessing a durable network of more or less institutionalized relationships of mutual acquaintance and recognition"; in other words, the network of connections and status within a hierarchy of a given field. The acquisition and maintenance of status and relationships within a field can enhance the ability of those who possess it to accumulate other forms of capital. For example, better educational qualifications, membership of groups, title, professional reputation (all forms of social capital) can lead to greater opportunities to accumulate economic or cultural capital.

The following section looks at two fields of activity in more detail, to identify and understand the motivating effect of capital accumulation of actors within those fields: the BPD and the West Baltimore drugs trade.

A specific source of praise for *The Wire* has been its depiction of the structural forces and institutions which both compel and constrain the actions of various characters. David Simon explicitly stated in an interview with Nick

Hornby that *The Wire* aimed to turn the standard police procedural TV cop show on its head: "instead of the usual good guys chasing bad guys framework, questions would be raised about the very labels of good and bad, and, indeed, whether such distinctly moral notions were really the point." Simon more explicitly identifies *The Wire* as a focal device which is "in its larger themes, a show about politics and sociology and, at risk of boring viewers with the very notion, macroeconomics. And frankly, it is an angry show" (Vest 172). Yet, while all those characters depicted in *The Wire* are necessarily participants in wider society, there does exist an ontological hiatus which separates them from it: that is, the protagonists do not occupy a place in American society as such, but rather hold positions within particular fields of activity, with American society itself a larger configuration of these different fields. Rather, the characters occupy worlds, these fields of activity, apparently separate from those of other characters: thus, the various Baltimores experienced by Jimmy McNulty (Dominic West), Tommy Carcetti (Aidan Gillen), Reginald "Bubbles" Cousins (Andre Royo), Frank Sobotka (Chris Bauer), Omar Little (Michael K. Williams), Namond Brice (Julito McCullum), Rhona Pearlman (Deirdre Lovejoy) and Russell "Stringer" Bell (Idris Elba), while inter-related, are all different. Nevertheless, these fields of activity are woven together in a nexus of relations, overlapping and coming into contact with one another, while also being constitutive elements of the city of Baltimore.

It is from these flashpoints of contact between the various fields that many of *The Wire*'s most dramatic story arcs emerge: McNulty's crusade against the Barksdale crew in Season One; Stan Valchek's (Al Brown) vendetta against Sobotka in Season Two; Stringer's dealings with the political sphere and property developers during his attempts to become legitimate in Season Three; Howard "Bunny" Colvin's (Robert Wisdom) academic research in the Baltimore school system in Season Four; and the consequences of a cash-starved city administration on morale and performance in the BPD in Season Five.

In essence, what is being proposed here is not a fragmentation of American society, but rather that American society is a configuration of different arenas of social activity, each characterized by its own codes of conduct and each constituted by the specific forms of capital deemed worthy of actors operating within those fields. While this diagnosis, at first, seems to agree with Simon's notion that "America is a country which is utterly divided when it comes to its society, its economy, its politics" (Simon), there is a strong argument that common values are detectable across all of these groups; values which bring these disparate fields together through shared understandings and common values to constitute America itself.

All the Pieces Matter: Structure and Agency

Prior to examining the various forms of capital and the commonalities of values across disparate fields of activity, it is essential to explore how the accumulation of social, cultural and economic capital influences, and indeed directs, the activity of agents within a field. Such a process can be misinterpreted as overstating the role of structure as being all-powerful. However, it is important to recognize that social structures themselves are constantly changing in response to political, social, cultural, demographic, legal, technological and environmental changes. These changes lead to what Craig Calhoun (292) has referred to as "structured improvisations" whereby individual agents respond to the transformations of their field of activity. This concept offers a nuanced explanation of the dialectical relationship between structure and agency that helps bridge the major problem in the social sciences as identified by Bourdieu: the antimony of structure and agency.

Such structured improvisations are demonstrated throughout *The Wire* as the various characters respond creatively, intelligently and with ingenuity to emerging problems in order to continue accumulating the various forms of capital of their given field. Furthermore, it is one such example of ingenuity on which the first season of *The Wire* is based: the Barksdale crew's use of pagers, payphones and codes to avoid police monitoring of their illegal activity.

The Barksdale crew devise counter-strategies to respond to advances in technology and police strategies to tap cellphones. The use of pagers and payphones, alongside strict instructions for their lieutenants to not talk business on the phone:

WEE-BAY: What's the rule?
D'ANGELO: I know the rule
WEE-BAY: Say it!
D'ANGELO: Don't talk in the car. Or on the phone, or in any place that ain't ours and to anybody that ain't us, but it was just you, yo. It's your fuckin' truck. Don't talk in the car [1.01].

Similarly, in response to police tactics, drug dealing transactions are designed to involve a process where corner boys break the transaction into distinct parts, thus making evidence gathering and prosecution much more difficult, as illustrated by D'Angelo Barksdale's changes to the drug dealing operation under his control:

> This the way Ronnie Mo set it up? Yo, I mean, this is fucked up. Look, you can't serve your customers straight up after taking their money. Somebody snappin' pictures, they got the whole damn thing. See what I'm saying? You get paid, you send their ass off around the building yo, then you serve. We gotta start tightening up man, no more shortcuts [1.01].

These are simple examples of how social structures encourage intelligent, creative and ingenious responses to changing conditions within fields. While structural changes are responsible for these responses, the responses themselves are agential acts arising by the need to continue acquiring capital within the field of activity, in this case the narrow field being the Barksdale crew and, the broader field being the West Baltimore drug trade. Structure does not dictate action; it provides a framework of logic within which each individual actor can respond to challenges in an infinite number of ways provided they do so according in a manner which does not defy the logic of their field of activity.

While these examples are drawn from the first episodes of the first season, where the rules of the Baltimore drugs trade are necessarily made discernible to the viewer, there are many other examples whereby actors depicted in *The Wire* are responding to changing conditions of the fields in which they operate.

Season Two depicts the struggles of the port unions and the improvised responses of Frank Sobotka in engaging criminal activity to fund a lobbying campaign in the pursuit of two projects which will help secure the future of the port industry, as well as the related experiences of Nick and Ziggy Sobotka (Pablo Schreiber and James Ransone) as they are drawn into the drugs trade and theft from the port as legitimate work becomes an unreliable and insufficient source of income. It also shows Valchek's loss of face when his stained glass window is rejected by the local priest, leading to a personal vendetta against Frank Sobotka, a consequence of Valchek losing out to Sobotka in the accumulation of social capital within the Baltimore Polish Catholic community.

Bunny Colvin's misguided attempt to establish drug-tolerant zones in Season Three is the stand-out example of an actor responding to changes in his field in *The Wire*. The pressures brought to bear on Colvin and other divisional commanders are illustrated in the Comstat meetings chaired by Commissioner Ervin Burrell (Frankie Faison) and Deputy of Operations Bill Rawls (John Doman). What at first seems like a rebellious move by Colvin is actually a strategy to comply with Burrell's and Rawls' orders to keep murders down and achieve key performance indicators on other crime measurements. While certainly born of frustration and with a mischievous and insubordinate nature, Colvin's strategy is a structured improvisation that is intended to result in the achievement of goals laid down by the senior management of the BPD, albeit one which simultaneously allows Colvin to demonstrate his own conviction that "soldiering and policing ain't the same thing" (3.10).

Season Four sees Colvin paying the price for his Hamsterdam experiment and he ends up working on a research project to investigate and understand repeat violent offenders with Dr. David Parenti (Dan DeLuca), a professor of sociology from the University of Maryland. Season Four shows the viewer how the rules of the game peculiar to the West Baltimore drug trade and "the corners" are inscribed and inculcated at a very young age. Young boys and girls learn the rules of the "game," and learn to value certain forms of social, cultural and economic capital through their experiences at home, on the streets and in school. It reveals a process of socialization whereby West Baltimore youth develop skills required to navigate and survive in the ruthless environment in which they live. The story arcs following Namond, Michael Lee (Tristan Wilds), Dukie Weems (Jermaine Crawford) and Randy Wagstaff (Maestro Harrell) show how, with differing levels of success, each of these young teenagers fairs in navigating the unforgiving terrain of the West Baltimore corners.

The school funding crisis has profound effects in Season Five, leading McNulty to devise a harebrained scheme to divert funds to the ongoing investigation into the rising drug dealer Marlo Stanfield (Jamie Hector). Simultaneously, Baltimore Sun reporter Scott Templeton (Thomas McCarthy) runs into conflict with city desk editor Gus Haynes (Clark Johnson) when he breaks ethical codes of conduct and reporting policy. Templeton does this in pursuit of greater recognition for his reporting, which he receives from the editor and senior management, with the montage at the end of Season Five showing Templeton receiving the ultimate accolade of a Pulitzer prize for his story on the homeless.

The compelling and constraining power of social structures are evident in every story arc in *The Wire*. David Simon wrote, in his introduction to Rafael Alvarez's book *The Wire: Truth Be Told* about the ambitions of *The Wire*: "We were bored with good and evil. To the greatest possible extent, we were quick to renounce the theme" (Alvarez 3). It is this decision which necessitates the development of an understanding of the social structures which compel, constrain and influence the actions of *The Wire*'s sprawling array of characters, thus conveying how responses and actions of actors within a given field contribute to the reproduction and transformation of those very structures. Nowhere is this dialectical relationship between structure and agency more clearly demonstrated than in the final episode when Michael seems to take the place of Omar as a stick-up boy, and Dukie descends into heroin addiction to become the new Bubbles. Furthermore, it is this rejection of such simplistic characterizations of "good" or "evil" which allows characters such as Omar, McNulty, Bubbles, Ziggy or Stringer to resonate so deeply with viewers; they are characters with whom it is possible to empathize in spite of their immorality, greed, violent nature, ineptitude or personal failings.

The problematization of good and evil is perhaps most evident in the field of the BPD. This field, as McNulty is prone to point out at when venting his contempt for "the bosses," is itself fragmented, as demonstrated in the following argument with Lester Freamon (Clarke Peters):

> LESTER: You wanna talk about police work? I was doing the job when you were just dreaming on it. Daniels was out there too. And now you gonna fuck him when he pulled you off a goddamn boat?
> McNULTY: He's a boss. Fuck the bosses.
> LESTER: Maybe Daniels plays a few games to get by, but he's cost himself plenty for the sake of the job. He's earned some loyalty.
> McNULTY: Fuck loyalty, and fuck you, Lester. I never thought I'd hear that chain-of-command horseshit come out of your mouth.
> LESTER: Motherfucker, I spent a lot of time in a lot of weak units. More than you. Now this here may not be perfect, but it's a chance to be police [3.04].

It would be a mistake to regard McNulty's vendetta against Barksdale and Bell as anything other than an attempt to single himself out as "natural police": in conversation with Judge Phelan, McNulty assures Phelan "it's a career case your honor" (1.07), a revealing comment which is repeated at the end of the first season by Pearlman in conversation with McNulty. In this case, we can also detect the career ambitions of Pearlman to climb the ranks of the legal profession, and a fairly callous disregard for the victims of the violent crimes which form the case:

> I have to admit it Jimmy, this is a great case. And not just because of Greggs ... but because of how deep it goes. I mean the murders, the money. Jesus I feel like I've been drunk since that kid started talking to us.... You wanna try to go Federal with this? I am up for it. I get cross designated as an AUSA and we can really run with it. You know? Career fucking case [1.13].

David Simon recognizes the motivating power of capital accumulation, specifically social capital. He also links the characterization of McNulty to his experience working with real Baltimore Homicide detectives during his time as police reporter for the Baltimore Sun. Describing a "frightening aspect" of McNulty, he argues that "absolute truth of all the cops I've known" is that "the best you can hope for from a really good cop is that he cares about the game" (Rothkerch).

What is evident here is that the moralizing usually portrayed in police procedural dramas, where cops are solving murders primarily because they care, is conspicuous by its absence: in *The Wire* the homicide detectives are concerned, first and foremost, with their professional reputation, and subsequently with their clearance rate. Look elsewhere in the BPD and similar patterns can be observed. For example, the Western Drug Enforcement Unit, headed by Sergeant Ellis Carver (Seth Gilliam) in Season Three, consists of undisciplined police officers, including Carver himself, Thomas "Herc" Hauk (Domenick Lombardozzi), Anthony Colicchio (Benjamin Busch) and Kenneth Dozerman (Rick Otto), who pride themselves on a zero-tolerance, aggressive military-style approach to policing which they call "the western district way" (3.01). In fact, again in an interview following the completion of airing of Season Three, Simon (quoted in Vine) states that "the third season is also an allegory that draws explicit parallels between the War in Iraq and the national drug prohibition." This distinction is portrayed through the transformation of Carver from an ignorant, thuggish and indifferent law enforcer at the outset of Season Three. Carver's metamorphosis is initiated when Bunny Colvin lectures him on the nature of real police work and how "soldierin' and policin'? They ain't the same thing" and that Carver and his DEU team "ain't shit when it comes to policing" (3.10). Colvin's lecture has the desired effect and Carver's transformation to a conscientious and effective community police officer is played out over Seasons Three, Four and Five.

All in the Game: The West Baltimore Drug Trade

The "rules of the game" of the west Baltimore drugs trade are laid out primarily in Season One. Interactions between D'Angelo Barksdale and his young crew selling drugs in the Pit, consisting of Malik "Poot" Carr (Tray Chaney), Preston "Bodie" Broadus (J. D. Williams) and Wallace (Michael B. Jordan), show the viewer the various forms of capital that are pursued. Aside from the economic benefits that drug dealing brings, the social and cultural capital is also unveiled in a memorable scene where D'Angelo, nephew of Westside drug kingpin Avon Barksdale, finds Wallace and Bodie playing checkers with a chess set.

> WALLACE: So how do you get to be the king?
> D'ANGELO: It ain't like that. See, the king stay the king, a'ight? Everything stay who he is. Except for the pawns. Now, if the pawn make it all the way down to the other dude's side, he get to be queen. And like I said, the queen ain't no bitch. She got all the moves.
> BODIE: A'ight, so if I make it to the other end, I win.
> D'ANGELO: If you catch the other dude's king and trap it, then you win.
> BODIE: A'ight, but if I make it to the end, I'm top dog.
> D'ANGELO: Nah, yo, it ain't like that. Look, the pawns, man, in the game, they get capped quick. They be out the game early.
> BODIE: Unless they some smart-ass pawns [1.03].

What this dialogue reveals is the ambition of the young hoppers to rise through the ranks and their perception that the forms of capital in this field, including the money and the reputation for ruthlessness and a streetwise intelligence, are worth the risk of imprisonment, injury or even death.

In 4.08, Colvin notices patterns of behavior of some of the at-risk students he is working with, a discussion which illustrates the subtlety of inculcation of values, development of the skills, and the requisite understanding of the field which are achieved through a socialization process. These students are viewed as being disruptive and withdrawn from the educational process they are supposed to be engaged in at school, but Colvin highlights that all of the students are receiving an education and socialization for the field they are going to graduate to: the West Baltimore drug trade. He describes the school system as "practice for the corner" (4.08), and takes this discussion further in the same episode, posing the question "What makes a good corner boy?" which leads initially to a vibrant and enthusiastic discussion, notable as it stands in stark contrast to the usual atmosphere of the research project's experimental class. The students offer some striking insights into the mentality of the corner boys when faced with a hypothetical scenario where they a member of their crew is potentially stealing from them. Darnell argues against beating the offender, instead proposing they pay it back "out of his own cut ... if he a good worker, he know what he need to do. If he thinks about it, says it ain't his fault, then that nigger runnin' game on you" (4.08). Darnell then concedes that if it can be established that the person is stealing, then he should be beaten or "fucked up." When asked "Why?" by Colvin, Darnell responds, "There always people watchin'," looking for a sign of fragility and weakness. In Season One, it is such fragility and weakness which leads to the shooting of Wallace by Bodie and Poot. Prior to his death, D'Angelo takes Wallace to task over his wavering commitment in a warning that sadly came too late, instructing him, "You play it hard, you play it tight and you make sure niggers know you gonna stand by your people" (1.12). This ruthless and vengeful attitude is an essential characteristic of any actor in the West Baltimore drug trade, and to be known as someone fierce and unyielding is a form of social capital specific to the field.

In 4.10, Colvin homes in on the central argument being proposed here: that to operate in a field, whether it be the BPD, the Corners, City Hall, the port unions or any other sphere of activity, one must learn, absorb, accept and understand the "rules of the game" specific to that field through a process of socialization:

> You put a textbook in front of these kids, put a problem on the blackboard, teach them every problem in some statewide test, it won't matter. None of it. 'Cause they're not learning for our world; they're learning for theirs. They know exactly what it is they're training for and what it is everyone expects them to be. It's not about you or us or the test or the system. It's what they expect of themselves. Every single one of them know they're headed back to the corners. Their brothers and sisters, shit, their parents. They came through these same classrooms. We pretended to teach them, they pretended to learn and where'd they end up? Same damn corners. They're not fools, these kids. They don't know our world but they know their own. They see right through us [4.10].

Comparing Capital: BPD vs the Corners

As previously stated, Bourdieu's concept of the various forms of capital helps us distinguish between different fields, identifying differences. The table below lists some of the types of capital valued by actors in the two fields discussed above:

Figure 1—Comparison of Forms of Capital

Form of Capital	Baltimore Police Department	West Baltimore Drug Trade
Economic	Salary, pension, overtime.	Wages; "points on the package" or percentage cut of sales.
Social	Official Rank	Rank rising from lookout, hopper, on-the-money, running a corner or tower, or becoming an enforcer or "muscle."
Social	Being "natural police" e.g. Lester Freamon	Street smart intelligence, e.g. Stringer Bell, Omar Little, Proposition Joe.
Social	Clearance rate/arrest statistics	Kills/body count, "fierceness" and unforgiving nature. To be a "soldier."

Social	Loyalty and observing the principle of chain of command	Trustworthiness (to "stand tall" when arrested and say nothing); "do the years" if necessary.
Social	"Kin" to other police officers	Family ties to other "players"
Cultural	Ethnicity, e.g. opportunities for promotion for African Americans through Baltimore's affirmative action policy	Taste in clothing, fashion, cars, music, weapons.

At this point, it would be incredibly easy to agree with Simon's claim that America is now "a country now utterly divided when it comes its society, its economy, its politics." Yet, this conception of America as a configuration of different fields of activity would presuppose America has always been divided in this way. In fact, Simon acknowledges this disparity between "worlds," somewhat contradicting his notion of a single America being torn apart, when discussing the role of *The Wire*'s writing team: "the D'Angelo Barksdales and Frank Sobotkas live in *their worlds*; we visit from time to time with pens poised above splayed notes" (Alvarez 10).

How, then, can this contradiction be reconciled? How is it possible to save the American Dream for those evermore on the outside looking in? Are they excluded permanently from participating in the great American experiment? Is the American Dream doomed to failure? Thus far, this essay has identified the manner in which fields of activity can be differentiated: on the basis of the specific forms of capital available for accumulation within those fields. Yet, there are also striking similarities in terms of core values that suggest the American Dream still has life in it yet, if certain pressing issues concerning poverty, criminality, drug-abuse, wealth distribution, employment opportunities and urban regeneration can be more effectively addressed.

Gramsci, Hegemony and the American Dream

There are several broad themes which are woven through the fabric of *The Wire* and which reveal a basis for consent across social groups which appear, at first glance, to be on opposite sides of the fence: rule of law, competition and justice. These three main ideas are portrayed across many of the fields represented in *The Wire*, though perhaps not all in every field.

In Gramscian terms, these values can be described as hegemonic; that is, they have been successfully negotiated between the ruling elite and subaltern groups which make up American society. Hegemony, in the Gramscian sense, describes a situation where a ruling group or elite has their values, dispositions and interests represented, taken up and internalized by a variety of subaltern groups. It is more than brainwashing, more than the ideological domination of subaltern groups by a leading group, and more than simple persuasion, as Williams argues:

> If our social and political and cultural ideas and assumptions and habits were merely the result of specific manipulation, of a kind of overt training which might be simply ended or withdrawn, then the society would be very much easier to move and to change than in practice it has ever been or is [Williams 37].

Hegemony, in the Gramscian sense of the term, requires engagement between the leading and subaltern groups of a given society in an ongoing process of negotiation which serves to build consensus and promote social cohesion through articulating the interests of various subaltern groups under the leadership of the dominant group. Such an understanding of society may lead to both active, conscious support for the hegemonic situation and unconscious acquiescence when such hegemonic conditions are accepted as legitimate and normal.

There are several instances where characters on the wrong side of the law indicate an acceptance of and acquiescence to systems of rules. Namond attempts to be suspended from the experimental class in Season Four, and, when told this is not going to happen, complains that "I know the rules. You gotta suspend me. School gotta have rules" (4.06). Fruit, one of Marlo Stanfield's lieutenants, objects to the Western District initiative to move all dealing to the free-zones in Season Three: "Look. We grind and y'all try to stop us. Why you got to go fuck with the program?" (3.04).

Throughout all five seasons of *The Wire*, there is fundamental acceptance of rule of law and the processes and procedures which it entails. While *The Wire* portrays those who find themselves justifying their legal transgressions, whether it be Omar Little, Frank Sobotka, Bubbles or any other character involved in criminal activity, it also refuses to pass judgment on these protagonists, allowing the viewer to arrive at their own conclusion. This acceptance of rule of law appears to be doxic and hegemonic, as defined by Bourdieu and Gramsci respectively: doxic because it never occurs to the characters to question its legitimacy; hegemonic because rule of law is consented to universally, both consciously and unconsciously, even in instances where characters face grand jury, prosecution and imprisonment.

Each field has its own codes; its own concept of justice. This does not refer to the legal system, which is the state's codified interpretation of justice and which is based around the values and morality which the state seeks to render hegemonic, but rather to the deep-lying consensus that justice is a concept which is shared across all fields. How, why and for what reasons justice is administered are different for each field of activity. That the West Baltimore drug trade exists outside the boundaries of legitimate society requires it to administer its own justice and it is certainly possible to argue that justice itself does not exist in this field, instead being replaced with extra-judicial punishment, vengeance and retribution. However, there is a general acceptance that those who transgress the rules of the game in each field will be subject to punishment and that such punishment is justified and commonly understood as a legitimate consequence for breaking intersubjectively understood codes of conduct.

There are examples of such extra-judicial justice being meted out across all fields: McNulty is sent to the boat for ignoring the golden rule of adhering to "chain of command" (2.01); D'Angelo Barksdale is murdered by a prison inmate contracted by Stringer Bell (2.06); Randy Wagstaff becomes the target of assault and arson for being a "snitch" (4.11; 4.12); Bodie is eliminated for talking to the police (4.13); Stringer Bell is murdered for his involvement in the death of Brandon and attempt to kill Brother Mouzone (1.05; 2.11); Michael Lee's stepfather is brutally killed by Chris Partlow (Gbenga Akinnagbe) for intimated child abuse (4.10); the young corner boys in Season Four attack a rival group with urine-filled water balloons in retribution for beating up Dukie (4.01); and yellow paint is poured on officer Eddie Walker by the corner boys for his perceived overstepping of the mark (4.11). Raw and ruthless competition in the drugs trade is visible through the Barksdale Crew's antipathy towards Proposition Joe and the Eastside drug crews in Season One, and through their "war" with Marlo Stanfield's crew in Season Three. This is out-and-out competition over real estate, with high risks and high rewards; survival of the fittest, smartest and most ruthless. Yet it is a value which is couched in terms that resonate with widely-held beliefs on the nature of capitalism, perhaps most vividly through the mutual betrayal between Avon Barksdale and Stringer Bell in Season Three. Stringer sums this up succinctly in a graveyard rendezvous with Bunny Colvin to rat-out Avon Barksdale, justifying his betrayal of Barksdale with the statement that "it's just business" (3.11).

Stringer's attempts to bring a corporate mentality in Season Two, and his later efforts to transition to legitimate businessman, bring another dimension to *The Wire*'s account of drug crews. Barksdale and Bell both harbor ambitions to accumulate economic capital in the form of the profits generated by their illegal activities. Stringer, however, seems to wish to escape the boundaries of West Baltimore and move beyond the drug-dealing and front operations, such as the print shop and Orlando's strip club, to acquire economic capital in his own name, telling Barksdale shortly before his death:

> You know, Avon, you gotta think about what we got in this game for, man. Huh? Was it the rep? Was it so our names could ring out on some fucking ghetto street corner, man? No, man. There's games beyond the fucking game [3.10].

Proposition Joe coaches Marlo Stanfield on the laundering of money through the drug lawyer Maurice Levy (Michael Kostroff) in order to protect his profits. Prop Joe lectures Stringer Bell and, on at least two occasions, uses the phrase "buy for a dollar, sell for two" (2.07; 2.09) to encapsulate what he believes the Baltimore drug trade should be like. Even Fat Face Rick is caught in a minor scandal involving Council President Nerese Campbell in the opening episode of Season Five whereby he has acquired derelict property scheduled for redevelopment (5.01). It is clear that these men, despite their success in the drug trade, wish, to a greater or lesser extent, to become a legitimate part of American society or, at least, to straddle the line between criminality and legitimacy.

We see this acquiescence to the competitive vagaries of capitalism across all seasons. Even Season Two, which focuses on the plight of the unions, demonstrates a consensus with capitalism and American hegemony. The stevedores are proletarian, yet Frank Sobotka's efforts to save the union reveal that they are complicit in their own domination under the capitalist system. The stevedores take great pride in who they are; have their own codes and rules, and pursue their own forms of economic, social and cultural capital. Frank, in heated conversation with Bruce DiBiago, vents his anger at the degradation of the port industry and the introduction of technology to replace union workers:

> ... down here it's "who's your old man," till you got kids of your own, then it's "who's your son." But after the horror show I seen today. Robots! Piers full of Robots! My kid'll be lucky even if he's punchin' numbers five years from now. And while it don't mean shit to me I can't take my steak knives to DiBiago and Sons, it breaks my fuckin' heart that there's no future for the Sobotka's on the waterfront [2.07].

In contrast to the competitive nature of capitalism, we also see instances of cooperation. For example, Stringer Bell's efforts to establish a drug cartel in partnership with Proposition Joe and other drug kingpins, an initiative that is rejected in Season Three by Avon Barksdale and then in Season Four by Marlo Stanfield, shows an inherent contradiction of capitalism that cooperation can be preferable to competition in situations where mutual interest is served and agreement can be reached. As Proposition Joe comments in (3.05) "for a cold-ass crew of gangsters, y'all carried it like republicans and shit," referring to the cordial nature of the rival dealers in coming together for their mutual benefit.

Conclusion: Proposing the Concept of Extra-Hegemonic Activity

The Wire shows us instances whereby social groups which appear to be denied opportunities to participate in the American Dream nevertheless contribute to and benefit from its promises. Yet, while the responses of these groups, including the West Baltimore drug crews and the Locust Point stevedores, can be construed as illegal, they cannot be considered rebellion against American values. In many cases we see the motivations of various actors to maintain and extend their participation in the American Dream, even though they are increasingly excluded from legitimate routes to the realization of that goal. Their activities revolve around the accumulation of capital specific to the social institutions in which they primarily operate, complemented by a belief that anyone can achieve success if they apply themselves and work hard towards their goals. Of course, the different structures, conventions and practices of each field differentiate these fields, as does the type of capital available, yet there are several concepts which are common across all fields.

While David Simon and Ed Burns have clearly set out to lament several regrettable features of contemporary American society, what they unwittingly reveal is that participation in the American Dream is the one consistent motivation for every single group portrayed in *The Wire*. The actions and decisions of those involved in illegal activity cannot be construed as rebellion against the American Dream, but rather as a "structured improvisation," an attempt to continue participation and pursuit of goals despite exclusion from mainstream society and legitimate routes to success. These attempts can be seen in the callous, naked greed of kingpins like Avon, Stringer, Marlo and Prop Joe in the pursuit of wealth and reputation; in the desperation of the dockworkers to preserve their community and which drives them to theft; in the unethical journalism of Templeton in pursuit of greater recognition; and in the illegal attempt by Colvin to establish drug-tolerant zones in order to rescue his profession. At the root of all these actions is a commitment to the values at the heart of the American Dream, and although such examples may not conform to the methods prescribed by the state, they can be thought of as *extra-hege-*

monic: that is, as activities which aim to allow participation in the American Dream, but which reject the usual accepted and legitimate routes to participation as laid down by the state. *The Wire*, then, carries both ominous signs of the dysfunctional aspects of contemporary American society, but also that the bedrock of the American Dream, the values and aspirations associated with it, is arguably intact and unaffected. Such an argument gives hope to the notion that, even in spite of the major challenges faced by America in the early 21st century, the drive exhibited by the protagonists of *The Wire* suggests that the type of social decline depicted in the show can be arrested.

Works Cited

Alvarez, Rafael. *The Wire: Truth Be Told*. New York: Canongate, 2009.
Bourdieu, Pierre. "The Forms of Capital." *Handbook of Theory and Research for the Sociology of Education*. Ed. J. Richardson. New York: Greenwood, 1986. 241–258. Print.
Bourdieu, Pierre, and Loic Wacquant. *An Invitation to Reflexive Sociology*. Chicago: University of Chicago Press, 1992
Calhoun, Craig. "Pierre Bourdieu." *The Blackwell Companion to Major Social Theorists*. ed. G. Ritzer and Jeffrey Stepnisky. Cambridge, MA: Blackwell, 2011. 274–309. Print.
Gramsci, Antonio. *Selections from the Prison Notebooks of Antonio Gramsci*, 11th ed. New York: International, 1992.
Hornby, Nick. Interview with David Simon. *The Believer*. August 2007. Web. 18 November 2013.
Jenkins, Richard. *Pierre Bourdieu*. London: Routledge, 2003.
Rothkerch, Ian. "What drugs have not destroyed, the war on them has." Salonwww. 30 June 2002. Web. 15 November 2013.
Simon, David. "David Simon: 'There are now two Americas. My country is a horror show.'" *The Observer*. 8 December 2013. Web. 10 December 2013.
Vest, Jason. P. *The Wire, Deadwood, Homicide and NYPD Blue: Violence Is Power*: Santa Barbara: ABC-CLIO, 2011.
Vine, Richard. "Totally Wired." Guideblog, *The Guardian Unlimited*. 13 January 2005. Web. 10 December 2013.
Webb, Jen, Tony Schirato, and Geoff Danaher. *Understanding Bourdieu*. London: Sage, 2002.
Williams, Raymond. *Culture and Materialism: Selected Essays*. London: Verso, 2005.

"It's all in the game"
Citizenship as the "Missing Middle"[1]

Michael Lister

In this essay, I examine an oblique aspect of *The Wire*. I argue that citizenship is the missing middle of the celebrated HBO police procedural and that its absence is part of *The Wire*'s attempt to depict the consequences of a privatist, disengaged citizenry and thus to act as a prompt to civic engagement and participation.

The term citizen is only ever used in *The Wire* as a way of designating someone who is not in the drug trade, commonly referred to as "the game." The game, I will argue, is a term that comes to mean a number of different things, but underneath these different meanings, is a sense that it refers to competition, agency and the interaction with institutions. Thus, citizens are seen as lying outside of this realm. When this is added to the fact that "ordinary people" or citizens either do not feature prominently in the show, or do so only as passive victims or objects of institutions and other forces, the picture of citizenship that emerges in *The Wire* is a troubling one. It is one where citizens are absent, and there is a lack of civic engagement in public affairs. *The Wire* can thus be seen as a dystopian vision of "missing" citizenship.

The Wire has been lavished with praise as both entertainment and social commentary and analysis. Yet, despite many comments and views about the reality of *The Wire*, it remains a work of fiction; David Simon has repeatedly reinforced this: "It's fiction, I'm clear about that" (Simon, qtd. in Burkeman). It has frequently been compared to novels, particularly those of Dickens and Tolstoy. To an extent, this seems an appropriate comparison, as despite its televisual form, the structuring of the program (particularly the lack of dramatic arcs within episodes and the cumulative, developmental nature of the narrative) does seem novelistic. I.A. Richards describes a book as "a machine to think with" (qtd. in Porter Abbott 206) and indeed, although *The Wire* provides absorbing entertainment (albeit of a bleak, and at times dark, kind), its complexity compels the "reader" or the viewer to think, in a number of ways. The way that the narrative unfolds is complex and its poly-vocal and multi-strand structure requires the viewer to focus and concentrate; and indeed, that commentators of both left and right have found much in *The Wire* to support their world views attests to this lack of a definitive pedagogic message. It is also worth noting that Simon argues that one of the motivations for the focus of the Season Five on the media is the question as to why people are not aware of and talking about the problems and issues depicted in other series/scenes:

> Why [do] those problems seems so insolvable, why is it that we're not intensely aware of those problems? Why is the underclass so invisible? Why are the city schools so ineffective for so long? Why does the police department continue to embrace a dysfunctional drug war and manage to solve less and less crime with every year? And what is the political element doing about these things? You can ask the questions specifically of those institutions, but in the end, *the first question you have to ask is, what are we paying attention to?* [Simon, qtd. in McCabe, emphasis added].

I will go on to argue that this invitation or urging to contemplation is representative of a wider invocation to participation. *The Wire*, I will argue, presents a dystopian vision of a post-industrial city where citizens are defined by their absence and one of the major problems the city faces is that of the lack of civic virtue and engagement. Thus, *The Wire* is a call to recognize "missing" citizens and to think collectively about the challenges posed by this missing middle.

After a consideration of how the metaphor of the game features in *The Wire*, I will go onto how this relates to citizenship. Here I focus particularly on how citizens, in *The Wire*, are defined by being absent or outside of the game, concluding that this view, of absent or missing citizens, can be seen to act as a call to greater civic engagement.

"It's all in the game"

The term citizen is only ever used in *The Wire* in the context of the metaphor of the game. The game is one of the most frequently recurring motifs, themes and metaphors in *The Wire*. It is used in five distinct ways: in terms of the drug trade, as a claim to the equivalence of the drug trade with other "regular" or official institutions in Baltimore, as a comment on the constraints that individuals face, as institutional competition and finally, as a characterization of the struggle for agency and acquisition.

Thus, despite its initial usage in terms of the drug trade (to be "deep in the game" is to be heavily involved in the drug trade), the term grows to be used more and more outside of this original connotation. Politicians, the police and other characters often refer to their situations as "games." In part, this equation points to one of the major themes of *The Wire*, namely an equivalence (in structure, values and personnel to name but three aspects) between the institutions and organizations that make up the drug trade, and other institutions, particularly the police. This is a point made in a number of different respects, with characters in the drug trade and law enforcement being portrayed as not all that dissimilar. As the stick up artist Omar Little (Michael K. Williams) memorably states to the Barksdales' defense attorney Maurice Levy (Michael Kostroff) in the Season Two: "I got the shotgun. You got the briefcase. It's all in the game, though, right?" (2.01). Also worth noting is the view of Bill Zorzi, a writer and actor on the show, that "Politics is, after all, an insider's *game*" (qtd. in Alvarez 280, emphasis added).

The game, though, stands for more than a suggestion that the worlds of crime and law enforcement are not that dissimilar. David Simon has frequently, when asked to explain what *The Wire* is about, used language which invokes institutional or structural logics:

> We've basically taken the idea of Greek tragedy and applied it to the modern city state.... What we were trying to do was take the notion of Greek tragedy, of fated and doomed people, and instead of these Olympian gods, indifferent, venal selfish, hurling lightening bolts and hitting people in the ass for no reason— instead of these guys whipping it on Oedipus or Achilles, it's the postmodern institutions ... those are the indifferent gods [Simon, qtd. in Talbot, n.p.].

The point is also clearly made in Season Four, when Preston "Bodie" Broadus (J. D. Williams), a "soldier" or drug lieutenant expresses the idea that "this game is rigged man. We like them little bitches on a chessboard" (4.13). This statement echoes and draws the viewer back to a scene in the Season One where Bodie's then superior, D'Angelo Barksdale (Larry Gilliard, Jr.), explains the game of chess in terms of the drug trade (1.03). This sense of inevitability, of resignation to fates determined elsewhere, is seen in the way that at various moments, characters express the sentiment "It's all in the game." While at first, this statement seems to be invoked to explain why events occur in the drug trade (why, for example, someone gets beaten or murdered as a result of a particular action), as the series progress, other characters, such as corrupt politician Clay Davis (Isiah Whitlock, Jr.), invoke this same phrase. Indeed, it comes almost to stand as a proxy for a shrug of the shoulders and "that's life" as an explanation for events, which are sometimes the result of specific actions and other times seem random.[2]

Thus, a key notion, which underpins much of the five seasons, is the idea that individuals are heavily constrained in their choices and activities and that institutional logics can thwart the best of intentions, bending individual choices and decisions. In one sense, it is as good an exposition of the structure/agency dialectic as one is ever likely to see in modern entertainment media. Throughout the seasons, characters are shown struggling to achieve certain ends, working within, and sometimes against, institutional constraints. Sometimes, such as in the case of the police department, these are formal institutions, with (mostly) codified rules and norms; at other points, the institutions are more informal (the drug business, "the street"), and characters must both ascertain and learn to cope with the boundaries and rules. In both instances, characters are shown as both constrained and enabled by institutions. The rules of the game(s) facilitate certain characters to rise and others to fall. The institutional constraints privilege certain strategies over others, echoing Jessop's notion of "strategic selectivity," where the terrain is structured so that certain strategies are more likely to succeed than others. Thus, it is not the case that all actors, and all strategies, are equally constrained. What *The Wire* manages to graphically portray is that individuals' aims and ambitions are not all that matters. More than this, the show also depicts attempts (of varying success—indeed, it must be noted that *The Wire* while allowing for agency, does seem to lean towards structural determination) to change and reform the structural terrain and context. Whether this is Russell "Stringer" Bell's (Idris Elba) attempts to make the drug game about business rather than bodies, Major "Bunny" Colvin's (Robert Wisdom) attempts to decriminalize drugs in Hamsterdam, or Frank Sobotka's (Chris Bauer) attempts to preserve the dockworkers' employment and livelihoods, *The Wire* consistently depicts characters attempting to reform and change the structures and contexts around them. In this regard, when Sobotka is informed that "the writing is on the wall" for the longshoremen, his defiant response of "fuck the wall" (2.05), is perhaps one of the clearest, if ultimately futile, examples of attempts to shift the game.

Thus, as Talbot suggests, the game "emerges during the course of the show as a metaphor for the web of constraints that political and economic institutions impose upon the people trapped within them" (n.p.). As the drug dealer and aspiring property entrepreneur Bell argues, when trying to persuade Avon Barksdale (Wood Harris) that they should diversify out of the drug "game," "There's games beyond the fucking game" (3.10). The game thus comes to represent a number of things. At one level it stands for the struggle of individuals to assert themselves in the institutional context; that one has to play games ("the numbers game" of official statistics is a prominent and recurring example) in order to get on and to survive. Yet it also seems to represent the conflict across and between institutions; the ways in which the institutions of the drug trade, police and local government interact and compete.

It is interesting to reflect on quite what the game is in terms of its aims, or how one can "win." In one sense, *The Wire* suggests that the game is impossible and that one cannot win. In Season Four, the statement is clearly made when Roland "Prez" Pryzbylewski (Jim True-Frost) states, "No one wins, the other side just loses more slowly" (4.04). As noted above, the game is about agency and exerting influence, but these are power games are futile in that no one seems to win. Even if they do seem to win, as Thomas Carcetti (Aidan Gillen) does when he defeats the incumbent Clarence Royce (Glynn Turman) in the Democratic primary, their capacity for agency remains heavily constrained. Despite Carcetti's electoral victory, his capacity to effect change is heavily circumscribed. Thus constraints, while omnipresent, are experienced differently.

The game also seems to be about acquisition; about, if not material gain, then certainly gain in other terms. Indeed, the notion of a game, even if it is one that does not seem to end or be won (and thus have clear winners and losers), does imply competition, as indicated by Avon Barksdale's injunction to "Play or you gonna get played" (2.04). Some characters, such as Omar and Davis, play for financial gain; some, such as Jimmy McNulty (Dominic West) and Carcetti, play for their own personal needs; some, such as Royce, Bill Rawls (John Doman) and Jay Landsman (Delaney Williams), play for career advancement in the police hierarchy, while Marla Daniels (Maria Broom) attempts to advance in the political sphere. While this characterization of their motivation is somewhat rigid, and their reasons for playing the game shift over the five seasons, all the characters who are portrayed as playing the game are seen to be doing so for some kind of self-interested, personal benefit. For example, McNulty's sometimes obsessive pursuit of the Barksdale operation, and of Stringer Bell in particular, has less to do with serving justice than it has with satisfying his own need to prove his own abilities. In his case at least, the game is a somewhat individualistic engagement. Indeed, given its depiction of bureaucratic failure and how institutions fail despite the best efforts of the individuals involved as their logics produce sub optimal outcomes, *The Wire* could be seen (and has been by some conservative critics), as representing some tenets of public choice theory[3]; another game metaphor awaits.

To sum up, in *The Wire*, the metaphor of the game is used in five distinct senses. Aside from the original use as a description of the drug trade, it also represents the equivalence between the drug trade and the "normal" institutions in the city, the institutional constraints individuals encounter, institutional competition and a struggle for agency and acquisition.

The Missing Middle?

One fascinating aspect of *The Wire*'s use of the game metaphor, which comes to stand as a metaphor for many of the show's broader thematic points, concerns the way in which the language of citizen and citizenship is used in relation to it. The term citizen is only ever employed as a way of defining someone who lies outside the game. This usage is clearly illustrated in this example of two of the detectives, McNulty and "Bunk" Moreland (Wendell Pierce) interviewing a suspect for the murder of a witness:

> MCNULTY: And it's not like you did anything real bad—throwing a couple of hot ones at Pooh Blanchard. I mean, no one's going to miss that motherfucker right?
> BUNK: But you know the man who got killed this time? You know who that poor son of a bitch was?
> MCNULTY: A citizen
> BUNK: Worked every goddamn day of his life [1.02].

Omar invokes a similar distinction when stating that he has "never put my gun on no citizen" (2.06) and Reginald "Bubs" Cousins (Andre Royo), the addict turned police informant, uses the term in the same way when asked if there is anyone in West Baltimore that he does not know, and responds, "Just citizens" (3.10). At one level, the distinction goes back to the original meaning of the game metaphor, the drug trade. The term citizen is used to refer to someone not in the drug trade; a taxpayer who has a job, and is not a drug dealer or a drug user. One might be tempted to pass over this interesting semantic aspect of *The Wire* if it was not for two further aspects. The first is that *The Wire* is a very carefully composed piece which gives the impression that, while there may be scenes that are not central to moving the narrative onwards, and which may only be there to evoke mood or character, nothing is present by accident. To view it as an accident would be a strange reading of such a meticulously composed narrative and social cartography.

The second issue is that if texts and narratives like *The Wire* can indeed be thought of as machines to think with, then some of the most thought provoking aspects can be the silences and omissions. One such absence, and one that I find striking is the almost total absence of citizens, or "ordinary people."[4] The world depicted in *The Wire* is one of a game across and between the core (in the form of state institutions such as the police, local political offices and the educational system) and the margins (those in the drug trade, addicts and the dispossessed). Absent almost entirely are "ordinary" citizens.[5] One could argue, of course, that many of the individuals who staff the state institutions are themselves citizens, middle class, "ordinary people" in that they are taxpayers with jobs. However, I would contend that their characterization is almost wholly in terms of their roles within the state. Very few of the characters are afforded much of a private life, and when such aspects are shown, it is invariably to enrich our understanding of their behavior in their formal, state, role.

I argue that citizens are almost entirely absent, and that where they do appear, they do so only fleetingly, and in passive roles. Citizens appear as frustrated and besieged attendees at local community meetings where nothing gets done, or, worse still as victims of the game in the form of murdered witnesses. If, as Omar says, "the game is out there. And it's either play or get played" (1.07), then in *The Wire*, it seems citizens, as non-players of the game, are getting played. Of course, one might argue that the missing middle (class) is simply a geographical aspect of American cities (and maybe many western urban locales), with regard to which *The Wire* is entirely accurate in its depiction.

Yet, taken with the above reflections on the deliberate and recurring use of citizen, as someone who is not in the game, a picture of citizenship does emerge in *The Wire*. Citizens, in the sense of individuals emanating from, or participating in some kind of civil society, are mostly absent (interesting in itself in a program dedicated to providing an accurate representation of the life of an American city) and divorced from the game of agency and institutional interactions, or indeed, the many "games" where other characters strive for agency and purpose. It is a hollowed out picture of citizenship, a passive conception where citizens have very little to do with urban life and urban interactions, other than as passive victims. Returning to the analysis of the game metaphor above, this also implies that citizens lack agency; that they are "being played," by the various institutions depicted in *The*

Wire. The term citizen, in its original meaning, meant not the member of a nation state, but a member of a particular city. In French, *citoyen* referred to membership of a city. David Simon has pointed out that ultimately, *The Wire* is about the city (Simon, "The Wire was not about McNulty"), yet it is a city without citizens.

It is interesting at this point to pause to consider quite what is missing; if citizens are indeed absent from *The Wire*, what is not there and what does this mean? There is a sense in which individual rights are lost or diminished in *The Wire*, or as Alvarez (46) puts it, "*The Wire* is making a case for the motivations of people trying to get by in a society in which individual institutions have more rights than human beings." Yet *The Wire* does not present a world in which individualism is under threat; it presents a world where individualism has become rampant and that this threatens the rights and protections of marginal groups and individuals. An oft-cited crisis around citizenship is one of identity and cohesion; under the conditions of globalization, identities become fluid and unstable and that this has unsettling effects on communities and individuals (see Turner; Scobey; Joppke). In *The Wire*, citizenship in this sense is either absent or diminished, yet I wish to focus on something else.

Citizenship has been seen, from its republican roots onwards,[6] as involving participation; to be a citizen is to participate in the life of one's political community. For republicans, freedom requires citizens to participate in government; a failure to participate will result in laws and decisions, which ordinary people have had no hand in authoring, being made which impact and impinge upon them (Pettit; Skinner). Furthermore, if people do not participate, political power will come to reside with factions and cliques, with inevitably deleterious consequences. Indeed, a passing glance back at the *Federalist Papers* (Hamilton, Maddison and Jay), reveals that such beliefs and propositions lie at the very heart of the founding of the American state. It is this sense of citizenship which *The Wire* depicts as glaringly absent. Without individuals' participation in political and social life, all kinds of negative consequences follow. The liberal thinker John Rawls phrases the position thus:

> The idea is that without widespread participation in democratic politics by a vigorous and informed citizen body, and certainly with a general retreat into private life, even the most well defined political institutions will fall into the hands of those who seek to dominate and impose their will through the state apparatus either for the sake of power and military glory or for reasons of class and economic interest, not to mention expansionist religious fervour and nationalist fanaticism. The safety of democratic liberties requires the active participation of

citizens who possess the political virtues needed to maintain a constitutional regime [Rawls 272].

It is this kind of privatism, and the consequences thereof, which is depicted in *The Wire*. Institutions do seem to fall into the hands of those who would use them for their own purposes as individuals retreat beyond the public into the private sphere. Indeed, one could argue that this is one of the fundamental problems on display in *The Wire*, namely the absence of an ethos of public good in public institutions and furthermore, their exploitation to fulfill private agendas and goals. Arguably, this is only possible in a context of limited civic engagement. This absence is seen in comments such as that by Marla Daniels to her husband, that he should not get involved in the games played in the police department and should retreat to private law practice: "The game is rigged, but you cannot lose if you do not play" (1.02).

This "missing middle" is something that David Simon has commented upon, specifically in terms of this accusation that the Baltimore portrayed in *The Wire* is partial and that it ignores, in particular, the black middle class that exists there. It links to the notion that *The Wire* is a portrayal of the "other" America. Acknowledging that the "real" Baltimore is not exhausted by the depictions in *The Wire*, and that there are more positive aspects to it, Simon maintains that some of the places portrayed in *The Wire* are true to life:

> And yet there are places in Baltimore where *The Wire* is not at all hyperbole, where all of the depicted tragedy and waste and dysfunction are fixed, certain and constant. And that place is, I might add, about 20 blocks from where I live. That is the context of *The Wire* and that is the only context in which Baltimore—and by reasonable extension, urban America—can be fairly regarded. *There are two Americas—separate, unequal, and no longer even acknowledging each other except on the barest cultural terms. In the one nation, new millionaires are minted every day. In the other, human beings no longer necessary to our economy, to our society, are being devalued and destroyed* [Simon "The escalating breakdown," emphasis added].

Bringing these aspects together, what emerges is a view of *The Wire* offering not just a critique of the drug war, urban problems and the policy responses, but also a critique of western privatist citizenship. The fundamental disconnect between citizens in *The Wire* is starkly illuminated by the virtual exclusion of "ordinary citizens." There are some occasions when this disconnect is spoken to directly. In a brilliant scene, McNulty takes Bubs to his son's football match in a leafy suburb. The discomfort of the character in such an environment is shown, but, in an effective piece of editing, when McNulty drops Bubs off, the leafy normality of a child's school football game is brutally contrasted to the deprivation of the area where Bubs calls home: "thin line between heaven and here," he says as he gets out of the car (1.04).

While there are forms of public participation depicted in *The Wire*, these do not seem to aim at a collective good. The drug co-op, for example, that Joseph "Proposition Joe" Stewart (Robert F. Chew) forms and chairs, stands as an example of this, yet it is not *political* participation and it is not underpinned by civic virtue, a concern with the public good, but rather with a concern for the preservation of private good and economic gain. Similarly, while there are depictions of citizens being involved in civic affairs, such as the residents who attend community meetings in order to harangue the police, this involvement is neither widespread, nor is there effective influence on public institutions as "powerless" citizens make the same complaints about the slow death of their communities. In this sense, citizens lack agency and the structural terrain on which they live and exist, is one with few opportunities for political expression. It is interesting to note that one of the main instances of direct political participation by a major character (outside of the political "game"), when Randy Wagstaff (Maestro Harrell) delivers election flyers across the Westside, is motivated by finance and the $50 he is paid (4.06).

When the term citizen is used, it seems, as noted above, that the prime quality which marks someone out as a citizen is that they work, that they are in gainful employment rather than the drug game. It seems, therefore, that in the world depicted in *The Wire*, civic virtue and public participation are neither present, nor are they seen as core characteristics of the citizen, who is, rather, defined in primarily economic terms. Indeed, this economic foundation to the concept of citizenship which underpins *The Wire* and the corrosive effects of this are noted by Simon. He makes the argument that the logics and structures which underpin economic activity spill into other areas: "We saw there were elements in the culture that were parasitic and self-aggrandising, that the greed and rapaciousness of a society that exalted profit and free markets to the exclusion of any other social framework would be burdened by that level of greed" (Simon, "The Wire was not about McNulty"). He goes on to point to that this rampant (economic) individualism has contributed to a decline in civic virtue and cohesion and a sense of contempt for "offering citizens anything approximating a sense of communal purpose" (Simon, "The Wire was not about McNulty").

Thus, in *The Wire* citizens are defined in economic terms, yet this economy has encouraged a retreat from collective endeavor and civic virtue. Citizens are seen to be outside the "games," to be powerless and frequently victims of a game being played out by, in, and across institutions over which they exercise little or no influence. This is indeed a disturbing and depiction of citizenship, yet more worryingly still, one that perhaps resonates with viewers who are fearful, overwhelmed by public problems, distrustful of political actors and institutions, and who instead retreat inwards to the private sphere. What is perhaps somewhat ambiguous, to return to the language of structure and agency, is the explanation for this state of affairs; is it one where a structural context so limits the means for significant civic engagement, that citizens turn away, inwards to private concerns? Or has rampant individualism led to a state of ossified public institutions, which are then ripe for certain individuals to use for their own personal gains? Or some dialectic interplay of the two?

Thus the absence of citizens and "ordinary people" is not a problem (in the sense of something which undermines the veracity or impact of its narrative, as Atlas and Dreier argue) for *The Wire*. It is a very deliberate narrative device to illustrate social fragmentation. As Simon states, "at all points, when filming our drama, we understood that we were arguing the case of one America to the other" (Simon "The escalating breakdown"). One wonders, therefore, whether *The Wire* represents a challenge to citizens, or, rather a call to citizenship. Is *The Wire*, as well as depicting the problems of urban decay and distemper, also a picture of a broken citizenship? As a picture of urban decay, *The Wire* is somewhat overwhelming; there seems to be no way out. Indeed, the blunt (and given the subtlety of what has gone before, slightly heavy-handed) end to the show in Season Five makes plain that the game just goes on. Yet such a pessimistic conclusion would be to ignore some of the important aspects of *The Wire*. Rather is the story not that, *if nothing is done to change things*, the game rolls on and on? As Simon and Burns write in a new afterword to *The Corner*:

> This is the America we have built and paid for, and therefore the America that all of us deserve. Perhaps it is possible to pay for something more, for something better. But not without first acknowledging honestly the depth and complexity of the problem itself [Simon & Burns 627–8].

The picture painted by *The Wire* is a troubling one; indeed, how could it be otherwise? It is particularly troubling because, despite the fact that *The Wire* is sometimes criticized for being partisan (Bowden, n.p.), it resists any simple (or any) policy solutions (while both of the main writers, Simon and Burns are very clearly in favor of decriminalizing drugs, the outcomes of this policy choice as displayed in the series in terms of Hamsterdam, are ambiguous). It does not pretend to have any answers. There are no obvious solutions lying out there, there are no white knights who will come in and rescue us (Carcetti is a wonderfully ambivalent character in this respect).

The absence of citizens in *The Wire* is, I contend, an omission which speaks to fundamental fissures and fractures within contemporary polities; one of which is the tendency to privatism in many western, liberal, capitalist economies. This seems to reflect the response of many (such as Marla Daniels, noted above) to the seemingly intractable nature of cycles of decay. This may sound like it is slipping towards another work which made use of game metaphors. But while Robert Putnam's *Bowling Alone* might have meticulously depicted the minutiae of the decline of civic participation in America, the portrayal in *The Wire* of the consequences is visceral. Indeed, by creating such vivid characters to populate the fictional narrative, one effect is to bridge the gaps that currently mark many western liberal capitalist polities and to make real the consequences of, among other things, a lack of civic engagement. As Jones argues, "On *The Wire* there really is no such thing as 'them.' There is only us." It is possible, therefore, that despite occluding citizenship, *The Wire* represents one of the most vibrant and urgent calls for it. If public institutions are all too frequently lacking in a public good ethos, and exploited for narrow individual gains, it seems to fall back to citizens to do something about it. While there may be few "simple" solutions overtly advocated to the problems illuminated in *The Wire*, it might be that one step towards such answers lies in one of the elements missing.

Conclusion

The Wire is an extremely dense and complex piece of storytelling, with a strong air of verisimilitude. At its best it marries careful depiction of complex urban problems, with sensitive and luminous characterization which renders social problems vivid; as more than simple statistics. The rhetoric of the game abounds in *The Wire* and this metaphor is one of competition, of institutions, and of agency. In conjunction with the virtual absence of ordinary people, civil society or citizens, I find it intriguing that the term citizen is used to designate someone outside of the game. It seems to me that among all the failure and problems shown in *The Wire*, one that is very subtly portrayed is the failure or absence of citizenship. One of the problems in *The Wire* is that the citizens of this "missing middle," although let down by their institutions, are not involved with them and in them. Burns and Simon may overstate their case in this depiction (and Atlas and Dreier level precisely this accusation, suggesting that there is far more civic engagement in West Baltimore than is portrayed) yet the point is that it invites the viewer/reader to think and to consider. As mentioned earlier, it is perhaps in this area that *The Wire*'s greatest contribution lies; as a compelling and vivid narrative which resists easy answers and thus draws the viewer/reader into a contemplation of contemporary urban politics and a call to a more active and engaged citizenry.

NOTES

1. Earlier versions of this paper were presented to the "Aesthetics and International Relations: Exploring the Frontiers of Visual and Cultural Politics" workshop, held at the University of Birmingham 11/07/09 and the "Reading *the Wire*" panel at the ECPR Conference in Potsdam 10/09/09. I am very grateful to Jill Steans and Debbie Lisle and the BISA Art & Politics Working Group for their comments and for organizing these sessions. I would also like to thank editors Justin Gest, Oz Hassan, Rico Isaacs, Lee Jarvis, David Norman and Emily Pia for feedback and comments. The usual disclaimers apply.
2. See also Anderson (373–4), who argues that the phrase "the game is the game" functions as a tautology that serves to reinforce the inescapability of certain outcomes.
3. Public Choice Theory is a derivative of Rational Choice Theory, and much work in this tradition has focused on how public institutions produce sub-optimal outcomes by, for example, public employees seeking to maximize their department budget, even if this comes at the expense of efficiency.
4. It is worth noting that this is obviously not the only omission in the show. Women, for example, are perhaps underrepresented.
5. This is not to suggest, of course, that members of the drug gangs, the addicts and the dispossessed are not citizens. Although it is interesting to note that characters like Bubs do not view themselves as citizens.
6. Here meant in the sense of political philosophy of engaged and responsible citizenship, rather than as referring to the Republican Party.

WORKS CITED

Alvarez, R. *The Wire: Truth Be Told*. London: Cannongate, 2009. Print.
Anderson, P. A. "'The Game Is the Game': Tautology and Allegory in *The Wire*" *Criticism*, 52, 3–4 (2010): pp. 373–398. Print.
Atlas, J., and P. Dreier. "Is *The Wire* too cynical?" *Dissent* (Summer 2008). Print.
Bowden, M. "The Angriest Man in Television," *The Atlantic*, Jan/Feb 2008. Print.
Burkeman, O. (2009) "Arrogant? Moi?" *The Guardian*, 28/02/09. Print.
Hamilton, A., J. Madison, and J. Jay. *The Federalist Papers*. 1788. New York: Signet Classic, 2003. Print.
Jessop, B. *State Power*. London: Polity Press, 2007. Print.
Jones, K. "Down in the hole." *Sight and Sound* (May 2008). Print.
Joppke, C. "The Retreat of Multiculturalism in the Liberal State: Theory and Policy." *British Journal of Sociology* 55, 2 (2004): 237–57. Print.
McCabe, B. "Case Closed. David Simon: *The Wire* Exit Interview." *Baltimore City Paper*, 12/3/08. Available online at http://www.citypaper.com/news/story.asp?id=15437 .
Pettit, P. *Republicanism: A Theory of Freedom and Government*. Oxford: Clarendon Press, 1997. Print.
Porter Abbott, H. *The Cambridge Introduction to Narrative*. Cambridge: Cambridge University Press, 2008. Print.
Putnam, R. *Bowling Alone: The Collapse and Revival of American Community*. New York: Simon & Schuster, 2000. Print.

Rawls, J. "The Priority of Right and Ideas of the Good." *Philosophy and Public Affairs* 17, 4 (1988): 251–76. Print.
Scobey, D. "The Specter of Citizenship." *Citizenship Studies*, 5, 1 (2001): 11–26
Simon, D. *The Culture Show*, BBC, 15/07/08.
_____. "The escalating breakdown of urban society across the U.S.." *The Guardian*, 6/09/08. Print.
_____. (2009) "The Wire was not about McNulty..." *The Big Issue*, 30/10/09. Print.
_____, and E. Burns. *The Corner: A Year in the Life of an Innercity Neighbourhood*. 1997. Edinburgh: Canongate, 2009. Print.
Skinner, Q. "Machiavelli on the Maintenance of Liberty." *Politics*, 18, 2 (1983): 3–15. Print.
Talbot, M. "Stealing Life: The crusader behind *"The Wire."* *The New Yorker*, 22/10/07. Print.
Turner, B. "The Erosion of Citizenship." *British Journal of Sociology* 52, 2 (1991): 189–209. Print.

PART TWO

"The Target": The War on Drugs and Its Cost

The Corners of Crime

ROBERT ANDERSSON, JØRGEN BRUHN
and ANNE GJELSVIK

"What is the answer?" "I am not sure, but whatever it is, it can't be a lie."—Major Howard "Bunny" Colvin

Using cop-shows as social commentary is relatively rare; doing it in the way it is done in *The Wire* is exceptional. Whereas HBO originally considered *The Wire* to be a standard police procedural, creator David Simon has often been quoted as saying that *The Wire* is "a visual novel" that was conceived of as "storytelling that speaks to our current condition" (2009, 4). Much of the academic attention the program has accrued, however, has come from television researchers who have been most interested in the series' narrative and aesthetic achievements while the representation of crime has only been discussed rather briefly by criminologists and social science scholars (see, for instance, Mittell *Television*; Potter and Marshall).

In their article "*The Wire* and the World," Helena Sheehan and Sheamus Sweeney fittingly described the series as a panoramic, provoking and political depiction of a post-industrial America in decay (Sheehan and Sweeney). With its open structure, *The Wire* poses complicated political and ideological questions rather than attempting to deliver more or less clear-cut answers or solutions to the problems represented. By doing so, the show can be seen as a different form of crime fiction than typical crime shows (Bruhn and Gjelsvik). In this sense, the particular focus is on the series' representations of the "War on Drugs," the intricate relations between social institutions and the reasons behind crime, and on crime solving. David Simon has frequently been openly critical of the War on Drugs, for instance when he described the conflict as a "war on the poor" and a social control mechanism that in fact makes American cities less safe (Vuillamy and Ray). Simon continues to be involved in the public debate, one example of this being his participation in the critically acclaimed documentary *The House I Live In* (Jarecki, 2012).

The aim of this chapter is to discuss *The Wire* as a commentary on current crime politics, a politics that has manifested itself in a War on Drugs, mass imprisonment, and zero-tolerance policing. Our argument is that *The Wire* critiques a policy that frames the drug problem as an individual problem that can be erased by expunging the criminal individual, by instead presenting the viewer with a harm reduction perspective wherein drugs are an inescapable feature of contemporary society. As such, the problem cannot be completely eliminated, but the harm caused by drug use can be reduced. Our approach to such questions is through a combination of disciplines, and therefore also perspectives, which have not been combined until now. In order to describe central aspects of the series, we employ a multi-disciplinary approach that includes media-historical aspects, criminology, literary theory and sociology. Consequently, this chapter discusses *The Wire* both as an aesthetic phenomenon (which must be analyzed by way of narratology and thematic analysis) and as a representation of societal facts (which demands analysis based on sociological, historical and criminological perspectives). The paper asks what *The Wire* is reacting to, in terms of crime-preventing politics and contemporary American urban developments, and what questions *The Wire* poses, via criticism and fictive narration. The paper also discusses the possibilities of fictional "investigations" such as *The Wire*, compared to conventional criminological research and debate, and we discuss the series against two different forms of policing, zero-tolerance and harm reduction.

More specifically, the discussion focuses on the representation of "Hamsterdam" (a confined "free zone" where the police do not intervene against drug-dealing or use of drugs), which is seen as the series' attempt to investigate, in fictional form, the possibility of legalizing drugs. The series questions whether such an initiative actually minimizes drug-related crime and whether it could have positive consequences, not only for drug addicts but also for the surrounding society. We sketch the background and the development of the establishing of a free zone and discuss the results of the experiment, by drawing on M.M. Bakhtin's idea of polyphony.

Our analysis shows that, following the entire "poetics" or design of *The Wire*, the series debates criminological questions by posing questions rather than answers. Consequently, the failure of the free zone (described below) does not entail a total refusal of the idea of legalizing drugs.

Context: U.S. Crime Policy

The Wire comments on a United States wherein the inner city life of post-industrial cities like Baltimore is experiencing an ongoing process of decay, where entire city areas are taken over by "the game," that is, the drug trade. Standing guard against the decay is a police department that relies on brute force and proactive police work that consists of constantly harassing the players of the game. In order to understand the setting of *The Wire*, it is necessary to consider the trajectory of American crime policy. What are the origins of the bleak picture painted in *The Wire*?

Firstly, it is important to understand the ideological notion of the African American culture (or, rather, subculture) as a culture of poverty that brought with it the emergence of an entire underclass. Secondly, it is important to understand how the root causes of crime, such as social and economic structures, became redundant to this picture. Thirdly, one must comprehend how the policing strategy known as "zero-tolerance" could become a viable and rational solution to crime. The following looks at the phenomena of mass imprisonment.

Since the 1980s, the U.S. has created a unique penal form that has been conceptualized as "mass imprisonment" (Garland, J. Simon). Whereas comparable countries have a prison population ranging from 44 to 150 per 100,000 people, the rate in the U.S. is 750 per 100,000 people (Walmsley). Mass imprisonment has three distinct features: its scope, its categorical application and its increasingly warehouse-like or even waste management-like qualities. Simon (141) writes that, "[i]f present [imprisonment] trends continue, nearly one in 15 Americans born in 2001 will serve time in prison during their lifetimes." An even more incriminating picture emerges if these figures are broken down by ethnicity; based on current trends, one in three African Americans and one in seven Hispanics will serve time in prison (Bonczar in J. Simon). On this basis, "[t]he odds of an African American man going to prison today are higher than the odds he will go to college, get married, or go into the military" (J. Simon 141). At the heart of this process is the so-called War on Drugs. The clampdown on drugs depicted in *The Wire* is causing the mass imprisonment.

The War on Drugs dramatized in *The Wire* is part of a conservative political reaction to what was depicted as a lenient welfare society that pampered its citizenry by being permissive. According to Lilly et al. (234) this conservative turn in crime policy was a reaction to a social order seen to have been caused by "bleeding-heart liberals" and political movements like the feminist and civil rights movements; a politics of excess that had come to corrupt American policy during the 1960s. Richard Nixon's law-and-order and the War on Drugs was thus a politics conceived of to end a period that, brought on by what was considered to be a morally decadent, secular culture relying on liberal welfare-state policies, was seen to have made social dependents out of the poor and minorities.

From this period emerged the idea of a new social phenomenon, this being the underclass, a new stratum of society defined as "[...] a caste of people free from basic wants but almost totally dependent upon the state, with little hope of breaking free" (Anderson 56). Alongside this development came the depiction of inner-city deprivation as something caused by a culture of poverty. This cultural explanation claimed that the poor have a unique value system and that they would remain in poverty because they would adapt to the burdens of poverty. The conceptualization of poverty among minorities as a culture of poverty started with the Moynihan Report, *The Negro Family: The Case For National Action* (1965). The report claimed that the root causes of African American poverty in America were hard to solve because of the relative absence of nuclear families. Without the means to support a family, the report claimed, African American men would ultimately become alienated from their roles as husbands and fathers. This, in turn, would cause an increase in divorce rates, abandonment and out-of-wedlock births. What emerges from this is an idea of an underclass primarily made up of minorities that inhabit the inner cities of the U.S. due to a culture of poverty, which is infected by drug abuse.

According to Lilly et al. (244 ff.) this led in the 1980s to cultural explanations of poverty and the blame placed on the liberal welfare state merging with a conservative criminology that explained crime in terms of biology, human nature and intelligence. This was a criminology built on the consistent denial of the importance of any form of economic inequality or disadvantages as the root cause of crime. Crime was viewed either as a rational choice or as the result of biological inferiority. Disregarding the root causes of crime was a central factor in the establishment of Reagan's War on Drugs and zero-tolerance policing. When crime is depicted as something that emanates from individual shortcomings caused by biological or intellectual inferiority, there is no room left to blame society. One of *The Wire*'s unique features, as a crime show, is its emphasis on the root causes of crime. Sometimes the show can almost be read as a filmed criminological textbook on theories of crime. Whereas other mainstream crime dramas, such as *CSI* or *Criminal Minds,* totally invest in the prevailing conservative criminological understanding of crime as individual pathology, *The Wire*'s narrative only stresses the social and economic structures that have shaped urban African American life.

The framing of crime as an individual problem, rather than a social problem, is a prerequisite for the law-and-order politics that is synonymous with the War on Drugs. This war incorporates a style of policing now known as zero-tolerance policing (Wacquant). The War on Drugs targets every type of drug handling as a criminal act, upon which the police come down hard. The interesting feature in this policy is that this not only *combats* crime, but has become a way of *preventing* crime. This preventive capacity emerges out of the framing of crime as an individual problem. Consequently, different strategies that aim to remove potential culprits are also framed as crime prevention (Andersson and Nilsson). *The Wire* questions the assumptions behind this policy, as well as the policy in itself. The opposite of a zero-tolerance approach to the drug problem is harm reduction. Therefore, the Hamsterdam project exemplifies harm reduction and, as such, questions the U.S. government's War on Drugs. Consequently, Hamsterdam can be seen a case of peacekeeping policing, a harm-reduction policing strategy that builds on keeping the peace by not clamping down on unlawful behavior that does not threaten the peace on the streets: in other words, the opposite of zero-tolerance policing. Peacekeeping policing, even though an old feature in policing, can thus be seen as a sort of harm reduction in that it does advocate minimizing the control damages in that it builds on assessing the negative effects of the use of forceful law enforcement on social order. When Major Howard "Bunny" Colvin (Robert Wisdom) delivers a speech explaining to his officers why they should pursue the Hamsterdam "free zone" project, he addresses what policing should or should not be and exemplifies it with the brown paper bag used to conceal the unlawful public consumption of alcohol (3.04). While zero-tolerance policing cracks down on illegal as well as semi-illegal acts, and thus would not accept public drinking even if concealed by the brown paper bags, peacekeeping policing is about maintaining the peace; as long as the peace is kept, a police officer keen on keeping the peace should overlook the case of public consumption of alcohol. The benefit of Hamsterdam as a form of peacekeeping policing, therefore, is that it maintains peace on the streets.

An Aesthetics for Crime Problem Solving

In many respects, *The Wire* is well situated within a realistic tradition of American crime fiction, with predecessors such as Sidney Lumet's film *Prince of the City* (1981), and television shows such as NBC's *Hill Street Blues* (Steven Boccho 1981–1987) and, in particular, *Homicide: Life on the Street* (Paul Attansio 1993–1999). Telling a story not about criminals, but about contemporary society, it follows that the cast of characters is not limited to police and criminals. In Season Four, for instance, children and teachers play important roles. The perspectives are also broader. The main issues in *Hill Street Blues* were the work and lives of the police officers. In *The Wire*, however, the main topic is crime and the way it links several sectors of the community. Brian G. Rose has described the show is a "direct assault against the cop show, the most venerable of TV genres" (Rose 82).

The Wire stands out in contrast to other contemporary crime series' goal-oriented and fast forward dramaturgy. First and foremost, compared to contemporary crime-solving narratives, things take time. In contrast to, for instance, *CSI*'s rapid searches in digital archives of fingerprints and DNA samples, it takes several episodes just to set up a relatively simple wire-tap. It takes the detectives hours to type reports on typewriters and long lists of unsolved cases are always visible on the investigators' whiteboard. Kjetil Sandvik has stressed the substantial differences between the depiction of forensics in fiction and in real life, where the tedious work of the technicians is the rule, as opposed to the exceptionally quick findings on crime sites that are so common in crime fiction (Sandvik 298–299).

Although, as the name suggests, *CSI* does investigate *crime scenes* (at least, in the original series set in Las Vegas), these series focus primarily on physical evidence. Such investigations, to a much larger extent, take place in the minds of the criminalists and in the laboratory. In *The Wire*, the police work is situated where the crime takes place, and once again, *The Wire* clearly indicates the failure of a police strategy focusing on "the stats" instead of pragmatic, harm reducing policing in actual contexts. This focus on actual experience in specific settings may explain one of the most striking features of the series, namely its extended use of locations. While series such as *CSI Miami* or *CSI: NY* include the names of the respective location cities in their titles, *The Wire*'s representation of Baltimore becomes one of its main elements. It could even be argued that Baltimore is a character—or *the* character—in the series (Marshall and Potter 13, D.Simon 3). For instance, most of Season Two takes place at the docks of the Port of Baltimore and Season Four is centered around the fictional Edward J. Tilghman Middle School. Using M.M. Bakhtin's concept of the chronotope, we might say that *The Wire* offers a realistic version of time and space as compared to the conventional cop shows' "adventure"-like time-space contexts (see Bruhn and Gjelsvik for a discussion of the important role of "the streets" of Baltimore from a Bakhtinian point of view).

In addition, the show does not make it easy for a casual viewer to catch up with the show: episodes do not open with recaps of previous storylines, and neither do they usually provide the closure or climaxes that viewers tend to expect (Rose 87). Instead of offering a solution to an investigation or the closure of a case, an episode usually ends by focusing on the situation for one of its many characters. As Detective Ellis Carver (Seth Gilliam) tellingly remarks in the very first episode, the War on Drugs has no ending. In a similar way, the closure of a season is typically constructed as a montage of the situations for several characters.

Although the war does not come to an end, and crime mysteries are not solved, the series does suggest solutions to the drug problems, most directly in the Hamsterdam theme in Season Three. The Hamsterdam storyline occupies the centerpiece (in several senses of the word) of the entire series. Not only is the experiment central to Seasons Three, but it also occupies a central thematic or argumentative place because it shows how the conventional methods of fighting drugs are useless, while at the same time stressing that there are no easy solutions to the complicated drug problem. The Hamsterdam experiment is initiated as the result of the failure of War on Drugs, which, it could be said, is the overarching subject of the entire series. At the same time, it is one of the very few examples of problems being dealt with proactively, as a way of trying to solve problems rather than simply minimizing the catastrophe.[1]

Establishing the "free zone" (which comes to be known as Hamsterdam)[2] is the idea of Major Colvin. It is important to note that Colvin's unconventional plan is not inspired by, for instance, European concepts on drug legislation or on academic discussions or ideas; it is meant as a purely practical method, which, as he repeats throughout Season Three, is intended to "save what is left to save" in his neighborhoods. In 3.04 he rallies the dealers to make clear that the drug-dealing corners of the Western districts for which he is responsible will henceforth be cleared from the drug trade, whereas three small parts of the inner city will be a "free zone." It takes significant efforts for Colvin to convince the dealers as well as his staff. The police officers Carver and Thomas "Herc" Hauk (Domenick Lombardozzi) clearly exemplify the conflicting sentiments towards the experiment among the police; whereas Carver may symbolize the hope for a new, thoughtful generation of police officers, Herc's resistance parallels the confusion of the dealers, whose routines are also interrupted: as one of the dealers asks, "Why you got to go and fuck with the program?" Threats of violence and extreme vigor are used to convince the dealers but, having finally moved the dealers to the "free zone," a new problem arises. This is astutely described by Alvarez (235): "now the problem strikes at the foundation of capitalism: no customers." Consequently, the police are forced to make one of several concessions to their conventional work: using police vehicles to transport drug customers to the free zone.

After five weeks, the project receives media coverage that prompts the administration to shut down the free zone and even demolish the entire blocks. The representation of this four- or five-week period has a narrative plot of its own; after initial hesitation, the free zones flourish and, as such, it results in substantially lowered crime rates for the entire city, dramatically enhanced conditions of living in the neighborhoods that are rid of the drug trade, and it even functions as what seems to be a win-win situation for the drug addicts, who have easy access to drugs in an environment without violence and with social workers handing out clean needles, AIDS tests and condoms. The "Homecoming" episode (3.06) depicts a regular piece of televisual American utopia with signs of a flourishing community: children play in the streets, elderly people walk the neighborhood and tend to their stoops in safety.[3] According to Bubbles' (Andre Royo) former using partner Johnny Weeks (Leo Fitzpatrick), "this is a soldier's paradise" (3.07), but following the more reasonable viewpoint of Bubbles, viewers understand that Hamsterdam is not a paradise, but rather a kind of hell; a safe and lively society is made possible *outside* Hamsterdam, but Hamsterdam itself has its own terrible problems.

Bubbles' visit to Amsterdam is an important high point in the Hamsterdam narrative: dark, intense, horrifying, and—unlike the extremely verbal series—almost without words. The protracted image of depravity and decay, as early as in episode 3.08, makes it only a question of time before the experiment will be stopped.

Witnessing Hamsterdam

The Hamsterdam storyline has several implications within the fictional universe. It arouses debates among police officers as well as politicians concerning the nature, goal and results of the War on Drugs, and, as discussed below, the series forces viewers to reflect upon the ethical and ideological difficulties inherent in the "experiment." Thus, the Hamsterdam theme exemplifies the narrative structure of *The Wire*, in which a complicated phenomenon is methodically prepared, worked through and evaluated through human interest, political, criminological and psychological perspectives. Furthermore it exemplifies *The Wire*'s structural strategy of weaving several plots together simultaneously. Characters known from other contexts partake in the experiment, and characters from a number of plot lines become embroiled in its politics (for example, it draws in the rival Barksdale and Stanfield drug organizations). The Hamsterdam experiment is encountered and represented through a number of "witnesses" who make different assessments of the Hamsterdam experience.

It has been noted often that *The Wire* is intellectually demanding (Gjelsvik, Mittell *Complexity*) and it seems as though the directors of the series have been well aware of the risk of the Hamsterdam string being considered too much of a political exemplification, rather than as engaging television. The underlying ideas concerning the legalization of drugs are presented in what Bakhtin describes as a polyphonic structure; that is, differing ideas and existential viewpoints are presented as incarnated antagonists instead of as pure ideas, devoid of relation to a real world. Whereas Bakhtin's polyphony is strongly tied to uttering verbal truths, a TV series (even one as cognitive as *The Wire* is at times) must "show" ideas, not as facts in themselves (for instance, the success or failure rate of the experiment) but rather as the impact of the ideas. Such an impact is only partly verbalized in a verbo-visual medium such as television; it is primarily shown visually. This why the series employs a series of witnesses to testify to the impact of Hamsterdam: viewers encounter the experiment by watching the witnesses seeing and sensing, making sense of Hamsterdam.

The temptation to support the experiment with multiple references to external sources is resisted; instead, the strategy of the creators of the series is to make a double representation consisting of a visually-orientated "witness" position on one hand, and a more rational, discursive stratum involving all the verbalized assessments on the other.

When analyzing Hamsterdam, it is evident that the authors and directors have worked consciously with individuals who have "witnessed" the experiment. In 3.08, the Deacon walks silently through the free zone, after which he presents some of his essential doubts to Colvin. We also see the amazed Omar Little (Michael K. Williams) analyzing the area from his car for opportunities to rob dealers, believing that it must be a trap. The police are often seen in the unaccustomed role of bystanders, *watching* the scenery. In episode 3.11, Councilman Tommy Carcetti (Aiden Gillen) is even brought down to watch it. When he hesitates to approach the scene (feeling outside his normal habitat) Colvin encourages Carcetti to do it on his own so that the politician can make his own assessment of the experiment instead of relying on media reports or the official police version of the events.

Characteristic in these scenes is how people walk through the free zone on their own, observing without talking or acting. The act of seeing substitutes for the viewer's engagement with Hamsterdam. The witnesses are "guides" who function as the "extended eye of the viewer whose presence and perceptual activity are conjured and in a sense made visible."[4] In this way, the witnesses see what goes on, thereby delivering a point of view in which viewers can partake, which may again be understood as an aspect of the polyphony of the series. This particular setting becomes overwhelmingly intense in one particular visual testimony, where we follow Bubbles entering what feels like a Dantesque Inferno.

Bubbles functions as a mediator between several worlds. Starting as a drug addict forced to frequent the Western district in order to make money and buy drugs, he later moves home to live in the basement of his sister's house while he tries to get clean. In a moving scene in the final episode of Season Five, Bubbles leaves the basement and takes his place at his sister's table, finally being cured and accepted. He is a paid informer on friendly terms with the female police officer Kima Greggs (Sonja Sohn), and he is (probably)[5] a homosexual with younger men as partners. Bubbles is one of the most important figures in *The Wire* and it is no coincidence, therefore, that he is the most important witness to the Hamsterdam experiment.

Bubbles' trip to what feels like a strange subterranean world is introduced with an extreme close-up in which viewers can clearly see Bubbles' exasperation as he watches material destruction, and the miserable life of the drug addicts, hearing the drug dealers, seeing prostitutes and even meeting small children living on the street. According to dramatic convention, the extreme close-up functions as the moment of truth (Koskinen 110), the moment at which viewers can "read" the face of a character. As such, it is difficult for viewers to distance themselves from Bubbles' experiences; for instance, when he is threatened and faced with a desperate man who comes very close to him, the man feels very close to the spectator too. People are half naked, everybody seems to be in a perpetual fight, or close to a fight, and by shifting the perspective to the police, we learn that violence is indeed an important result of the experiment, which seems to illustrate a Hobbesian struggle of everyone against everyone else. The choked Bubbles even meets his former partner, the younger drug addict Johnny, who looks very badly treated, complaining about the terrible itching on his arms but also seeing Hamsterdam as a "soldier's paradise." Johnny refuses to follow Bubbles, who begs him to "take a break" for the sake of his health. Unsurprisingly, when Hamsterdam is shut down, the body of Johnny is found in one of the vacant houses, badly gnawed by rats; a frightening symbol of the human costs of drugs.

Bubbles' visual testimony, in its wordless horror, is a strong argument against the Hamsterdam experiment, whereas the positive aspects of Hamsterdam are almost exaggeratedly represented in scenes from well-functioning, daytime-lit neighborhoods with children playing in the streets and grown-ups taking care of everyday business, as mentioned above. Consequently, it could be argued that, whereas Major Colvin is the figure who inaugurates and supports Hamsterdam, the visual testimony of Bubbles clarifies how the costs of the experiment are too high. From this point on, it is Bubbles who "closes" the project. It is logical, therefore, that it is these two figures who in a short and rather cryptic conversation, evaluate the project together, looking over the torn-down rubbles of the vacant houses.

> BUBBLES: That's something, huh? Like they just took a big eraser and rubbed across it.
> COLVIN: Yeah.
> [Pause]
> BUBBLES: Yeah, but before, a dope fiend come down here, cop a little something, ain't nary a soul hassle him. Hoppers [dealers] and police, they just let him be.
> COLVIN: Was a good thing, huh?
> [Pause]
> BUBBLES: I'm just saying.
> [Pause]
> BUBBLES (to his new companion): You probably don't know, but it's rough out there, baby. Cops be banging on you, hoppers be messing with you [3.12].

Colvin hopes for an unequivocal answer from Bubbles, guaranteeing a kind of posthumous reputation of his experiment. However, Bubbles cannot affirm the undying fame of Hamsterdam. "I'm just saying," is his short answer, even if he also acknowledges the easier life for a "dope fiend" under the former liberal Hamsterdam "administration." Viewers tend to remember, with Bubbles, his trip to the underworld several episodes before.

Conclusion

The results, as well as the legacy of the Hamsterdam experiment, are hard to evaluate: the politicians in charge and the high-ranking police-officers strongly denounce the entire experiment. However, these decision makers themselves have not directly witnessed the experiment. Colvin, in the above-mentioned conversation with the Deacon, takes a much more positive view and offers an inconclusive position on the outcome. Bubbles, as a prime witness, loses his friend in Hamsterdam and he seems to see and understand that the costs of legalizing drugs in limited areas are very high.

The War on Drugs is a discourse that frames all discussions regarding how to address the drug problem. This becomes apparent in the results of the Hamsterdam project (here understood as evaluation from the surrounding society). Colvin's high-paying job offer at Johns Hopkins University is retracted as a consequence of the Hamsterdam project. The discursive framing of the War on Drugs disqualifies anyone associated with what can be regarded as liberal drug attitudes, and the university board knows the dangers of having any such person on their staff.

The political implications of being associated with liberal attitudes to drugs are something that Carcetti, the mayoral candidate, is acutely aware of. Knowing that support for Colvin's Hamsterdam project would probably be political suicide, Carcetti sides with the winning side of the discourse—those who champion the War on Drugs as a success. By showing how crime policy is a field in which careers can be made and unmade, the series sheds light on the War on Drugs as a crime policy discourse with a major impact. Carcetti's political career is also strongly tied to his use of crime policy in his campaign for mayor, where crime policy is part of his career-making, and therefore his crime policy adheres directly to the dominating discourses without questioning them. *The Wire* offers no easy answers. The disillusionment and futile violence of normal police work focused on fighting the results of the drug trade, not the reasons behind them (as discussed among the police in 3.05) is no less true after the episode, but the pictures of blossoming drug-free areas during the experiment linger and cannot be neglected. The series seems to have reservations about the specific results of the isolated experiment and instead proposes a wider, more comprehensive explanation to the problem of crime and drug dealing in civic surroundings; namely, that it is part of a larger tendency towards urban decay.

Consequently, the Hamsterdam episode must also be seen in the larger urban planning discussion that runs through the series. The use of the city, and the importance of streets, the corners and the houses in the setting, has been mentioned above and is vital for the ideological ideas of the series. The visual high point of the transformation of the cityscape and the urban environment is the demolition of parts of the Projects. Part of the series' criticism of political inefficiency (not to mention lust for power and corruption) concerns the inability to take care of the city in its most basic ways. Peter Clandfield has suggested that Season Three offers two "very different, yet comparably unofficial, redevelopment initiatives": Colvin's Hamsterdam project and Stringer Bell's real estate investments. (Clandfield 42).

In other words: the politicians are the only agents who are not doing anything to change the city. Only when Major Colvin's experiment becomes known do the politicians act. Even then, they do not act proactively, like Major Colvin (and the gangster "Stringer" Bell when investing drug money into property), but reactively. As Carcetti claims with "rhetorical bombast," "We turned away from those streets in West Baltimore: the poor, the sick, the swollen underclass of our city trapped in the wreckage of neighborhoods which were once so prized, communities which we've failed to defend, which we have surrendered to the horrors of the drug trade" (quoted in Alff 32).

Accordingly, the real truth of the Hamsterdam experiment, as well as the ideological position to be inferred from the series, probably lies somewhere between the somewhat idealistic or even naive attempt of Colvin (and the profit-oriented counter-parallel attempt from Stringer Bell) and the cynical political populism of Carcetti. *The Wire* offers an alternative to the traditional answer to the "Whodunnit" question in traditional crime fiction. It offers "truth" in the form of a question.

Notes

1. Colvin's work in the public school in Season Four displays parts of a similar attempt to solve problems (by dividing children into different groups with different needs) instead of using tired models.
2. The name "Hamsterdam" comes from a misunderstanding: the experiment is presented as something resembling the liberal, harm-reduction policies of Switzerland and the Netherlands. These parallels prompt one of the dealers to reply: "I ain't going to no Hamsterdam" (3.04).
3. The "utopian" scenes of *The Wire* are comparable to the flashback scenes in *The Corner* (HBO 2000), where the contemporary destruction of the neighborhoods (as a result of the drug trade and the War on Drugs in combination) represents both a golden past and the dream of a possible future. *The Corner* was the Simon and Burns' earlier TV series that may be seen as a low-budget and even more radical representation of life on the streets than *The Wire*.
4. The quote relates to Johan in Ingmar Bergman's *The Silence*. See Koskinen 118.
5. Bubbles' protective friendships with younger men may not be homosexual but only intensely loving. In Season Five, however, the relationship between Bubbles and the reporter from *The Baltimore Sun* seems to be based on both curiosity and some kind of attraction.

Works Cited

Alff, David M. "Yesterday's Tomorrow Today: Baltimore and the Promise of Reform." *The Wire: Urban Decay and American Television*. Marshall and Potter 23–36. Print.

Alvarez, Rafael. *The Wire: Truth Be Told*. Edinburgh: Continuum, 2010. Print.
Anderson, Martin. *Welfare: The Political Economy of Welfare Reform in the United States*. Stanford, CA: Hoover Institute Press, 1979. Print.
Andersson, Robert, and Roddy Nilsson. *Svensk kriminalpolitik*. Malmö: Liber, 2009. Print.
Bakhtin, M. M. *Problems of Dostoevsky's Poetics*. Minneapolis: University of Minnesota Press, 1984. Print.
Bruhn, Jørgen, and Anne Gjelsvik. "David Simon's Novel Cop Show." *New Review of Film and Television*, 11, no. 2 (2011). Print.
Clandfield, Peter. "'We Ain't Got No Yard': Crime, Development, and Urban Environment." Marshall and Potter 37–49. Print.
Garland, David. *Culture of Control: Crime and Social Order in Contemporary Society*. Oxford: Oxford University Press, 2001. Print.
Gjelsvik, Anne. "The Wire og den nye serialiteten." *Fingeravtryk, studier i krimi og det kriminelle*. Ed. Riber Christensen Jørgen and Kim Toft Hansen. Aalborg: Aalborg universitetsforlag, 2010. Print.
Koskinen, Maaret. *Ingmar Bergman's The Silence: Pictures in the Typewriter, Writings on the Screen*. Seattle: University of Washington Press / Copenhagen: Museum Tusculanum Press, 2010. Print.
Lilly, Robert, Francis Cullen and Richard Ball. *Criminological Theory: Context and Consequences*, 4th ed. London: Sage, 2007. Print.
_____, and _____, eds. *The Wire: Urban Decay and American Television*. New York and London: Continuum, 2009. Print.
Mittell, Jason. "Narrative Complexity in Contemporary American Television." *The Velvet Light Trap* 58 (2006): 29–40. Print.
_____. *Television and American Culture*. New York: Oxford University Press, 2010. Print.
Potter, Tiffany, and C.W. Marshall. "'I am the American Dream!' Modern Urban Tragedy and the Borders of Fiction." Marshall and Potter 1–14. Print.
Rose, Brian G. "*The Wire.*" *The Essential HBO Reader*. Ed. Gary R. Edgerton and Jeffrey P. Jones. Lexington: University Press of Kentucky, 2008, 82–91. Print.
Sandvik Kjetil. "Convergence of Place and Plot." *Fingeravtryk, studier i krimi og det kriminelle*. Ed. Jørgen Riber Christensen and Hansen Kim Toft. Aalborg: Aalborg universitetsforlag, 2010, 298–299. Print.
Sheehan, Helena, and Seamus Sweeney. "*The Wire* and the World: Narrative and Metanarrative." *Jump Cut: A Review of Contemporary Media*, 24 August 2009. Web.
Simon, David. "Prologue." *The Wire Truth Be Told*. Ed. Rafael Alvarez. Edinburgh: Canongate, 2009, 1–32. Print.
Simon, Jonathan. *Governing Through Crime: How the War on Crime Transformed American Democracy and Created a Culture of Fear*. Oxford: Oxford University Press. 2007. Print.
United States Department of Labor. *The Negro Family: The Case for National Action*. Office of Policy Planning and Research, 1965. Print.
Vulliamy, Ed, and Saptharsi Ray. "David Simon, Creator of *The Wire*, Says New U.S. Drug Laws Help Only 'White, Middle-class Kids.'" *The Observer*, 25 May 2013. Web.
Walmsley, Roy. "World Prison Population List," 8th ed. 2009. Web.

The Paper Bag Compromise
Hiding the Problem of Drug Dependency in Hamsterdam

J. D. Taylor

"Sometimes the gods are uncooperative."—Major Howard "Bunny" Colvin (3.03)

In Season Three of *The Wire,* Major Howard "Bunny" Colvin (Robert Wisdom) experiments with a desperate solution to West Baltimore's irrepressible drug-related crime: drug legalization in three abandoned and derelict neighborhoods. Dealers and users are transported by police into the free zones of "Hamsterdam," nicknamed after the Dutch city known for its liberal drug laws. As a result, felony rates decline by up to 14 percent, while drug-users and sex-workers are able to access medical treatment. Drugs are sold and consumed freely, so long as users adhere to Colvin's social contract: no violence. Yet what also occurs is an intentionally hellish vision of brutality and lawlessness, as children become ensnared in the disorder and misery of the "free zone," which is ultimately shut down after violence and political scandal.

Colvin's "Hamsterdam" experiment offers a powerfully ambivalent portrayal of the consequences of drug legalization in urban post–9/11 America, and the story of its rise and fall encompasses the entirety of Season Three. In this essay I propose that the significance and interest of this story-arc lies not in legalization itself but in the sociopolitical and ethical rationale that leads Colvin to construct it. I reassemble David Simon's own tantalizing clues about Greek tragedy and the failure of the "War on Drugs" to re-situate Colvin as a noble but inevitably thwarted hero whose vain attempts at "reform," the self-addressed theme of this season, imply the vast sets of forces and institutions which thrive on the corruption and misery of "the game" which *The Wire* dramatizes. Ever wary to avoid explicit political critique, *The Wire*, through Colvin's failure, instead indicates that reform of institutions as they currently stand will be abortive and ineffective without a more substantial political and economic transformation of American society. Colvin's social pragmatism effects merely a temporary truce or social contract, reducing felonies and murders in the Western District in exchange for limited drugs legalization and no violence among dealers. The significance of this potent yet abortive intervention is discussed in the first section.

To do real police work, "the kind that's actually worth taking a bullet for" (3.02), Colvin faces the War on Drugs naturalistically, and using a similar conceptual approach as "Natural Law" political philosophers like Jean-Jacques Rousseau, Thomas Hobbes, but most coherently, Benedictus de Spinoza, who scorned other political theorists for viewing human societies "not as they are, but as they would like them to be" (*Political Treatise* 680). Colvin shares much of Spinoza's political naturalism, understanding human societies as things of nature, whose stability and happiness are ensured in the security, opportunity and peace of its constituent parts, and the importance of this post–9/11 political naturalism are analyzed in the second section.

Yet Colvin is neither merely a tragic foil nor a hard-headed realist: as I argue, his Hamsterdam experiment and his impossible gesture towards a social contract (in the form of "paper bag compromise") allow *The Wire* to consider urban post–9/11 American society from two critical perspectives: naturalistically (in the sense of its political and social ecology), leading to an abundance of analogies to nature and ecosystems, analyzed in the second section. This leads to a withering critique of the institutions, legal and illegal, which have failed to provide for basic social needs in postindustrial Baltimore yet which continue to thrive in the grotesque and excessive failure of the War on Drugs, which is analyzed in the third section. The tragedy of this struggle, and of the struggle of Colvin to establish a place of compromise within it, leads to the season's second critical perspective, a metaphorical one, from the impossible utopia (whose literal meaning is "non-place") of Hamsterdam, and of the dramatic divine struggle of individuals against corrupt institutions, assessed in the fourth section. Colvin's subversive intervention will consist not in breaking existing laws, but in legitimizing unwritten laws regarding the game and entrenched social problems of drug use, poverty and unemployment. Through a philosophical detour through the naturalistic ethics of Spinoza, the fifth and final section of the chapter scrutinizes the efficacy and limits of a social contract, and attempts to go beyond the producers' own ambivalence about Colvin's initiative to consider how institutional reforms might aid the problem of drug dependency.

"The word from on high"

As writer David Simon notes in his episode commentary to 3.01, the overarching theme of Season Three is "reform." Yet what is largely operative in this season is the failure of reformers and the impossibility of reform, portrayed through two different leaders on separate sides of the game (3.11). Russell "Stringer" Bell (Idris Elba) and Major Colvin attempt in vain to reform the institutions that employ and empower them to control, with different priorities, the Baltimore drug trade. In both cases, their attempts at reform involve a naturalistic confrontation with the realities of the drug trade and a desire to remove its more violent and socially-damaging effects. For Stringer, this involves an attempt to transfer drug money into property and remove some of the street violence from the game, both within the Barksdale organization and through entering into a co-operative with other Baltimore drug gangs. For Colvin, this occurs in the move to transfer the focus of policing in the Western District from undercover drug stings and corner-raids to improving and protecting communities, through an audacious program of drugs decriminalization. Like Stringer's initiative, Colvin's actions stem from a desire to remove street violence from the game. The experiment becomes Hamsterdam, and is one of the most memorable story arcs of the show.

In both cases, their attempts at reform are ultimately thwarted by pre-existing and new institutional forces invested in perpetuating this system: these include Avon Barksdale's (Wood Harris) escalating territorial war against Marlo Stansfield's (Jamie Hector) organization, the double-dealing scams of State Senator Clayton "Clay" Davis (Isiah Whitlock, Jr.) or, for Colvin, in Commissioner Ervin Burrell (Frankie Faison) and Mayor Clarence Royce's (Glynn Turman) self-serving schemes for political survival. These intentional obstructions to reform and serve to show the powerful set of modern American institutional forces which act as a "Fate" against which these tragic heroes vainly struggle. As writer George Pelecanos notes, Colvin is "the central guy in this season" (3.11, DVD commentary), and his actions are either directly or indirectly pivotal in the establishment of Hamsterdam, the political rise of Councilman Thomas "Tommy" Carcetti (Aiden Gillen), the wire case of Lieutenant Cedric Daniels (Lance Reddick), and ultimately to the betrayal of Avon. As Pelecanos wryly notes, "in true *Wire* fashion, he pays the price for it." Like all *Wire* heroes, Colvin becomes locked into an unwinnable struggle but his heroism lies in his belief that reform can be possible, however unthinkable. Against Žižek's critique of *The Wire* as insufficiently radical in its attachment to realism (2012), I propose instead that one of *The Wire*'s most subversive interventions into post–9/11 American culture is in the depiction of its characters like Colvin (or like Detective James "Jimmy" McNulty's [Dominic West] faked serial killer investigation in Season Five) to think through and beyond the rules of realism and the capitalist real and, in the process, to produce new realities. Confronted with the fate-like impasse of the game, Colvin, Bell and McNulty each strive in various ways to effect reform without (ostensibly) breaking the rules of the game. In the process, they both subversively legitimize those corrupt processes of the game left unreformed while, for a brief time, indicating weakened fissures and alternative possibilities within what is considered real. This ideological dimension of reality becomes increasingly thinned as characters like Colvin haphazardly yet substantially transform institutions from minor, conservative or ethically-just premises, often obeying the fact or "spirit" of the laws beyond just observing the rule or "letter" of them. These unthinkable story-arcs serve to undermine how thinkable, or acceptable, the contemporary stalemate on the War on Drugs and how a more fundamental social war against the urban poor has operated in the United States.

In order to assess how this operates in Colvin's case, I turn to Hamsterdam and the most radical premise of Colvin's reform: the legitimization of drug use. For Colvin, drug use is an effect of the natural social environment, and is thus one which police should work around rather than target. It is also an affect or emotive expression of the suffering and problems in these communities caused by greater social issues. As viewers may recall, a combination of disasters in the first two episodes of Season Three lead to the creation of Hamsterdam. The failures of the current police approach, basically undertaken in accordance with the principles of the U.S. War on Drugs, are indicated by a futile police helicopter chase of a boy acting as a decoy, who later appears in custody badly beaten, but without any drugs. Driving around the once-genteel and proud African American streets of the Western District, Colvin views the decades-long failure of basic social infrastructure like policing, healthcare, housing and social services to aid communities. Instead of reducing the harm of drugs, young "hoppers" rush up to passing cars, including Colvin's, to engage in the only trade still thriving locally. The streets have returned to a violent pre-civil state where the authority of the laws is regularly undermined, and can no longer be effectively enforced: a damning comment on the intensifying failure of successive federal governments to tackle inner city problems of education, employment and basic infrastructure out of which new underground economies have naturally festered. The following day, one of his officers is shot in an undercover sting-op, and the incident reminds Colvin that, in his time, a good night is an "absence of negative." Policing has lost its preventative function. With his retirement and a safe job at Johns Hopkins University looming, Colvin existentially ponders on a broader crisis of the city and on what can he do to address the deeper impact of drugs on the city. Thinking out loud, he says to his friend, the Deacon (Melvin Williams):

> Here's the thing, six months now I'm gone.... But you know what? The shit out there. The city is worse than when I first came on. So what does that say about me? About my life? [3.02].

The Deacon replies that "drugs are a force of nature." Metaphors of ecology and nature are essential to understanding Hamsterdam. At first Colvin seems unconvinced, but through a series of inquisitorial COMSTAT police chief meetings, it becomes apparent that he will have to redefine crime in some capacity or otherwise lose his job. When "the word from on high" demands that felonies be reduced by 5 percent and murders capped at 275, Colvin is confronted with the bald corruption of modern policing into political functionalism. As Deputy Commander William Rawls (John Doman) remarks: "Any of you who can't bring in the numbers we need will be replaced by someone who can" (3.01).

Colvin is situated at the center of the dilemma. He could follow his colleagues and legitimately redefine recorded crime by "juking" his stats, and in the process protect his career. This is what the other commanders do, and *The Wire*'s comment is that this is the only credible option. But Colvin remains stung by his observations and by the Deacon's advice: after all, re-classifying felonies into lesser crimes is what Colvin earlier calls "turning wine into water" (3.02). Instead, Colvin's reform is to redefine not crime itself but the criminalization of just one aspect, drugs. This is the least radical or pervasive redefinition of crime by any of the commanders, yet it is the most subversive. For, if drugs are a force of nature, then they are the effect of specific causes and affects of particular problems in human societies as understood in terms of naturalism: they cannot be subtracted from or taken out of the context of the environment in which they exist. In order to analyze this naturalism more deeply, I now turn to one of its stimulating and provocative articulations in the thought of Spinoza.

"Like one of those nature shows"

In his 1670 *Theological-Political Treatise* (*TPT*), Spinoza argued that what preceded civil society was a universal "state of nature," without any moral laws, justice or rights, where one individual's desire to stay alive or increase their power naturally comes into conflict with another. Here, paraphrasing St. Paul, "there is no sin before law is established" and "each individual thing has the sovereign right to do everything that it can do, or the right of each thing extends so far as its determined power extends" (*TPT* 195–7). This state of nature exists before civil society, and societal breakdowns lead to a return to this naturally violent, self-seeking state, "the war of all against all" in the words of Spinoza's contemporary Thomas Hobbes (30). Spinoza's argument differed from that of Hobbes, however, in that he did not pessimistically endorse the validity of this natural struggle, but explained how and why human societies first formed out of a desire for self-protection and greater quality of life that could only be ensured by mutual assistance in a civil society. Where laws and institutions collapse, these societies will naturally revert to this original struggle. The war of all against all is like the game, a force that naturally permeates beneath legitimate society, decreasingly contained by the faltering institutions which *The Wire* portrays over its five seasons. What Spinoza suggests is that in order to bind individuals together into communities, a social contract functions in which individuals obey the laws of the sovereign power in exchange for security, shelter, and the various benefits of citizenship.

In Baltimore, the social contract is held in place by the local and federal government. However, where that contract fails, other societies function according to their own social contracts, such as those put in place less conventionally, but equally significantly, by a maverick police chief who physically moves drug-sellers and users into three abandoned neighborhoods where drugs are de-criminalized under his supervision, or a by gang-leader who provides the only paid employment and opportunity for valor for young men acting as the sole income-earners in impoverished households. But while Hobbes developed an earlier and more well-known concept of the social contract as being an absolute transfer of power from subject to sovereign, secured by verbal expression of submission, it is Spinoza's development of the contract which remains more relevant and insightful. For Spinoza, the social contract is no formal event or agreement, but instead inscribes a socio-political rule: the requirement of "common consent" by subjects to legitimize the power of the ruler, which can only be realized through the expression, or management, of the basic desires of those that are ruled. Each person has a natural right (equivalent to their power) to electively obey or disobey a sovereign. An effective sovereign secures the "word" of their subjects by promising and effectively demonstrating that it can allow and protect sufficient freedom for subjects to pursue their own desires while maintaining civil stability. If it can manage this rare balance, the sovereign will create the conditions for present and future stability by possessing the unanimous support of the subjects. Like any composition of forces, Spinoza's model of society will survive for as long as it can maintain its own being without any larger forces overwhelming it (*TPT* 73; *Ethics* 251–255; *Political Treatise* 688). Spinoza's social contract is incisive and revelatory in that it empties politics of all moral or juridical imperatives: to represent and express the power of subjects is to share in it. While Colvin makes no attempt to act as a political sovereign of the troubled corners, his response to "the word from on high" is akin to the social contract at its most brutal stage: in order to take control of the re-naturalizing disorder of the corners, he presents a basic agreement with hoppers, dealers and users, which is that they move to the "free zone," and perpetrate *no violence*. In turn, they are free to do as they wish. To his police officers and to communities, he presents this social contract as the "paper-bag compromise."

In 3.02, Colvin addresses a packed meeting of his district police supervisors. He brings with him, and places on his lectern, a small rectangular paper bag, the kind that street-drinkers would normally use to conceal a bottle of beer. He explains that the bag and bottle illustrate "a great moment of civic compromise. That small wrinkle-ass paper-bag allowed the corner boys to have their drink in peace, and it gave us permission to go and do police work" (3.02). The paper-bag compromise represents an unwritten social contract between the urban poor ("the corner is, and it was, and it always will be the poor man's lounge") and the police. If they do not openly flaunt public laws, the police will overlook any possible transgression in order to do real police work. If the paper-bag could conceal urban street-drinking, largely by the poor, so that police officers could tackle more serious offenders, its equivalent with the drug trade on the Baltimore street corners would require some similar concealment. Given that the narcotics trade is already an underground economy, Colvin's "free zone" herds together drug-sellers, dealers, and addicts in three abandoned districts of West Baltimore, in a collective paper-bag, of the arrest-free zone.

Colvin's paper-bag compromise conceals the problem of drugs to the benefit of busy police and innocuous users, but legitimizes the fact of drug use as a compromised choice, that is, as a lesser evil. In doing so, Colvin adheres to the three laws of human nature in civil society outlined by Spinoza in his description of the social contract. He argues that all things will naturally seek their own advantage or "conatus" (drug use and trade will continue despite prosecutions, for as long as it remains an accessible outlet for suffering or economic opportunity); that when faced with two options, a person will select the lesser evil or greater good of two (more serious felonies should be pursued over minor drug arrests); and that the security of societies consists in the collective welfare of its people or constituent parts (as a retiring policeman, Colvin is determined that his legacy should be established in clean corners and safer communities, and not merely in "giving Rawls his stats" (3.03) (cf. Spinoza *TPT* 195–201). Colvin's social contract has one condition in return for the *de facto* legalization of drugs, which is that there should be no violence within the free zone. He explains his "new system" to the dealers using the carrot and stick analogy, that as long as they do not return to their old corners, and later, as long as there is no serious violence or killings in the free zones, "you're free to make your drops, collect what need collecting, won't nobody bother you" (3.05). In this temporary suspension of law, a new social contract is established that is based on a verbal agreement. There are frequent references to this: Colvin announces in the same scene that "you got my word on it"; Carver later berates a Hamsterdam crowd after a fight breaks out that the "only rule is no fighting, no cutting, no shooting!" (3.07); and later, he vainly appeals to the dealers after the murder in Hamsterdam: "I'm saying the rules got broke. My people kept their promises ... they were as good as their word" (3.09). Of course, an attempt at compromise about drug legalization may seem completely against the logic of the metaphor of warfare upon which the War on Drugs is waged: "you made them an offer?" asks a disgusted Rawls once Colvin's renegade scheme has become known (3.10). As with the war against terrorism which the series attempts to mirror (Simon, commentary to 3.01), for the sake of war continuing there can be no dialog with the enemy and no official social contract: such a reform would necessarily confer legitimacy on the concealed and unwritten laws of the game.

As the narrative follows Colvin and his assistant Lieutenant Dennis Mello (Jay Landsman) across Baltimore in 3.03, this trope of concealing/unconcealing plays out: Hamsterdam simultaneously hides the drug problem from commercial, residential and school areas as well as from police high command. Colvin repeatedly misinforms his staff, and later Daniels' Major Crimes Unit and a *Baltimore Sun* journalist, that this is a "new strategic plan" (3.03) and "tactical deployment" (3.07) to round-up and entrap the major drug-sellers. However, just as the paper-bag conceals a social problem without tackling its cause, on a collective scale Colvin's concealment of legalized drugs from the rest of society accommodates a social problem while doing nothing for its social causes. Just as mass incarceration for drugs offenses, which vastly disproportionately impacts poor black Americans, has led in effect to a concealment of urban poverty and unemployment through prisons, so at the same time Hamsterdam conceals West Baltimore's drug problems in an abandoned and largely invisible series of neighborhoods. In a broader sense, its act of concealment also ghettoizes and hides the deeper problems of an impoverished, unemployed urban underclass, particularly its large number of idle school-age boys ("hoppers") previously employed by the drug-dealers as look-outs. Colvin's project increasingly veers towards collapse early on for not providing for the social needs of both hoppers and addicts, with a number of improvised gestures, from "unemployment insurance" payments and a basketball hoop for idle hoppers, or a needle-exchange and public health support.

This problem becomes clearer as the Hamsterdam experiment develops. In 3.07, following a desperate scene which shows violence, abandoned children, lack of electricity and water, and open drug usage and sex work, flaunting the usual visual codes of civil order, a fight breaks out in Hamsterdam. While Carver helps break it up, Detective Thomas "Herc" Hauk (Domenick Lombardozzi) refuses to involve himself in "playing nurse-maid to a bunch of goddamn animals" (3.07). Later, when Carver points out the large number of idle children, Herc compares it to the state of nature: "it's like one of those nature shows. You mess with the environment, some species get fucked out of their habitat." This motif of nature is used by Carver later to describe the vulnerability of the hoppers to "stickup crews" as like being trapped in a "lamb pen," surrounded by "wolves" (3.08). Mirroring Herc's negative naturalism, Carver worries that "we got fifty, sixty kids on the inside been fight or flight since they popped out the chute ... all these ex-runners, ex-lookouts, that shit worries me as much as any carnivores out there." While Carver attempts to address the environmental determinative causes that will drive young boys into further crime, through setting up a basketball game, encouraging some hoppers to participate in Dennis "Cutty" Wise's (Chad L. Coleman) new boxing gym, even organizing a welfare initiative for the boys from the proceeds of dealers, Herc condemns their nature, "like roaches when you turn the lights on" (3.09), bound to scurry back to their corners once the project ends.

However, at the same time, this act of concealing also mirrors an unconcealing: the act of hiding drug use in Hamsterdam—the application of the "paper bag" to the problem—is also a tacit acknowledgment of the problem. Colvin's initiative does not attempt to prohibit consumption, an impossible enterprise given his resources, but to reduce its impact and improve life in the remainder of the district. It treats drug addiction without any notion of warfare: the greater common good is sought. Colvin repeatedly gives up on concealing the truth of felonies. When in local team-meeting in preparation for COMSTAT, Colvin rejects a suggestion to re-classify felonies into minor crimes: "Fuck this. Do it clean. Don't massage anything ... we give them the fucking truth.... Fuck them if they can't take a joke" (3.03). In the following episode, Colvin addresses a community meeting where residents are furious about drug crime and daily harassment. Again, the expectation is that Colvin should at least pretend to have reduced crime, or be devising initiatives to do this. Such a gesture would, however, conceal the impossibility of actually removing the whole problem. Against the grain, he offers no answers to the residents: "I can't promise you it's gonna get any better.... This here is the world we got, people. It's about time all of us had the good sense to at least admit that much" (3.04). In response to this admission, one of the members of the community asks him what his answer to the problem is, to which he replies: "I'm not sure, but whatever it is, it can't be a lie." Colvin's response comes with a knowing smile: the paper-bag compromise of the arrest-free zones does not lie about addiction.

As David Simon notes, Hamsterdam is about "societal and political triage, where you reach some sort of accommodation with a social problem rather than pretend you're actually controlling it" (3.03, DVD commentary). At the same time, unconcealing the problem of drug addiction by concentrating all its victims in one location leads to the unforgettably grim and hellish scenes of violence and loss of dignity as witnessed by Reginald "Bubs" Cousins (Andre Royo) walking through Hamsterdam in 3.07, and later in 3.12. Yet one should be careful not to conclude that legalization might lead to some hellish scenario: the "village of pain" which Colvin creates, to use the Deacon's phrase (3.08), is one in which an already existing problem is no longer dispersed, but concentrated in one place and made plainly visible. As Colvin remarks to Carcetti later during his journey from peaceful, revitalized communities to the degradation of the free zones, what he sees "ain't pretty" (3.12), but it enables a reduction in crime rates, the regeneration of previously-harassed neighborhoods, and drug treatment and HIV prevention initiatives to reach an at-risk community. In typical *Wire* fashion, Hamsterdam offers a pairing and mirroring of concealment/unconcealment without prescribing a moral answer. The problem for Colvin will be that to make peace with an enemy in the War on Drugs will be far too unpalatable for politicians, police officers and drug-sellers, who each in turn contribute to the demise of Hamsterdam, through either serving their own political ambitions (Carcetti 3.12), compromised loyalties to Colvin (Carver's dragging of a murder victim outside of the free zone 3.09, and Herc's betrayal to the *Sun* newspaper, 3.10), or abandoning the no-violence pledge of the free zone (in one boy's tragically meaningless shooting of another for laughing at his shoes, 3.09).

"This so-called drug war"

From the outset of Season One, *The Wire* offers a consistent and powerful social and moral critique of the War on Drugs waged by successive political administrations since President Richard Nixon first "declared war" on "public enemy number one," illegal narcotics, on 18 June 1971 (*The House I Live In*). Carver in 1.01 questions how something can be called a "war" if it never ends. Simon explains in an insightful 2007 interview with Nick Hornby that the show was pitched to HBO from the outset as the "anti cop-show," abandoning the harmful moral pretensions of good police against bad criminals in the drug war. Instead, as he states here and repeatedly in other interviews, he is "unalterably opposed to drug prohibition; what began as a war against illicit drugs generations ago has now mutated into a war on the American underclass, and what drugs have not destroyed in our inner cities, the war against them has" (Hornby par. 12). Carver's skepticism about whether it can even be called a "war" sets the scene, as police, dealers, addicts, children growing up in drug-afflicted areas, and later labor unionists, teachers, and ex-offenders are all ensnared in a futile collision of forces which the five seasons follows, the "other America" and the "America left behind" which Simon claims to represent (Hornby par. 9). As the disgraced ex-cop turned public school teacher Roland "Prez" Pryzbylewski (Jim True-Frost) notes with melancholy, "no one wins. One side just loses more slowly" (4.04). In a war that cannot be won, *The Wire* follows from numerous different vantages how this losing plays out. In this sense one can properly understand why David Simon and others have frequently compared the program to Greek tragedy (Hornby pars. 7–8, Žižek "Clash of Civilizations").

Colvin's Hamsterdam is therefore offered as one of the clearest critiques of this war, with the rare grace of a possible solution, albeit one the show is keen to underline is currently unworkable. Colvin himself explains to his loyal sergeant Carver his opinion on the failure of modern policing which is the war on drugs:

> You call something a war, and pretty soon everybody gonna be running around acting like warriors. They gonna be running around on a goddamn crusade, storming corners, slapping on cuffs, racking up body counts. And when you at war, you need a fucking enemy. And pretty soon, damn near everybody on every corner is your fucking enemy. And soon the neighborhood that you supposed to be policing, that's just occupied territory [3.10].

However, Colvin finds himself isolated from his own superiors and those he commands in rejecting this approach, the conflict in attitudes embodied both in the machismo of Rawls' raid on Hamsterdam to the soundtrack of Wagner's Ride of the Valkyries (an echo of *Apocalypse Now*) and in Herc and Officer Anthony Colicchio's (Benjamin Busch) understanding of police work as little more than "jack a crew and grab vials" (in Colvin's words, 3.10). When modern policing is little more than soldiering, "real police work," working with communities rather than against them, disappears. Echoing the sentiments of the show's writers Simon and Pelecanos (cf. 3.11, 3.12, DVD commentaries), Colvin remarks that "the worst thing about this so-called drug war, to my mind, it just ruined this job" (3.10). But once a war of attrition has begun, there is little clear way of ever ending it except for some drastic solution, and given the season's initial metaphor of the collapse of the twin towers of the Franklin Projects and 9/11, war must continue to be waged, whatever the cost, even if fought "on a lie" as Slim Charles (Anwan Glover) states to Avon in their own war against Marlo's organization (3.12). Extrication can be just as ugly and hellish, if not dangerous. Although Colvin has no equivalent peacemaker in Iraq or Afghanistan (one might picture a renegade American general who negotiates an informal power-share and ceasefire with local militia) the analogy is clear: destroying Franklin Towers simply shifts the violence of the game elsewhere. The "reform" is superficial, concerned only with "self-affirmation" in a groundless world where "rules" are cynically observed but the real facts of power are concealed (Virno 87), according to the logic of the corrupt "postmodern institutions" which Simon repeatedly has criticized (3.03 DVD commentary). While the war on drugs is fought on a lie (efficacy of prohibition and criminality of addiction) only Colvin dreams up a temporary truce or compromise. Part of the intrigue of Hamsterdam is the lingering possibility that such a reform may just succeed. It is with a sharp jolt that the viewer joins Mayor Royce, who is initially willing to let the Hamsterdam experiment run, observing scandalized television reports once it becomes publicly known and is awoken from considering any alternative: "what the fuck was I thinking?" (3.12).

Yet Colvin's social contract expresses itself in a different ethical register to the War on Drugs, in a similar way to that in which Spinoza's own social contract sought to define itself as something beyond a merely Hobbesian model of competitive egoism. This egoism is like that reanimated by early 21st century social Darwinism of contemporary neoliberalism, where economic might is right and wealth is a natural effect of hard work and ambition, with the urban poor justifiably marginalized as criminal, culpable failures. The criminality of drug use is the hegemonic assertion of the War on Drugs, and of the politicians which continue to support it, and is used to defend what *The Wire* critically portrays as an attack on, and criminalization of, largely Afro-American inner-city social life at a time of social and political upheaval in race relations and class demands. Industries of illegal narcotics and state incarcerations each imprison communities into generational cycles of suffering within de-industrializing and decaying cities, while at the same time putting to work a largely surplus labor pool. Colvin's gambit, following Spinoza, is to enable this social problem to be concealed in order to improve the standards and welfare of his communities and corners, rather than to legalize drugs or make any comment on them. After all, they are a "force of nature" and not the subject of his reform, which is to re-establish social order. But his heroic paper-bag social contract cannot possibly survive the wrath of the game.

"The gods will not save you"

As Simon notes pessimistically in the DVD commentary to 3.12, "this country's too invested in the failed policy of the drug war to ever seriously contemplate an honest turn" (3.12, DVD commentary). In the failure to reform, the victims of war are not the commanders or politicians, all of whom remain in their posts by the end of the season, but the rank and file soldiers among the police, hoppers and drug gangs' "muscle" killed or wounded across the series. This has led some critics to interpret the program as offering an outlook too bleak and cynical (see Atlas and Dreier in this volume) to be considered politically effective. In contrast others, such as Thompson (110–1), have rightly emphasized the significance of the heroism of certain individuals in struggling against the current of institutional corruption. McNulty, Colvin, and Detective Lester Freamon (Clarke Peters) all exhibit such a heroism, but in the system portrayed in *The Wire*, these acts are necessarily tragic. While Toscano and Kinkle (pars. 10–14) are right to detect a critique of financial capitalism in *The Wire*, it would be misleading to claim that the program offers a political alternative. While the critiques of corrupt institutions are compelling, *The Wire* offers only an exposure of this corruption without prescribing any alternative. Colvin's Hamsterdam project is bulldozed as soon as it is publicly exposed, as police commanders and politicians scramble to save their own careers in the fear of a potential public backlash. Despite the failure of Hamsterdam, however, *The Wire* conveys a potent political message through the dramatic mechanism of tragedy.

While the tragic nature of *The Wire* has already been identified by Simon himself, as well as Žižek and others, less attention has been paid to its specific deployment. The most epic framing of tragedy actually occurs in the COMSTAT meetings of Season Three, in which the protagonist Colvin faces the antagonistic forces of Burrell, Rawls, and their inert, futile war. A number of religious and classic metaphors are consciously deployed in these scenes. This first occurs early in 3.03, when Major Marvin Taylor (Barnett Lloyd) is demoted by Burrell after being unable to address the high crime rates in his district. Having removed Taylor, Burrell asks: "Anyone else having trouble with the writing on the wall?" This image is drawn from the Book of Daniel, a mysterious prophetic sign that the final king of Babylon, Belshazzar, will be killed and his city destroyed. Colvin later evokes a similar divine motif when facing Rawls at another COMSTAT meeting, before his creation of Hamsterdam leads to a fall in crime, at which he presents "clean" recorded crimerates. The failure to bring down the crime rate leads Colvin to declare that "sometimes the gods are uncooperative." As he utters this, Burrell hurries into the room after being further pressured to reduce crime and, seemingly, does not hear what Colvin says. Despite this, he too expresses the heavy influence of the gods to drive human affairs soon after: "the gods are fucking you, you find a way to fuck them back. It's Baltimore, gentlemen. The gods will not save you" (3.03). However, at a later meeting Colvin can offer what Burrell and Rawls desire: a 12 percent reduction in crime over the previous four weeks, following the establishment of Hamsterdam. "Sometimes the gods do listen, sir," he suggests. "Not in the Western, they don't," Rawls replies (3.08).

As Simon later explains, "stealing" from the Greek tragedians allows *The Wire* to create "doomed and fated protagonists who confront a rigged game and their own mortality ... fated by indifferent gods" (Hornby par. 7). Chris Love has closely analyzed this use of Greek tragedy, and claims that in the case of Hamsterdam, Colvin confuses his gods. Rather than cynically assenting to the inevitable gods of "urban crime" of Baltimore's drug trade, and falling in line with his institution ("It's Baltimore, gentlemen"), Colvin instead attempts to appease and "fuck back" the "gods" which, in his confused perception, are Burrell and Rawls (497). While this is a compelling close reading, Colvin's paper-bag compromise is far more than just an attempt to get back at his commanders. It is one solution to the damage of the war on drugs on his district, and one that he later admits to Carcetti was not heavily analyzed. "I just did it" (3.12), he states, indicating that the experiment was simply an attempt to reassign his police units towards "real police work." At the same time, it emulates the stories of Oedipus and Antigone through its hapless protagonist vainly attempting to alter the passage of fate. The "gods" instead represent overwhelming institutional forces, which includes the forceful machinations within police, politics and the drugs trade. The gods may seem to cooperate, but this is only an illusory veil when an individual does not challenge their circumstances. The interest of the gods in the welfare of the urban underclass in the Western District is clearly absent. In such a tragic game, to fuck back the gods is simply to survive, as Burrell improbably does by the end of the season. Yet when the powerful leaders in policing and political institutions are determined only to war against drug crime-rates for the sake of political appearances and careerist self-interests, Colvin is the tragic hero who is sacrificed at the end. In turn, he can at least enjoy the private satisfaction of doing what he felt was "right" (3.12). When faced with the wrath of the gods, both McNulty and Colvin on different occasions (3.04 and 3.07) utter the same doomed, yet heroic, war-cry: "fuck the bosses."

"It's a different world down there"

While Season Three presents the impossibility of Colvin's victory against the gods of postmodern institutions, in this final part I turn to explore a claim made earlier, that the subversive power of the Hamsterdam reform and the paper-bag social contract lies in its abiding attachment to, and legitimization of, the facts and natural laws of the game. Colvin can give Rawls his stats while improving life in his communities, without coming into major friction with the drug-sellers on the corners. Like other Baltimore commanders under pressure from the statistical demands of Rawls and Burrell, exemplified in the COMSTAT meetings, he instead redefines crime not in the bureaucratic realm of record-keeping, but in creating a physical place where, concealed, a non-place (*utopia*), is the site within which drug trade can continue to operate along its own natural laws. Yet, while openly reckoning with drugs as a "force of nature," Colvin's utopia is presented from the outset as startlingly otherworldly.

Richard Price, series writer of 3.02, states that Hamsterdam represents the transition from utopia to dystopia, of what "a nightmare an idea can become, no matter how good the intentions" (3.02, DVD commentary). However, this modern definition of utopia as an ideal place is misleading in this instance. Against Clandfield (43) and Jameson (372) it would be a mistake to consider Hamsterdam as an ideal utopia. The squalor of the derelict houses on Vincent Street, the young age of the drug-sellers, the abandoned children left behind, as well as the one remaining elderly resident all point to the inadequacy of the solution. Hamsterdam is not established in one swoop, and it requires several measures across the season, from herding in addicts to setting up a public health program, to make it even remotely functional. It is utopia in the sense of being a non-place, of being an other-world in which, briefly, the rules of the game and the facts of its societal damage are enabled to coexist without contradiction, in a space concealed from a police command and a popular press who are locked into perpetuating the destructive attrition of the War on Drugs. Throughout the season there are other-worldly terms for the free zones: "Gandhi-world" (3.08), "Jurassic park" (3.08), "a soldier's paradise" (3.07), and simply "hell" (3.08). The most memorable name is the corruption of Amsterdam as "Hamsterdam" (3.03). The hoppers who provide the name have no idea of the whereabouts of Amsterdam or Switzerland, the examples which Colicchio gives as places where this kind of toleration has been carried out before. The only thing that is real is "Hamsterdam," a twisting from what is familiar into an initiative unlike any other, an experiment that is impossible from the very outset. Colvin first refers to it as a "joke" (3.03), its results a "statistical aberration" (3.07), and Mello and Rawls ask him, before and after the experiment, if he's "lost his mind" (3.04, 3.10).

If Colvin has lost his mind, other characters struggle to focus their minds on the implications of the initiative. After Avon's first failed attack on Marlo, Stringer narrates to him what he has observed of Hamsterdam: "they got crews over there, twirling dope and coke like the shit was candy. Kids with a lemonade stand, it's a different world down there" (3.06). Such a world might represent the possibility of drugs being just "business," a world in which perhaps he too might advance on more rational, economic grounds. However, his peregrinations are lost on the distracted Avon who dismisses the possibility of sending their crews there. This ambivalence and inability is also expressed by Bubs at the close of the season. I challenge Williams' (536–7) claim that this final "Dickensian" scene of the season constitutes a "recognition of virtue," or that it testifies to Colvin's failure (Nannicelli 202n): instead, following Klein (183), I argue that this scene is entirely devoid of melodrama in its lack of musical accompaniment. Bubs in fact cannot actually tell Colvin whether it was a "good thing" or not (3.12). Hamsterdam thus poses one unthinkable world without endorsing it. The institutional power of the gods has rendered from the outside the impossibility, or otherness, of such an initiative. In his affirmation of the brutalized humanity of the addicts, something which has not been particularly aided by the Hamsterdam project, considering the death of his partner Johnny Weeks (Leo Fitzpatrick) (3.12), Bubs gives no actual answer on the initiative itself. Colvin thanks him at least for that, but as Bubs walks away, the season leaves behind Colvin to continue wandering through the ruins of his utopia, and the impossibility of such an "outrageous," mind-spinning strategy. While Spinoza would suggest the importance of understanding the causes of drug dependency or urban poverty, Colvin's approach is necessarily limited to triage and pragmatically reducing short-term social harm. What he nobly sets out to do is to reduce the impact of a phenomenon that is beyond his control. When he attempts to justify the "hell" he has created to the Deacon, Colvin does not realize that he himself has gone beyond his own boundaries: "Look, I'm a police. So I can lock a man up or I can move his ass of the corner. Now if you want anything more than that, you're in the wrong shop" (3.08). Colvin's angry reply indicates the limit of *The Wire*'s own treatment of Hamsterdam. To simply concede that institutions will always be corrupt, as Simon does, is, in effect, to permit them to carry on as they are, without civil scrutiny. The construction of civil society begins with its institutions. Proposing institutional changes, or devising new institutions and constitutions that express collective desire and the common welfare of the city, or even a common agreement between one group of urban residents, and the police, as Colvin's paper-bag social contract attempts, is one viable political route that Spinoza argues for, and to which Hamsterdam, in its very impossibility, attempts to make some compromise with. There is a certain relief in the story-arc as Hamsterdam is closed down, but lacking is an ethical consideration of whether Colvin's other-worldly utopia is worth the civil cost of drug legalization.[1] Violence and deaths are substantially reduced, but *The Wire* is unable to make any conclusive ethical statement about these unthinkable utopias beyond Bubs' ambiguous reply to Colvin in the rubble of Hamsterdam when he asks for his verdict: "I'm just saying." This ambivalence raises the question of what conditions are acceptable in order to create social compromise. In order to make such a reckoning, one must face the game legitimately, as a "force of nature," and in the process legitimize it, something which few reformers would ever dream of and, against the gods, none have so far succeeded.

The "moral midgetry" of the wider season is confirmed in one brief Hamsterdam scene during a survey of the large number of idle children. The camera shows an adolescent boy drinking beer out of a paper bag, Colvin's very image of civic compromise. Such a concealment is redundant in Hamsterdam, and Colvin's paper-bag compromise may have addressed the symptom but not the cause: the desperate unsupervised life of children who have had to fight or flee from birth, the poverty and deprivation of their communities, and the total lack of opportunities or stable family figures in their lives. Colvin's absurd solution is to give the boys jobs as "auxiliary cops," provided with police bicycles and radios. While *The Wire* depicts the failure of America's War on Drugs, total legalization without attending to its social causes also results in disaster. As Spinoza would explain, the social contract can only manage, without improving, the collective lot of humanity. Only through understanding the social causes of our actions, and attempting to re-direct them by education, toleration and building peaceful communities, can societies move beyond hiding problems to overcoming them. Like Colvin's Hamsterdam, this first requires America to face its civil problems collectively, however politically unpalatable for Burrell, Royce, Carcetti, or post 9/11 culture more broadly.

Notes

1. This lack of firm judgment can be compared to the effective decriminalization of drug-selling in Season Four in HBO prison drama *Oz* through a "no violence" social contract between Em City Unit Manager Martin Querns (Reg E. Cathey) and Simon Adebisi (Adewale Akinnuoye-Agbaje).

Works Cited

Alvarez, Rafael. *The Wire: Truth Be Told*. New York: Pocket, 2004. Print.
Atlas, John, and Peter Dreier. "Is *The Wire* Too Cynical?" *Dissent*, 25 March 2008. Print.
Beilenson, Peter L.. and Patrick A. McGuire. *Tapping into the Wire: The Real Urban Crisis*. Baltimore: Johns Hopkins University Press, 2012. Print.
Brown, Adrienne. "Constrained Frequencies: *The Wire* and the Limits of Listening." *Criticism* 52. 3–4 (Summer-Fall 2010): 441–459. Print.
Clandfield, Peter. "'We Ain't Got No Yard': Crime, Development and Urban Environment." *The Wire: Urban Decay and American Television*. Eds. Tiffany Potter and C.W. Marshall. New York: Continuum, 2009. 37–49. Print.
Hobbes, Thomas. *On the Citizen*. Ed. And trans. Richard Tuck and Michael Silverthorne. Cambridge: Cambridge University Press, 1998. Print.
Hornby, Nick. "Interview with David Simon." *The Believer*. August 2007. Web. www.believermag.com/issues/200708/?read=interview_simon. URL accessed 13/9/13.
The House I Live In. Dir. Eugene Jarecki. 2012. Film. Charlotte Street Films.
Jameson, Fredric. "Realism and Utopia in *The Wire*." *Criticism* 52.3–4 (Summer-Fall 2010): 359–372.
Klein, Amanda Ann. "'The Dickensian Aspect': Melodrama, Viewer Engagement, and the

Socially Conscious Text." *The Wire: Urban Decay and American Television*. Eds. Tiffany Potter and C.W. Marshall. New York: Continuum, 2009. 177–189. Print.

Love, Chris. "Greek Gods on Baltimore: Greek Tragedy and *The Wire*." *Criticism* 52.3–4 (Summer-Fall 2010): 487–507. Print.

McMillan, Lance. "Drug Markets, Fringe Markets, and the Lessons of Hamsterdam." *Washington and Lee Law Review* 69.2 (2012): 849–891. Print.

Nannicelli, Ted. "It's All Connected: Televisual Narrative Complexity." *The Wire: Urban Decay and American Television*. Eds. Tiffany Potter and C.W. Marshall. New York: Continuum, 2009. 190–202. Print.

Spiedel, Linda. *Surveilling The Wire: Interrogating the U.S. Television Crime Drama*. PhD thesis. Roehampton University, 2011. Print.

Spinoza, Benedictus de. "Ethics"; "Political Treatise." *Complete Works*. Ed. Michael L. Morgan, trans. Samuel Shirley. Indianapolis: Hackett, 2002. Print.

_____. *Theological Political Treatise*. Ed. Jonathan Israel, trans. Jonathan Israel and Michael Silverthorne. Cambridge: Cambridge University Press, 2007. Print.

Toscano, Alberto, and Jeff Kinkle. "Baltimore as World and Representation: Cognitive Mapping and Capitalism in *The Wire*." *Dossier*. 8 April 2009. Web. http://dossierjournal.com/read/theory/baltimore-as-world-and-representation-cognitive-mapping-and-capitalism-in-the-wire. URL accessed 15/9/13.

Thompson, Kecia Driver. "'Deserve Got Nothing to Do with It': Black Urban Experience and the Naturalist Tradition in *The Wire*." *Studies in American Naturalism* 7.1 (Summer 2012): 80–120. Print.

Virno, Paolo. *A Grammar of the Multitude: For an Analysis of Contemporary Forms of Life*. Trans. Isabella Bertoletti, James Cascaito and Andrea Casson. Los Angeles: Semiotext(e), 2004. Print.

Williams, Linda. "Mega-Melodrama! Vertical and Horizontal Suspensions of the 'Classical.'" *Modern Drama* 55.4 (Winter 2012): 523–543. Print.

The Wire: The Complete HBO Series 1–5. Dir: Various. 2008. HBO. DVD.

Žižek, Slavoj. "*The Wire* or the Clash of Civilizations in One Country." Talk at Birkbeck, University of London, 24 February 2012. Audio.

Insurgency, Accidental Guerrillas and Gang Culture

TIFFANY POTTER and TOBIAS SIRZYK

According to David Kilcullen, former senior advisor to United States general David Petraeus in Iraq, the effectiveness of any insurgency depends upon its capacity to gain support from the members of the local population who are initially uninterested in the cause, but can be provoked to fight and persuaded to change sides. Kilcullen calls these individuals "accidental guerrillas." For an accidental guerrilla, allegiance is typically dictated not by greed or by a particular grievance, but rather by the need to associate with whichever side can best increase access to the means of survival. This essay argues that the modern tactics of insurgency outlined by Kilcullen in his book *The Accidental Guerrilla: Fighting Small Wars in the Midst of a Big One* are similar to those used by the drug cartels depicted in *The Wire*. The application of Kilcullen's model of insurgency illuminates the methods used by both the Stanfield and Barksdale organizations to recruit "soldiers" and to sustain their power bases on their side of the War on Drugs. Committed fighters, such as cartel leaders Avon Barksdale (Wood Harris) and Marlo Stanfield (Jamie Hector) use insurgent tactics to gain power, in part through the support of accidental guerrillas in West Baltimore. Both the Barksdale and Stanfield organizations use the insurgent's tools of security, wealth, coercion and violence to recruit gang members and to dissuade them from changing allegiances.

In its humanization of the individuals involved in the drug trade and its criticism of the political motivations behind the War on Drugs, *The Wire* provides both individual and organizational examples of a peculiarly Americanized version of war, insurgency, and accidental guerrillas. The series depicts in some detail the rise of Marlo Stanfield's operation, and the evolution of the organization and its members quite directly parallels the four stages of what Kilcullen terms "Accidental Guerrilla Syndrome": infection, contagion, intervention and rejection. Within the rival Barksdale organization—fully formed when the narrative begins—the character arcs of D'Angelo Barksdale (Larry Gilliard, Jr.), Preston "Bodie" Broadus (J.D. Williams), Michael Lee (Tristan Wilds), and Namond Brice (Julito McCullum) suggest the existence of accidental guerrillas within *The Wire*'s representation of gang culture, and illuminate the methods by which an accidental guerrilla can be persuaded to fight and change sides: Michael, Namond and D'Angelo are all accidental guerrillas with changing loyalties, with the respective stories of childhood friends Michael and Namond representing the at times contradictory implications of Accidental Guerrilla Syndrome. In contrast, the loyal corner boy Bodie provides an example of a committed fighter, whose allegiances to the Barksdale organization remain constant regardless of changes in territory, superseding even his loyalty to friends, an initial stabilizer of his gang membership. As narrative circles expand, the small wars between rival individual ideologies and gangs operate in parallel to the larger War on Drugs that is so explicitly critiqued throughout the five seasons of *The Wire*. The series depicts the attempts of several social institutions to combat the influence of the drug trade as defensive acts of war, framed in American discourses of counterinsurgency. *The Wire*, then, takes the conventional metaphor of a "War on Drugs" and literalizes it, writing Baltimore's corner boys as participants in a war as significant, as political, and potentially as deadly as those fought in response to 9/11, except that the war of *The Wire* is one that young men have no choice but to fight, as cultural and economic systems enforce allegiances of violence upon those limited in economic and geographic mobility. The series offers a counterintuitive rendering of drug dealers as often unwilling insurgent soldiers, and of law enforcement, education, and social security systems as counterinsurgent interventions that fail for the same reasons that military interventions do. Through its representations of insurgency, counterinsurgency and accidental guerrillas, *The Wire* destabilizes the conventional narrative of the War on Drugs, as drug-addicted, violent criminals come to be understood as child soldiers who have no choice but to fight for their lives.

Models of Insurgency and Guerrilla Warfare

Insurgency is conventionally defined as a condition of revolt, against a government, that is less than an organized revolution, and is recognized as being more than mere belligerency. The drug wars of *The Wire* are not revolutions designed to overthrow local or national governments. However, they do involve controlled armed conflict (often between rival gangs, such as the turf war between the Barksdale and Stanfield organizations) and sustained, organized illegal activity, both of which are common markers of insurgencies. Both the Barskdale and Stanfield organizations successfully use guerrilla tactics to solidify their power bases. Insurgencies and guerrilla warfare could initially be considered two distinct entities: guerrilla warfare as a tactic of war, insurgency as a political movement. However, insurgencies have evolved to the point that modern day insurgencies typically incorporate the use of guerrilla warfare tactics. During the most recent Iraq war, for example, insurgent groups such as al Qaeda Iraq established base areas in local communities and used quick strike actions (such as car bombings) to attack enemy forces (Kilcullen 141). Both the use of quick strike attacks and the ability to maintain support within civilian areas are examples of guerrilla tactics to maintain an insurgent community.

One of the earliest twentieth-century considerations of guerrilla tactics is Mao Tse-Tung's *On Guerrilla Warfare* which identified guerrilla warfare as a revolutionary tool used to overthrow, through the use of unorthodox modes of warfare, state or non-state actors who have a stronger traditional army, or greater numbers of troops, weapons and technology. Guerrilla warfare seeks to take advantage of the relative rigidity of traditional armies' clear and centralized chain of command. The decentralization of guerrilla units, in contrast, facilitates short, surprise attacks followed by quick withdrawals, with minimal information available to those outside of each unit (Petraeus and Amos 74). This restriction of information allows each unit to function independently of higher command such that in the case of capture, a guerrilla soldier will have less available information than a soldier from an orthodox army. Without the need to communicate with higher command prior to any action, decentralization allows each unit to make faster, at times spontaneous, decisions on when to attack, withdraw and hide.

Whereas traditional warfare revolves around the idea of achieving a swift, decisive victory, one of the main tactics of guerrilla warfare is the prolonging of conflict. According to Mao, this prolongment demoralizes enemy troops and can diminish an enemy's ability to maintain political and civilian support for the conflict. In Mao's view the two greatest factors in successful guerrilla warfare are its incorporation as a cog in a larger revolutionary political goal, and the gaining and maintaining of civilian support. Mao believed civilian support to be paramount, increasing guerrilla access to potential recruits, information, and thus increased security. Civilian support affords guerrilla fighters the ability to hide in plain sight, wearing similar clothing and blending in with peaceful civilians in population centers. Mao's theories on guerrilla warfare proved highly successful. Guerrilla tactics were used by Mao and other members of the Chinese United Front to help defeat the Japanese Empire during the Second Sino-Japanese War (1937–45). As Jonathan Spence documents, for example, the use of guerrilla warfare later helped Mao's communist army defeat Chang Kai-Shek's Kuomintang during the ensuing Chinese civil war. However, de-colonization, increased urbanization and a sharp decline in interstate warfare following the end of World War II served to change the landscape of guerrilla warfare. While Mao relied on rural peasant militias for his support, growing urbanization has increased the importance of achieving civilian support in urban areas.[1]

Recognizing the evolution of guerrilla warfare and insurgencies, Paul Staniland calls for reform in the ways states analyze warfare, arguing that guerrilla warfare is no longer exclusively a device of a black and white revolutionary struggle. No longer is one side's sole purpose to overthrow the other in order to institute political reform and gain what Staniland describes as a "monopoly of violence" (Staniland 243). As civil wars and ongoing conflicts in Sierra Leone and Burma have shown, conflict can be sparked over the control of natural resources and desire for wealth (diamond mines, drug trafficking routes, kidnappings for ransom, for example). As a result, what Mao termed guerrilla warfare and what is currently termed insurgency have come to have significant overlap.

Staniland argues that in many conflicts, state and non-state actors have both cooperative and conflict-driven relationships. Contrary to those in Mao's sense of guerrilla warfare, these actors are not always in direct conflict with each other, and will cooperate to varying degrees if something mutually beneficial can be attained. Staniland gives the example of modern day Burma, where warlords pay the local government for the ability to transport narcotics through government-controlled territory. Staniland asserts that the relationship between state and non-state actors is fluid, and that in order to better understand and combat an insurgency, understanding the nature and fluidity of wartime relationships between state and non-state actors is key. In many cases, Staniland argues, victory is not achieved "from the decisive shattering of other actors, but instead through their co-optation, coercion, and incorporation" (Staniland 254).

This change in wartime political orders is also discussed in Kilcullen's *The Accidental Guerrilla*. Kilcullen suggests that in any insurgency, individual members of the population may strive to avoid the conflict entirely, may demonstrate full commitment to the cause, or may become accidental guerrillas. Non-combatants are those members of the population who are unwilling or unable to fight and cannot be persuaded to do so. In *The Wire*, older women make up the most consistently-cited members of the non-combatant group, as exemplified by the scenes depicting Omar's grandmother in her Sunday church hat in Season Three and the near-universal recognition that she is an utterly inappropriate target for engagement of any kind.[2] Committed fighters are those members of the population who are committed to a specific cause, remaining loyal to one group throughout the duration of the conflict. Mao's revolutionary guerrilla fighters would fall under the category of committed fighters, as would cartel leaders such as Avon Barksdale and Marlo Stanfield. The third group, accidental guerrillas, are those who may be persuaded to change sides. In a state of conflict, the accidental guerrilla's defining goal is his or her own survival and the safety of loved ones (Kilcullen xiv). While guerrilla tactics may no longer be used purely for revolution as Mao conceived, maintaining civilian support remains of paramount importance. Kilcullen argues that gaining and maintaining the support of a population's accidental guerrillas is integral to any insurgency. Similarly, any successful counterinsurgency must revolve around bringing any accidental guerrillas on side. In Kilcullen's opinion, accidental guerrillas make up the majority of any population, and any successful counterinsurgency effort must be designed to ensure their safety. As the only members of the population whose loyalties can be swayed, accidental guerrillas represent the swing votes that determine the outcome of any insurgency. With the support of accidental guerrillas comes majority support, and with it the capacity to foster an insurgency or end one.

Insurgency

The rhetoric of war runs throughout gang culture as it is depicted in *The Wire*, and with some notable exceptions, the street "soldiers" of the drug organizations are always implicitly understood to be at risk of changing sides. Like insurgent groups, both the Barksdale and Stanfield crews gain and maintain the loyalty of their employees through the use of several different tactics of the sort outlined by Kilcullen, including *security, wealth, coercion* and *violence*. The use of wealth and its implied correlative security as a motivator is clear throughout the series. In Season One, for example, the viewer is offered glimpses of the relatively lavish lifestyle afforded D'Angelo Barksdale in his status as lieutenant. Socially awkward though the experience may be, he can visit an expensive restaurant, and he keeps separate apartments for himself and for his girlfriend Donette (Shamyl Brown) and their child. Both D'Angelo and his immediate family members are provided for by the organization, and even after D'Angelo goes to prison, Donette and their son continue to receive money from the Barskdale crew, maintaining her loyalty through domestic and economic security. The same gesture entails coercion, however, in the both implicit and explicit threat that Donette's support can be withdrawn at any time if she appears insufficiently loyal or obedient. Similarly, the Stanfield organization provides wealth and security to Michael Lee, which meets his need to protect his younger brother Aaron "Bug" Manigault (Keenon Brice) from domestic abuse. Michael is provided a new home for himself and his little brother, and the Stanfields show their willingness to further ensure the security of Michael and Bug by killing Michael's abusive stepfather (4.10). The message from both cartels appears to be a simple one: demonstrate loyalty to the organization and you will achieve wealth and security, a pitch appealing to the situational anxiety of the accidental guerrilla.

D'Angelo's loyalty, however, is never portrayed as entirely reliable, and the Barksdale organization's efforts to demand his loyalty are never guaranteed to be sufficient. D'Angelo enjoys the wealth provided by his position as a high ranking officer in the Barksdale crew, yet grows increasingly weary of the violence associated with the drug trade. He is nearly led by Detectives William "Bunk" Moreland (Wendell Pierce) and James "Jimmy" McNulty (Dominic West) into writing a (likely incriminating) letter of apology to the family of the murdered William Gant (Larry Hull), the man who testified against him. He briefly turns state witness following the revelation that Wallace (Michael B. Jordan) was killed on the orders of Russell "Stringer" Bell (Idris Elba), and he cuts off contact with Avon after Avon arranges for rat poison to be mixed in with the prison's heroin supply. In each case D'Angelo acts upon his conscience, allowing his personal feelings to affect his loyalty to the insurgent group he represents. Unlike a committed fighter, his loyalty to his crew is at times overridden by his loyalty to those he cares about, like Wallace, and his own personal code of morality. Not only is D'Angelo persuaded to change sides, but he is persuaded to do so more than once. His loyalties shift first from the Barksdale crew to the Baltimore Police Department, before eventually returning to the Barskdale organization following a visit from his mother, Brianna Barksdale (Michael Hyatt). Even after agreeing to do his jail time, D'Angelo's loyalties remain ambiguous, particularly after he cuts ties with Avon following the rat poison scheme. The knowledge of D'Angelo's wavering loyalty is precisely why Stringer orders D'Angelo's murder, eliminating the risk that he again turns informant (2.06), affirming the critical place of violence in the complicated system of social regulation in gang culture and insurgency.

Bodie Broadus also meets a violent end, but his character arc and role within the Barskdale crew are vastly different from those of D'Angelo. The audience is first introduced to Bodie as a low ranking member of D'Angelo's crew in Season One. Unlike D'Angelo, Bodie's lifestyle is not at all lavish. He makes less money than D'Angelo and lives with his grandmother. Unlike David Simon's docudrama *The Corner*, *The Wire* never asserts itself as a documentary representation of Baltimore street life, but Bodie's low economic standing, despite the risk he takes, is typical of low-level soldiers in drug-distribution networks. Sudhir Venkates' study of drug dealers during the late 1990s concluded that a typical street-level dealer in Bodie's position (the majority of employees in the drug trade), was earning between $3.30 and $7 an hour. Despite an average salary at or below Maryland's year 2000 minimum wage, however, the opportunity for wealth within the drug trade is still higher than what is typically available to teens and pre-teens in *The Wire*'s version of West Baltimore. As a memorable scene between Duquan "Dukie" Weems (Jermaine Crawford) and Malik "Poot" Carr (Tray Chaney) in Season Five illustrates, there may be other jobs in Baltimore, but they are not necessarily available to young men at the age when a change of life path might be possible. Seeking a way out, fifteen-year-old Dukie is told by Poot, now selling shoes at Footlocker, that his employer requires a minimum working age of seventeen: "so I guess you need to bang a little longer, then come back, see if we got something" (5.08).

As Venkates documents, enlistment in the drug trade also offers the opportunity to rise up the ranks and eventually become one of the highly paid bosses or lieutenants, one of the few opportunities for a wage of upwards of one hundred thousand dollars per year available to a populace largely lacking high school education. As Major Howard "Bunny" Colvin (Robert Wisdom) tells Dr. David Parenti (Dan DeLuca) in Season Four, the majority of violent youths are out of social systems' reach by the time they are eighteen, having already spent years working in the drug trade (4.03). Wealth in and of itself represents a form of security, offering an escape from poverty to those children and teenagers willing to enlist with the Barksdale or Stanfield crews.

Bodie exemplifies a good-faith attempt to climb the drug ladder. Starting out as a low ranking member of D'Angelo's crew, Bodie is gradually promoted up the ranks, eventually running a corner of his own. He is uncompromisingly loyal to the Barksdales. Unlike D'Angelo's, Bodie's devotion to the cartel is not superseded by his friendships. Whereas D'Angelo turns state witness following the revelation of Wallace's murder, Bodie is the one who, along with Poot, carries out the act (1.12). In the moment he is emotionally distraught, but with Poot's urging, Bodie is able to prove his loyalty by shooting his lifelong friend. Bodie is referred to as a "soldier" by both Stringer and McNulty, and he embodies the unflinching loyalty that Kilcullen identifies as characteristic of fighters deeply loyal to an insurgency (xiv).

Bodie's eventual coercion into dealing for the Stanfields—given the offer of staying and dealing for Marlo or being violently displaced—takes place only after the Barksdale crew is destroyed and Bodie is left with no other option. Even then, he is not loyal to the Stanfield gang, agreeing to become a police informant following Little Kevin's murder. Although this change in sides could be qualified as representative of the actions of an accidental guerrilla, Bodie's agreement to inform for McNulty shows that he is still committed to the Barksdales and the drug game. He agrees to "snitch" because he believes that the Stanfield crew has violated the rules of the game by failing to support its workers. Whereas Bodie agreed to murder Wallace after he was presented with evidence pointing to Wallace's guilt, Bodie believes that the Stanfields murdered Little Kevin without any of the same information. As Bodie tells McNulty, "Marlo and their kind, they gotta fall" (4.13). Unlike D'Angelo, whose decision to snitch comes out of a personal connection with a fallen loved one and an increasingly conscious rejection of the rules of the game, Bodie's decision to snitch arises from Marlo's failure to play by those same rules. Bodie abides not by a personal code of morality, but by the code used by the Barksdales. Even though the crew to which he was committed is no longer in power, Bodie remains loyal to the Barksdale organization, refusing to snitch on his personal crew or any of the Barksdales (4.13).

Although Bodie agrees to work with the police, to the Barksdale crew he remains a committed fighter. This is an example of the cooperative relationships that can exist between states and insurgents. Bodie remains loyal to his own insurgent group (his drug corner and any remaining Barskdales), but he and McNulty agree to work together in order to achieve a mutually beneficial goal, the destruction of the Stanfield organization. There are several other examples in *The Wire* of these sorts of concurrently cooperative and conflictual relationships that Staniland associates with insurgency and counter insurgency. As Jason Read has considered, one particularly poignant example of these multi-dimensional relationships, members of the Barskdale crew are investigated and at times arrested by the police during the course of Seasons One and Three, yet at the same time Stringer Bell is nurturing a relationship with Senator Clay Davis (Isiah Whitlock, Jr.), bribing him to arrange construction deals, but remaining powerless and privately ridiculed because he does not know the rules of the larger political game. Similarly, the advent of the New Day Co-Op is a cooperative relationship between rival non-state actors.

Both the Barksdales and Stanfields use violence and the threat of ostracization to coerce the population in their geographies of power into obeying them and refraining from contacting law enforcement. The Barksdales kill William Gant, D'Angelo and Wallace for snitching. Marlo Stanfield's soldiers firebomb the home of Randy Wagstaff (Maestro Harrell) for snitching, and kill Bodie and Little Kevin (Tyrell Baker) simply because there is a possibility that they are informants. Like insurgency groups in other communities in conflict zones, the cartels help to impose a culture of ostracization upon suspected snitches and collaborators. The community is coerced into rejecting police or other aid, knowing they will be punished violently by the cartels for seeking outside intervention. In the insurgent group, association with a potential snitch is also considered taboo, and to risk association is to risk encountering a similarly violent punishment. Randy is attacked and ostracized by the majority of his schoolmates following his act of snitching, while Michael catches flack for defending him (4.11). Poot and Bodie are persuaded to kill Wallace after being told that Wallace is a snitch (1.12) and risk being rendered suspect themselves if they fail in their task. In a scene that confirms the negative connotation of being a snitch, Bodie begins a conversation with McNulty by telling him, "I ain't no snitch," before ultimately agreeing to become a police informant (4.13).

Accidental Guerrillas

Although the Barksdales are already an established criminal power at the beginning of the series, *The Wire* chronicles the rise of the Stanfield organization from low-level player to the most powerful of the Baltimore drug cartels. In several significant ways, Marlo's rise to power parallels the four stages of the Accidental Guerrilla Syndrome in more conventional models of insurgency. The first stage, *infection*, is characterized by the establishing of a presence in a remote, ungoverned, or conflict-affected area. These "groups opportunistically exploit breakdowns in the rule of law, poor governance, or pre-existing conflict" (Kilcullen 35). When Marlo is first introduced in Season Three, as an emerging competitor to the Barksdales in West Baltimore, the community is portrayed as an area riddled with crime. Although there is a police presence (and therefore a government presence) in the area, the streets of West Baltimore are depicted as fundamentally self-governing. Any interaction with the police is considered taboo and met with force, while members of the population go to the drug kings for help with individual protection, money, and even community infrastructure, as when Michael goes to Marlo for help with his stepfather and Dennis "Cutty" Wise (Chad L. Coleman) asks Avon to help pay for a new boxing gym.

As Kilcullen documents, in the infection stage, the insurgent group will seek to build relationships with members of the local community (35). After rising to power following the arrest of Avon at the end of Season Three, Marlo distributes money among the neighborhood children in order to gain their favor and loyalty (4.02). Michael, however, refuses to accept the money, later telling the other "boys of summer," the teenagers around whom Season Four revolves, that he did not want to feel indebted to anyone (4.02). Michael demonstrates the initial reluctance to join an insurgent group that Kilcullen argues insurgencies and their opponents need to overcome in order to gain the support of accidental guerrillas (Kilcullen 36). Namond, on the other hand, accepts the money, demonstrating the split between reluctance and acceptance among the accidental guerrilla population towards new insurgents during the infection stage. When Michael is initially introduced in the fourth season he resists any substantive associations with the drug trade. He works for Bodie in order to earn enough money for school clothes and supplies but refuses to continue working after school starts and he has earned what he needs to sustain himself and his younger brother. Enlisting full time with a criminal enterprise would run counter to those needs and the need for security that they represent. Enlistment would also raise the chances of Michael being arrested, eliminating his ability to care for Bug, while also increasing the likelihood that Michael will be engaged in violent activity on a day-to-day basis (which after joining Marlo's crew later in the season, he is).

Fellow student Namond at first appears to be on the opposite end of the spectrum. Beyond the few days he allows Michael to work his job, Namond sells drugs for Bodie's crew when he isn't attending school. Despite his status as the son of former Barskdale enforcer Roland "Wee-Bey" Brice (Hassan Johnson), Namond soon shows himself to be too sensitive to deal with the violence of West Baltimore (a characterization considered with nuance by Georgia Christgau). Namond is afraid to come to Michael's aid when he is being beaten by the terrace boys at the start of Season Four, and despite his brash talk, his basic needs appear to be maintaining his personal safety and avoiding violence. His association with Marlo and gang culture grants him the sense of security that he seeks in response to being neglected and abused by his mother. During conflict, the insurgent group seeks to benefit from the needs and insecurities of community members to establish its importance to individuals (creating loyalty) and to the larger community (creating a tacit obligation that each individual go along with the insurgent group for the greater good).

The second phase of the Accidental Guerrilla Syndrome is *contagion*, characterized by the spread of violence and influence to other areas beyond the initial area of infection by an insurgent group (Kilcullen 36). Following his victory over the Barksdales and gifts to the local children, Marlo proceeds to cement his hold on West Baltimore. He expands his control by cracking down on any possible dissidents: Chris and Snoop kill any remaining enemies within West Baltimore (as well as those even suspected of talking to the police) and hide their bodies in the vacant housing. The influence of Marlo's insurgent-like group spreads in this phase, as evidenced by Marlo's forced takeover of Bodie's corners, increasing the amount of territory he holds in West Baltimore. Similarly, "Prop" Joe Stewart's (Robert F. Chew) initial attempts to have Marlo join the New-Day co-op hint at Marlo's increasing influence, as Joe believes that Marlo's crew is the only one with enough muscle to take on the New York crew dealing drugs in East Baltimore (4.03). After joining the co-op later in the season, Marlo takes on the New York crew and begins to gain territory in East Baltimore (4.09). This spread of violence and influence is representative of the contagion phase of the Accidental Guerrilla Syndrome.

Through his use of violence and fear, Marlo is able to further increase his influence by controlling the flow of information among the populace of East and West Baltimore. As Marques documents, the intelligence supplied by the populace is integral to any guerrilla group: "Guerrilla forces rarely have sophisticated intelligence gathering technology and must rely almost completely on human intelligence" (Marques 21). Ensuring the support of any accidental guerrillas not only increases the ranks of supporters for an insurgent group, but also minimizes the flow of information and fighters available to its enemy. Marlo is able to limit the amount of information leaked to the police through his treatment of snitches, while also making it harder for the police to attract informants and gain support within the urban populace. By levying heavy costs upon any potential informant, the Stanfield organization uses tactics of fear as a means to minimize civilian interaction with the enemy. Marlo reinforces his control over civilian information through his violent treatment of snitches, as evidenced by his ruthless attack on Randy's house as well as the violence and stigmatization Randy encounters at school following his act of snitching (4.11).

The narrative of the expansion of the geographical area of Marlo's influence and the increasing control that he wields over community perceptions evolve in parallel to the needs of accidental guerrillas Michael and Namond. At the same time that Marlo is beginning to add to his drug empire and his status in the intra- and inter-community drug wars, Michael's stepfather returns home from prison (4.08). Although Michael is still resistant to joining Marlo's gang, the return of Michael's stepfather causes the spread of his basic needs beyond simply providing for himself and his little brother. He now believes he has to get rid of his stepfather in order to maintain Bug's safety. As Marlo Stanfield's operation begins to change during the contagion stage so too do the basic needs of Michael Lee: he begins to realize that he may need outside help to get rid of his stepfather (4.09).

Namond's situation similarly becomes darker. After Brianna Barksdale stops sending Wee-Bay's family money, Namond's mother De'Londa Brice (Sandi McCree) forces Namond to take on more responsibility in the drug trade, arranging for him to receive a drug package of his own to sell in order to support the family (4.06). Namond, however, proves ineffective at his new job, giving Michael's mother a vial of heroin at a discount and refusing to beat up Kenard (Thuliso Dingwall) after Namond finds out that Kenard stole from him. Both his enforced criminality and his ineffectiveness render Namond vulnerable to Marlo's insurgency as it continues though the expansionist contagion stage.

The third stage of the Accidental Guerrilla Syndrome, *intervention*, is characterized by outside forces intervening in the contagion area. External forces begin to take action against the insurgent presence in response to their acts of violence and growing strength (Kilcullen 37). In the case of *The Wire*, that large scale intervention can be seen in the reaction of the Baltimore Police Department (BPD) to Marlo's growing power. After gaining information from wiretaps on the Stanfield organization, the BPD launches a series of raids (4.05). According to Kilcullen, in cases of Accidental Guerrilla Syndrome this act of intervention serves to alienate the population instead of gaining their support for the outside agency that sees itself as protecting them. Reasons for this could be resentment caused by collateral damage (the intervening forces resulting in accidental harm being done to the local population), the outsiders' presence in their community and/or their failure to successfully overthrow the insurgent force: "Local people ... will always tend to side with closer against more distant relatives, with local against external actors" (Kilcullen 38). In other words, according to Kilcullen, West Baltimore residents would be more likely to support the drug dealers who live and work as their neighbors, than to support the police department whose presence is less consistent. The raids launched by the BPD prove unsuccessful, as few arrests are made and no drugs are uncovered (4.05). In any insurgency, the failure of one side to meet the basic safety needs of a possible accidental guerrilla is what causes that person to become one (Kilcullen 38).

Michael's domestic circumstance forces him to seek the intervention of an external actor to help with his security needs. He does have other options beyond going to Marlo for aid, but he has little confidence in other actors' ability to help him. Michael considers going to the school system, social services, or the police for help, but none of these options elicits any confidence. In the same way that the BPD attempts to do what it sees as good—but without establishing trust, and thus remaining an outside intervenor—Cutty offers help but Michael does not trust him, questioning his motives (4.09). Cutty's actions towards Michael appear to be benevolent, but by so readily offering aid, he has the opposite effect. Instead of gaining Michael's support, Cutty's attempts to intervene further alienate Michael, driving him toward Marlo's now widely-established organization, offering an effective example of the potential risks of intervention even from within a community in conflict.

The failure of Baltimore's social institutions to convey a sense of protection and security to Michael makes him feel that he has no choice but to go to Marlo for help (4.10). The scene in which Michael goes to Marlo's court to ask for his aid suggests that the divide between safety that can be provided by Marlo and that which can be provided through legal means is too large, whether that legal means takes the form of social services, the education system, as embodied in Roland "*Prez*" Pryzbylewski (Jim True-Frost) or the community, as represented by Cutty. As a result, he considers Marlo to be his only real option as indicated by his stating to Marlo, "I got a problem I can't bring to no one else" (4.10).

During this same time period Namond is placed in the experimental class under the supervision of Major Howard "Bunny" Colvin (Robert Wisdom). Namond takes an interest in the class and begins to make strides academically, earning Colvin's praise. However, Namond continues to deal drugs and is eventually arrested by Sergeant Carver (Seth Gilliam) (4.10). The movement of Namond from Prez's class to the experimental class represents a form of outside intervention by the school system (anti-gang, and by parallel anti-insurgent), while Namond's arrest later in the season represents a second form, police intervention. Although intervention often results in the alienation of a population, the progress Namond makes while in the experimental class and in his relationship with Colvin following his arrest represent the exception to the rule. Instead of alienating Namond from Colvin and the realm outside of the drug game, it is De'Londa's reaction to the police intervention that serves to alienate Namond from his mother. In an attempt to toughen Namond up, De'Londa kicks him out of the house following his arrest. This expulsion enables Namond to stay with the Colvins, where Bunny realizes that Namond could have a bright future if his circumstances were to change. The portrayal of Namond represents a rare example in the conflict zones of *The Wire* of a successful intervention.

An insurgency or counterinsurgency operation fails when one side alienates the potential accidental guerrillas in a population. The alienation that emerges in the intervention phase snowballs in the fourth and final stage of the Accidental Guerrilla Syndrome, the *rejection* phase. After intervention causes the population to feel alienated from external actors, rejection is the phase in which potential accidental guerrillas emerge as actual accidental guerrillas. The failed process of intervention by external actors causes the population to lose confidence in the ability of non-insurgent actors to meet their basic security needs. "The more the ... group can paint itself as similar to the local people and the more it can appear as their defender against outsiders, the stronger this phenomenon becomes" (Kilcullen 38).

The drug wars in *The Wire* manifest this process in Michael's actions once he decides to approach Marlo for help. After Chris and Snoop kill his stepfather, Michael begins training as an enforcer in the Stanfield organization and is given his own drug corner to run and protect. Whereas earlier in Season Four Michael was reluctant to be consistently associated with the drug trade, his enlistment with Marlo represents a rejection of those initial beliefs in the service of security. He alienates himself from Cutty and Namond, getting into a fight with Namond in Cutty's gym that causes Cutty to ban him (4.12). Even after Cutty comes again to offer his help, Michael continues to refuse his intervention, just as he continues to reject more formal social services. In an example of the Accidental Guerrilla Syndrome as work, Michael's conscious refusal can be read as the accidental guerrilla's rejection of external help from those not associated with the side of the conflict with which he has begun to align himself. Michael's case illustrates the failure of the social system and government institutions at attracting the drug wars' accidental guerrillas, while reinforcing the success of Marlo Stanfield's organization in attracting them. As Kilcullen states, the ability of an insurgent or government group to provide for an accidental guerrilla's needs directly influences the guerrilla's allegiance: "Political actors who enjoy substantial territorial control can protect civilians who live in that territory ... giving survival-oriented civilians a strong incentive to collaborate with them, irrespective of their true or initial preferences (Kilcullen 68). Michael's attempts and failures to meet his needs for security in the first half of Season Four suggest that the social system cannot meet his needs, while Marlo and his organization can, further establishing their social and psychological dominance, especially among young men, in the community at the site of conflict.

That said, even after enlisting in Marlo's operation Michael does not convey the unwavering loyalty associated with committed fighters. As is true of any accidental guerrilla, Michael's allegiances are not set. Despite his being a member of the organization Randy is "snitching" on, he still protects Randy even after his friend is labeled a snitch. Michael comes to Randy's aid when he is intimidated at school and takes part in a fight to protect him (4.11). These actions are different from the depiction of committed fighters in *The Wire*. Michael's actions are representative of the complex levels of allegiance in play in cases of accidental guerrillas.[3] Michael supports the Stanfield organization and is willing to commit murder on its behalf, but he also shows support to his friends: even Michael's fight with Namond arises because Namond is bullying Dukie. Similarly, unlike committed fighter Bodie, who refuses to leave his corners unattended even when faced with impending death, Michael quickly sheds his role as corner boy and enforcer in Season Five after he realizes that Snoop intends to kill him. He abandons his allegiance to Marlo after his basic needs (now again his security) are threatened, and he becomes a stick up boy. To further reinforce this changing allegiance, the only robbery that we see Michael carry out is the stick up of Marlo's old bank (5.10).

The rising Stanfield organization is the primary beneficiary of attempts at intervention by external actors, as corner boys and boys of summer are forced to choose sides, and in effect become accidental insurgents. In the case of Namond, however, the intervention by state and non-state actors proves successful. By kicking him out of the house De'Londa fails to meet Namond's basic security needs, causing Namond to reject his mother's negative influence in favor of life with the Colvins after Bunny Colvin persuades Wee-Bey to grant them guardianship. Namond stops dealing drugs and commits himself to his schoolwork. He is not seen with the any of the boys of summer, or any other West Baltimore residents for the rest of the series. After he is adopted by the Colvins, Namond disappears from the series and the community it depicts, and is seen only briefly, in a successful performance at a debate competition (5.09). Perhaps significantly, given that he is one of the only characters on the show who experiences a positive effect of intervention, Namond is last shown debating interventionary action for the African AIDS crisis.

The character arcs of Namond and Michael convey two opposing outcomes of the form of Accidental Guerrilla Syndrome that *The Wire* depicts in the drug conflict zone of West Baltimore: an accidental guerrilla can be pushed towards work for the drug cartels and a life in Baltimore's criminal underworld, or one can be pushed away. However, in *The Wire*'s version of West Baltimore very few of the characters that are introduced manage to reject the influence of the cartels and the larger drug game. D'Angelo attempts to reject the Barksdales, but is killed for doing so, and Namond is the only one of the four boys of summer to escape the influence of the drug trade: Randy is hardened by his time in the group home and rejects communication with the police; Michael becomes a stick up boy; and Dukie becomes a drug addict.

More often than not in *The Wire*, the intervention strategies of the American government's War on Drugs fail to result in any positive changes to a character's standard of living or quality of life (Simon and Mulholland). Analyzed through the lens of counterinsurgency doctrine, the failure of the War on Drugs is evident. According to the Kilcullen, "Effective counterinsurgency provides human security to the population where they live, twenty four hours a day," and the approach to security must be comprehensive, incorporating "political, security, economic and informational components" (Kilcullen 266). The comprehensive failure of the social system is evident in *The Wire*. Although Namond is protected by Carver and Colvin, state protection services are portrayed as inconsistent at best, incapable of providing the twenty-four hour security that is needed. The police department fails to protect Randy, D'Angelo or Bodie. Social services also fail to protect Randy, and do not elicit any confidence in Michael as an adequate means of security for Bug. The education system fails Dukie by forcing him to attend high school despite his being unprepared. Furthermore, despite the success of Colvin's experimental class, the school system refuses any structural reforms that might provide a different kind of security. For practical economic security, there are almost no legal jobs available to *The Wire*'s young men.

At a larger level, it is important to note the high priority placed by insurgent groups on control of information circulation, as Season Five of *The Wire* hypothesizes that the power of information is being abandoned by institutions that have the potential to protect by investigation and information dissemination: the downsizing of Baltimore's newspapers renders them unable to document systemic failures to protect American citizens. As Ryan Brooks also documents, throughout the series, the possibility of political security is rendered laughable as anything other than a mirage of manipulated statistics enforced by Mayor Clarence Royce (Glynn Turman) and Commissioner Ervin Burrell (Frankie Faison). Mayor Thomas 'Tommy' Carcetti (Aiden Gillen) initially seeks to be of a different sort, yet devolves into the same actions as his predecessor by the end of the series, forcing Cedric Daniels (Lance Reddick) to step down as police commissioner after he refuses to manipulate crime statistics, and replacing him with corrupt agent Major Stanislaus Valchek (Al Brown).

American counterinsurgency doctrine emphasizes the importance of maintaining continuity in leadership among key personnel and allowing them the authority and resources to implement "a consistent set of policies that can be developed and applied over time" (Kilcullen 266). The five seasons of *The Wire* depict multiple changes to Baltimore's political and police leadership (from Royce to Carcetti to Nerese Campbell (Marlyne Barrett) and from Burrell to Daniels to Valchek). Each new leader is portrayed as having a different leadership style, with different priorities and levels of competence. A deficit in funding for the school system in Season Four results in a lack of educational supplies and a rigid mandate towards ineffective test-based learning. Budget cuts to the police department and *Baltimore Sun* in Season Five prevent the police from gaining legitimate wiretaps on Marlo Stanfield and the *Sun* from performing its social mission. Queried by the *New Yorker* on this dark view of the systems that are supposed to protect Americans, David Simon has asserted that *The Wire* outlines the ways in which human beings are devalued in contemporary capitalist America: "Every single moment on the planet, from here on out, human beings are worth less" (quoted in Talbot 1). The lack of continuity in leadership, authority and resources in *The Wire* reinforces the ineffectiveness of Baltimore's institutions in maintaining population safety. The series emphasizes the uphill battle being fought by Baltimore's social institutions against the tactics of insurgency used by the city's criminal underworld, and the War on Drugs being fought in *The Wire* is portrayed as an entirely losing battle. Although there are the occasional exceptions like Namond, the failure of Baltimore's social institutions to maintain the individual safety of the population leaves potential accidental guerrillas with few options to meet their basic needs. In *The Wire,* the guerrilla tactics used by the drug cartels attract accidental guerrillas and committed fighters alike, while the stagnant interventionist counterinsurgency tactics of the governments of Baltimore and Maryland prove unsuccessful in combating them.

Notes

1. In his work on guerrilla warfare in urban environments, Patrick D. Marques argues that maintaining civilian support is still paramount to any insurgency but that the arena of battle has steadily shifted from rural areas to urban settings in the late twentieth and early twenty-first centuries. The terrain is different in a city, with buildings, communication centers, public transportation, narrow streets and back alleyways offering different methods of attack, concealment, and propaganda dissemination.

2. Omar's refusal to work with any gang marks him as a different kind of non-combatant, though his willingness to collaborate with police in the prosecution of Marquis "Bird" Hilton, a Barksdale soldier involved in the torture and murder of Omar's lover Brandon, renders him something of an accidental guerrilla in the larger War on Drugs.

3. An anecdote from Afghanistan in 2006 provided by Kilcullen illuminates an extreme version of the complex motivations of accidental guerrillas:

> The most intriguing thing about this battle was not the Taliban though; it was the behavior of the local people. One reason the patrol was so heavily pinned down was that its retreat, back down the only road along the valley floor, was cut off by a group of farmers who had been working in the fields and, seeing the ambush begin, rushed home to fetch their weapons and join in. Three nearby villages participated, with people coming from as far as 5 kilometers away; spontaneously marching to the sound of the guns. There is no evidence that the locals cooperated directly with the Taliban; indeed, it seems they had no directly political reason to get involved in the fight (several, questioned afterward, said they had no love for the Taliban and were generally well-disposed towards the Americans in the area). But, they said, when the battle was right there in front of them how could they not join in? Did we understand just how boring it was to be a teenager in a valley in central Afghanistan? This was the most exciting thing that had happened in their valley in years. It would have shamed them to stand by and wait it out, they said.

Works Cited

Beliveau, Ralph, and Laura Bolf-Beliveau. "Posing Problems and Picking Fights: Critical Pedagogy and the Corner Boys." *The Wire: Urban Decay and American Television*. Ed. Tiffany Potter and C.W. Marshall. New York: Continuum, 2009. 91–106. Print.

Blum, Lawrence. "'B5—it got all the dinks': Schools and Education on *The Wire*." *Darkmatter* 4 (2009). http://www.darkmatter101.org/site/category/journal/issues/4-the-wire/.

Brooks, Ryan. "The Narrative Production of 'Real Police.'" *The Wire: Urban Decay and American Television*. Ed. Tiffany Potter and C.W. Marshall. New York: Continuum, 2009. 64–77. Print.

Christgau, Georgia. "'These Are Not Your Children': *The Wire*'s Eighth Graders and Their Fate at Edward Tillman Middle School." *Darkmatter* 4 (2009). http://www.darkmatter101.org/site/category/journal/issues/4-the-wire/.

History of Minimum Wage in Maryland. Maryland Department of Labour, Licensing and Regulation. Online. Internet. 22 Feb. 2010. http://www.dllr.state.md.us/labor/wages/minwagehistory.shtml.

"Insurgency." *Oxford English Dictionary*. Web.

Kilcullen, David. *The Accidental Guerrilla: Fighting Small Wars in the Midst of a Big One*. New York: Oxford University Press, 2009. Print.

Marques, Patrick D. *Guerrilla Warfare Tactics in Urban Environments*. Dissertation, U.S. Army Command and General Staff College, Fort Leavenworth, Kansas, 2003. Web.

Petraeus, David H., and James Amos. *U.S Marine Corps Counterinsurgency Field Manual FM 3-24*. Chicago: University of Chicago Press, 2007. Print

Read, Jason. "Stringer Bell's Lament: Violence and Legitimacy in Contemporary Capitalism."

The Wire: Urban Decay and American Television. Ed. Tiffany Potter and C.W. Marshall. New York: Continuum, 2009. 122–134. Print.

Simon, David, and John Mulholland. "*The Wire* creator David Simon on what's behind the U.S. war on drugs." *The Guardian.com* 25 May 2013. Web.

Simon, David, and Edward Burns. *The Wire.* HBO. 2002–08.

Spence, Jonathan. *Mao Zedong: A Life.* New York: Viking, 1999. Print.

Staniland, Paul. "States, Insurgents, and Wartime Political Orders." *Perspectives on Politics* 10.2 (2012): 243–264. Print.

Talbot, Margaret. "Stealing Life: The Crusader Behind *The Wire*." *The New Yorker* 22 Oct. 2007. Web.

Tse-Tung, Mao. *On Guerrilla Warfare.* Washington, D.C: U.S Marine Corps, 1961. Web.

Venkates, Sudhir. *Off the Books: The Underground Economy of the Urban Poor.* Cambridge: Harvard University Press, 2006. Print.

The War on Drugs and the War on Terror

Arin Keeble

The pilot episode of *The Wire* subtly articulates a frustration that the hidden America it portrays—a swath of America that has been forgotten by its government and citizens—is being even further neglected in the aftermath of 9/11 as the nation turns its focus to terror. This first episode makes three significant allusions to what would come to be called The War on Terror through the introduction of its core surface-level subject, The War on Drugs. One of these allusions occurs in Orlando's, a strip bar that provides a "front" and base for the Barksdale organization. Directly following an exchange between Stringer Bell (Idris Elba) and D'Angelo Barksdale (Larry Gilliard, Jr.) during which Stringer is demanding a more ruthless and violent approach to the way D'Angelo manages his branch of the Barksdale drugs operation, the "low-rise" site, the camera lingers on a TV screen situated behind the bar which bears the headline, "America at War," in familiar post–9/11 iconography. This diegetic flourish, which closes the scene, serves as an ironic comment that highlights the way the continuing drugs conflict is occurring out of the spotlight in post–9/11 America; though it also works the other way, inviting comparison between these unconventional "wars." A second allusion to The War on Terror, which explicitly reinforces this idea that the drug war is being buried by post–9/11 policy shifts, occurs when Homicide Detective Jimmy McNulty (Dominic West) visits a contact in the FBI, Special Agent Terrance Fitzhugh (Doug Olear). Discussing a parallel drugs investigation, Fitzhugh tells McNulty explicitly that federal government resources previously allocated to the War on Drugs are all being reallocated to fight terror, "ever since those towers fell." (1.01) This is the first instance of a continuing strand of rhetoric about the "FBI reprioritizing from the war on drugs to the war on terror," which as Mark Chou states, becomes one of "*The Wire*'s most explicit and recurrent references" (Chou, par. 40). Finally, there is another more neutral link between these two "wars," which is established in an early dialogue between narcotics detectives Ellis Carver (Seth Gilliam), Thomas "Herc" Hauk (Domenick Lombardozzi) and Shakima Greggs (Sonja Sohn). In this scene the War on Drugs is evoked in conversation as an endless, futile and brutal conflict that is not accurately described by the term "war." With typical machismo, Herc is celebrating the aggressive tactics that he and partner Carver have made their hallmark and Kima replies with sarcasm: "fighting the War on Drugs, one brutality case at a time." Carver then counters by offering a wider criticism of the conflict: "you can't even call that shit a war." When Herc asks, "Why not?" Carver states flatly, "Wars end" (1.01).

Series creator David Simon has repeatedly made comments about his intention to critique the United States' War on Drugs—which he describes as a "brutal suppression of the underclass" – but it is hard not to link it here to America's newer global conflict, for several reasons, and in spite of the fact that this inaugural episode first aired in June 2002, three months before The U.S. Department of State issued the September 2002 National Security Strategy, the policy document that officially launched the War on Terror (2009, 11). Even when *The Wire* is explicitly critiquing America's disproportionate focus on terror, parallels are drawn. For example, in a scene in 4.01, in which the Western District officers are attending a mandatory training session on terrorism, the room erupts into hilarity when Officer Michael Santangelo (Michael Salconi) asks: "Even if those terrorists did fuck up the Western, could anybody even tell?" Again, while on one level, Santangelo's comments are designed to emphasize just how far removed the drug war is from the world of international terrorism, it also forces us to consider similarities in the violence-ravaged streets of Baltimore and the fields of international conflict in the War on Terror. The most prominent direct link between the two conflicts, made by Detective Carver in episode one, and continually emphasized throughout the series, is that which characterizes the War on Drugs as a futile and unending conflict. This characterization quickly became applicable to the War on Terror and became more and more prominent as *The Wire* played out, with particular parallels in the way the "enemies" in both conflicts were seen to have unclear identities, unclear and unstable structures of power, and to employ a range of guerrilla tactics.[1] Retrospectively, the portrayal of Herc and Carver, whose shaved heads, aggression and misogyny very clearly fit a certain stereotype of the American soldier, helps to establish this link, and Greggs' statement has a clear resonance in the sense that the War on Terror has comprised of a series of brutalities. Mostly though, with the backdrop of a government relying on retrograde ideas of international conflict and warfare, it is the simple question Carver raises, of what precisely constitutes a war, which resonates so powerfully within this moment of history, that is, as revanchist post–9/11 American foreign policy began to gather momentum.

The Wire's creative team were clearly unhappy with the way post–9/11 policy shifts pulled attention further away from the American forgotten, and from the institutional problems of the neo-liberal city which the program's surface story addresses. However, the examples above are merely subtle opening nods and while they are diegetic and fundamentally remain true to the program's realism, they are undoubtedly pregnant with the more complex narrative correlations that would play out over five seasons from 2002 to 2008—arguably the peak years of The War on Terror. This chapter will argue that two key aspects of the series' larger narrative allegorically respond to The War on Terror and, indeed, provide a politicized critical commentary that was for the most part absent in cultural production—particularly in television—during this period. The unique and multifaceted allegory of *The Wire* is particularly significant in the way it links America's hidden domestic problems with its very visible international conflicts. The first of these two allegorical strands is an aspect of the program that its creators have repeatedly emphasized (to the point that it has become a clichéd way of discussing the program), the idea that *The Wire* was deliberately conceived to trouble simplistic notions of good and evil, and heroes and villains: conceits that were, of course, at the heart of the George W. Bush Administration's nationalistic post–9/11 rhetoric. The second is the way larger series-long narrative of *The Wire* dramatizes the rise and decline of the Barksdale organization and the subsequent rise and development of the Marlo Stanfield group—both ostensibly "enemies" in the drug war being waged by the Baltimore Police Department and city government. This narrative demonstrates the way that, because of larger societal conditions and power systems, when one enemy organization is defeated or compromised, another emerges—a phenomenon often associated with terrorist cells and so called "rogue states" in The War on Terror. Moreover, each of the two drugs empires is characterized as a nebulous, unknowable or mutable enemy that seems to almost endlessly renew itself.

The Intradiegetic Allegory

My argument here that these two aspects of *The Wire*'s larger series-long narrative allegorically comment on the America's War on Terror, is made more compelling by the evident tension between the program's fetish for realism and authenticity, and what we can identify as national allegory. *The Wire*'s conspicuous attempt to be realistic and authentic is one of its most debated and contested characteristics, but however successful it is in this regard, and whatever value we place on its realism, it is my contention that it is this realism that enables it to operate as a particularly rich allegorical narrative. The documentary or journalistic ethos of *The Wire* relies to a large extent on its much-vaunted germination in Simon's own background as a Baltimore reporter and his celebrated reportage on the Baltimore drug trade. The program's claims to authenticity are strengthened by its equally-vaunted reliance on the professional experiences of co-creator Ed Burns, a former Baltimore homicide detective. The credibility that is afforded by the bibliographic history and mythology of the creators of *The Wire* was further consolidated by a casting policy that included the recruitment of many non-professional actors with relevant life experience, including policeman, politicians, dock workers, reporters, stickup men and gangsters. However, the extent to which the program is actually "journalistic," authentic or realistic is, as stated, contested. Frank Kelleter suggests the serial format of *The Wire* has perpetuated the mythology of its authenticity pointing out "that serial production overlaps with serial reception" and that

> a series, unlike a finished oeuvre, can observe its own effects on audiences as long as the narrative is running. Moreover, it can react to these observations, making adjustments in form and content [Kelleter 2012, 35].

This is undoubtedly the case with *The Wire*, and its particular brand of realism, especially in the later series, which give much emphasis to aspects of the program that blogs, journalists and scholarly articles had lauded in the earlier seasons. For example, the blurring of distinctions between fact and fiction through the use of non-professional actors and the employment of individuals who have participated in the drugs trade and gang cultures of Baltimore was taken to the extreme in the second half of the series through the much-discussed employment of individuals such as Felicia "Snoop" Pearson who plays Snoop in Seasons Four and Five, and who was a convicted murderer at age 14. This practice is reminiscent of the representation of the Algerian revolutionaries in Gillo Pontecorvo's celebrated anti-colonial film

The Battle of Algiers (1966). In fact, from the starless ensemble cast to the use of non-professional actors and participants from the actual conflict, and particularly in its conspicuous drive for a documentary realism and authenticity, *The Wire* is significantly indebted to Pontecorvo's film. Kelleter also makes the point that "the show's effect of authenticity depends on cancelling the presence of American television from its representational identity." In order to seem genuinely realistic then, "*The Wire* has to subtract its own (medium's) activities from the social world it depicts." (47) Not only, then, are *The Wire*'s storylines written by people who have reported and policed Baltimore's "urban crime environment," and portrayed by people who have lived and worked in this world, but they conspicuously avoid classic genre conceits of the police procedural, such as narrative closure, and heroism. But while this movement away from contrived or formulaic storylines might signify a heightened realism, it also results in the exclusion of what Michael Lister, in this volume, describes as "the missing middle," or the "citizens" of Baltimore, as Omar Little (Michael Kenneth Williams) would have it. It is certainly the case that this program, which has been widely celebrated as a "panoramic" representation of the neo-liberal city, is generally restricted to law enforcement, the drug economy, the political worlds, the stevedores and the journalists.

In another challenge to the realist imperatives of *The Wire*'s portrait of the neo-liberal city, Paul Allen Anderson points out that the program embraces allegory and symbolism just as readily as realism. Anderson examines the now-famous chess sequence in 1.03, where D'Angelo is explaining the abilities of each chess piece to his crew members, Wallace (Michael B. Jordan) and Bodie Broadus (J.D. Williams), by equating them to positions and roles in the Barksdale hierarchy. Crucially, as Anderson notes, D'Angelo emphasizes the hierarchical aspect of the pieces which is in stark contrast to the more "democratic" roles of checkers pieces (Wallace and Bodie were using the chess set to play checkers before D'Angelo intervened). The significance of this is that, firstly, checkers "evokes a social fantasy about the nongendered equality of opportunity as an achieved original position from which all players on the board begin their working lives." As Anderson explains:

> By contrast an explicit division of labor defines the game of chess. Half of a player's pieces are interchangeable soldiers (the pawns), whereas the remaining ones start as pairs with special abilities (rooks, knights, and bishops) or have singular importance (the irreplaceable king and his great protector the queen) [87].

The allegorical implication here is obvious and this kind of allegorical set-piece occurs throughout *The Wire*. Another notable early example occurs in

1.04 when members of "the detail," a special unit of detectives from the homicide and narcotics departments assigned to the Barksdale case, are apparently attempting to move a desk from one room of their dank basement office to another. After several minutes of pushing and pulling, the several individuals on each side of the desk realize that they had miscommunicated on whether they were trying to go into or out of the office, and had been pushing against each other the whole time. This evokes the series' larger picture of bureaucratic political or law enforcement institutions with roughly the same objectives unwittingly working against each other.

Another important aspect of Anderson's argument lies in his account of the tension between allegory, and what he identifies as "tautology" – the oft-repeated phrases such as "the game is the game," which resonate so powerfully with the futile existences and harsh realities of so many of the program's characters. But while tautologies reinforce the program's realism through a kind of stability or logic, allegory adds another dimension: as Anderson states, "an allegorical narrative ... *is what it is* and also *is what it is not*" (86). This is reminiscent of the way David Lodge describes the conventional understanding of allegory as a "mode of analogy" that presents "one thing or concept in terms of another thing or concept," while building a more complex notion of allegory in relation to realist narratives (361). Lodge notes that while "realism as a literary technique would appear to be opposed to analogical modes," in actuality, "analogical modes are allowed to permeate the apparently non-analogical mode of realism in the interest of meaning" (361). My stated contention here is that a similar dynamic exists in *The Wire*, in its depiction of the War on Drugs. However, *The Wire* adds another dimension to Lodge's formula as the realism of the narrative also enriches the allegory. This particular type of allegory as employed in *The Wire* is a mode that has been identified elsewhere by Gary Johnson, as an "intradiegetic" allegory (237). Before defining this particular type of allegory, Johnson firstly poses a question that is useful to any discussion of allegory: "is it [allegory] hermeneutic in nature rather than compositional—a way of reading, in other words?" (233). Allegory can, of course, be read either way—as intrinsically structural or as an interpretive framework used to "read" a text, and in an "intradiegetic allegory" it can be both. An intradiegetic allegory operates a "narrative nesting effect, a situation in which one narrative structure (the allegorical narrative) is embedded within another (the primary narrative)" (236). In *The Wire*, The War on Terror narrative is "nested" in the narrative through the many passing or critical allusions throughout the series, and then allegorized by the actual realistic narrative of The War on Drugs.

In *The Wire*, the frequent diegetic allusions to the War on Terror, such as the ones previously mentioned from the first episode, are comfortably embedded as anecdotes and asides in the realism of the War on Drugs narrative. They also build a bridge from the diegesis to the allegorical narrative "in the interest of meaning," or in order to add nuance and complexity to the allegory. The intradiegetic allegory of *The Wire*, then, not only offers a critical commentary on the War on Terror but also provides a platform for reflection in the sense that it engenders a kind of comparative dialogue between each narrative strand. Consequently, the allegorical narrative's critique of The War on Terror becomes even stronger through its connection to the series of failures and human causalities in the surface story of Baltimore's drug war, and the fact that America's new conflict has rendered it invisible to public. The ultimate conclusion of this allegory might be located in David Simon's more recent series Tremé (2009–2014) which is based on America's next major disaster, the flooding of New Orleans after Hurricane Katrina. The forgotten, largely African American citizens of New Orleans, who perished or whose lives were devastated by those events, were similarly invisible (before Katrina) to the underclass of Baltimore, and it is to the credit of *The Wire* that it is able to chronicle their plight while simultaneously allegorizing the War on Terror. The intradiagetic aspect of the series is clear: consider the language and terminology of The War on Terror in the passionate monologue about The War on Drugs from Major Bunny Colvin (Robert Wisdom) in season three:

> You call something a war, and pretty soon everybody gonna be running around acting like warriors. They gonna be running around on a goddamn crusade, storming corners, slapping on cuffs, racking up body counts. And when you at war, you need a fucking enemy. And pretty soon, damn near everybody on every corner is your fucking enemy. And soon the neighbourhood that you supposed to be policing, that's just occupied territory [3.10].

The allegorical resonance here is undeniable and the rhetoric about contrived enemies and occupation chimes precisely with criticism of the Bush Administration's foreign policy. The third season is particularly rife with diegetic references to the War on Terror and the critical edge to these becomes even stronger as the season reaches its nadir. In the final episode, rallying an emotionally damaged Avon Barksdale (Wood Harris), Slim Charles (Anwan Glover) discusses the importance of fighting the "war" between the Barksdale and Marlo Stanfield groups:

> Doesn't matter who did what to who at this point, the fact is we went to war and now there ain't no going back. I mean shit, that's what war is you know. Once

you in it, you in it. If it's a lie, then we fight on that lie, but you got to fight [3.12].

Is it possible to consider such a line, in an episode which first aired in 2005, without considering America's War in Iraq? Another example, which will be addressed in more detail, is the opening scene which depicts the falling of the Franklin Towers housing projects, which is well-analyzed by Elizabeth Bonjean who describes the way we are "transported back to 11 September" as the towers collapse and clouds of dust swirl around the blocks and down the surrounding streets (Bonjean 2009, 163). More subtly, one of the popular brands of heroin being sold throughout the season is called "WMD," connecting a street drug to the Weapons of Mass Destruction that so preoccupied the Bush Administration during the early years of the War on Terror: a literal and symbolic opiate. Even the satirical humor of *The Wire* utilizes this trope. In the penultimate episode of Season Three, when agent Fitzhugh is asked to pull strings with the FBI to get a wire tap activated immediately on Stringer Bell's phone, he inevitably relies on War on Terror policy shifts. When asked how he was able to do it, he rhetorically asks McNulty: "What is Stringer Bell's first name?" When McNulty responds correctly, by saying "Russell," Fitzhugh states, "Today its Ahmed," revealing his ruse for getting the FBI to prioritize the wire tap. These "embedded" references to the War on Terror or to Bush-era foreign policy enrich the two major strands of the series-long allegory by making direct reference to the allegorical subject in the realistic narrative of The War on Drugs.

Heroes and Villains

One of Simon's stated agendas in creating *The Wire* was disavowing simplistic notions of good and evil. He states in his 2009 account of the series that "we were bored with good and evil. To the greatest possible extent, we were quick to renounce the theme" (3). Simon also characterizes this part of his vision for the program as in specific contrast to the Bush Administration's rhetoric: "coating an elemental truth with the bright gloss of heroism and national sacrifice is the prerogative of the nation-state"(3). One could argue that, in terms of terror and terrorism, notions of good and evil are necessarily an issue of perspective. Depending on one's political or ideological allegiances, for example, "terrorists" might be seen as freedom fighters or revolutionaries, just as the Bush Administration's project of "spreading freedom" might be seen as occupation or imperialism. This semantic issue is compounded by fundamental questions of definition. Are, as Karen Festes asks rhetorically, "terrorists primarily criminals, warriors, or political protestors? It depends on the frame in the eyes of the beholder: the victim and bully perspectives" (2011, 76). The American socio-political climate in which *The Wire* first appeared, however, was not receptive to ambiguities of this kind. In the aftermath of 9/11, the American government set about ensuring that any ambiguity about the protagonists and antagonists in what President Bush characterized as a "changed world" of international conflict was quashed, establishing clear enemies, primarily the "axis of evil" in the Middle East or nation states which he accused of harboring terrorists or secretly developing "weapons of mass destruction" in order to "threaten the peace of the world" (2002, 103). The Bush Administration built a singular rhetoric that quickly became prevalent in mainstream culture and politics and was repeated continually in the many speeches the president delivered in the months and years after the attacks. "Terrorists" were the enemy and any individual or nation involved would be one too: "Either you are with us or you are with the terrorists.... From this day forward, any nation that continues to harbor or support terrorism will be regarded by the United States as a hostile regime" (Bush 2001, 65). Adam Hodges uses linguistic analysis to show how, through "narrative accrual," this rhetoric pervaded American culture: "the repeated narrations by the president of the United States effectively accumulate into a larger cultural narrative shared by many within the nation" (2011, 4). This rhetoric of good vs. evil, which pitted America and its allies against the "axis of evil," had clear aesthetic values, and the most dominant of these was the hyper-masculine image of the cowboy or frontiersman, an image that borrowed from America's national mythologies of the frontier, and from the president's Texan heritage. Politicians from both sides of the political spectrum were repeatedly seen in cowboy hats, hunting or fishing, or wielding shotguns in contrived photo opportunities that portrayed them as rugged, hyper-masculine leaders. Susan Faludi's trenchant study of post–9/11 masculinity, *The Terror Dream: What 9/11 Revealed About America* (2007), highlights this pattern of posturing:

> Why were our political and cultural stages suddenly packed with Lone Ranger leaders, Davy Crockett candidates, and John Wayne "manly men"? Why, in short, when confronted with an actual danger, did America call rewrite? [129].

Faludi's question cuts to the heart of America's post–9/11 reliance on a mythological frontier past, but also serves simply to remind us of the popularity of this rhetoric and aesthetic during the immediate post–9/11 years. With this hyperbolic national cultural backdrop, Simon's mission to "renounce" the theme of good and evil, and to depict the hidden America of *The Wire* in stark opposition to a mainstream culture fixated on mythological depictions of heroes and villains, has a certain logic.

The fact that all of *The Wire*'s characters are all fundamentally "flawed," is also part of its imperative of realism (in that characters are shown to be "human"), but it also conspicuously unites a large ensemble cast of otherwise very diverse characters through one common denominator. On the surface, *The Wire*'s depiction of morally ambiguous police detectives, politicians, stevedores, gangsters, organized criminals and junkies who participate variously in the War on Drugs is antithetical to the clearly defined protagonists and antagonists of the War on Terror almost to the point that it runs the risk of mirroring the singularity of the Bush rhetoric. However, *The Wire*'s complex and conflicted characters contain significant depth, and the gradations of sympathy engendered by particular characters is invariably guided by their relationship to institutions and their responses to institutional pressures. As Alasdair McMillan states, *The Wire* is "very sympathetic in its portrayal of individuals forced into compromising positions by institutions, and very critical of the ones doing the forcing" (2009, 62). Within this logic, *The Wire* does have a number of antiheroes who "are the rebellious, insubordinate characters who resist compromising when it matters most" (2009, 62). McMillan is discussing some of the police characters; McNulty, and Cedric Daniels (Lance Reddick) in particular. However, the most iconic antihero of the program, Omar Little, comes from the "criminal" or "illegitimate" world of *The Wire* – though Omar is also a character who is fiercely resistant to both the legitimate and illegitimate institutions of Baltimore.

As hard as the Bush Administration and a complicit, conservative media fought to maintain their rhetoric of good and evil and heroes and villains, inevitably, the complexities and ambiguities of war would begin to threaten its persuasive force. Against this backdrop, Omar, who it is worth noting, was originally going to be killed off in the first season but was deemed too important to lose, became integral to the series. On the surface, Omar is one of the clearest refutations of simple formulations of good and evil that the program offers: he is a criminal and a killer but also one of the only characters who operates within a strict moral code, who wouldn't harm a "citizen" and who is sensitive, and overtly emotional. However, Omar is also a deeply conflicted and tormented character and moving beyond being, simply, part of an "argument" against simplistic notions of good and evil or heroes and villains, Omar can be seen as emblematic of a wider conflictedness in American society of this time.

Omar was first conceived of as an archetypal American genre villain, a stick-up man, who according to co-creator Ed Burns, was partially modeled after several mythological Baltimore criminals that Burns describes as "mavericks"; "stickup boys with names like Apex and Ferdinand, Cadillac and Anthony" (Alvarez 2009, 313). Even more prominent then this archetype, Omar has many of the classic characteristics of a Western protagonist: like any number of Western heroes he is a maverick or rogue, often a loner, fiercely loyal, intelligent, resourceful and capable, possesses a strong moral code that disavows or disregards institutional law when necessary, and wears a dark overcoat which Alvarez describes variously as a "Jesse James style duster," or "Wild West duster," with a shotgun underneath (2009, 315). Tiffany Potter and C.W. Marshall also identify his temperament or outlook as particularly "Western," highlighting his "Wild West mentality," and describing him as "the lone frontiersman taming the wilderness of the drug trade" (2009, 4). Aesthetically, he is very distinct with his long facial scar, his duster and shotgun, his trademark nursery-rhyme whistle, "The Farmer in the Dell," and his oft-repeated mantras, "all in the game," or "oh, indeed." One memorable scene in the second season shows Detective Bunk Moreland (Wendell Pierce) witness some very small children taking turns dressing up as, and pretending to "be Omar" in a Baltimore ghetto version of Cowboys and Indians (2.03). As much as Simon wanted to turn away from mainstream notions of heroism, this characterization of Omar was certainly not accidental. Michael Kenneth Williams recounts how, in his first meeting with Simon, he was urged to watch two classic Westerns: Sam Peckinpah's *The Wild Bunch* (1969) and John Ford's *The Man Who Shot Liberty Vance* (1962), and the Western aesthetic values of *The Wire* do indeed go beyond the characterization of Omar. Many of the program's shootouts, such as the memorable opening to the 4.03, where a young child in an upstairs bedroom is killed by a ricocheting bullet, borrow heavily form the gunfights of classic Westerns, where competing gangs trade fire across open streets, running, shooting, and diving for cover. As Lynne Vitti states, "individual episodes of *The Wire* often evoke images of the classic American Western, with gunfights in the street, quick draw contests, holdups, sniping and shooting from behind buildings" (2009, 79). While this is certainly generally the case in *The Wire*, these scenes usually feature Omar.

There is never any doubt that Omar is a criminal and a killer, but he quickly becomes a moral anti-hero who never harms a "citizen" who is not in "the game," and who lives by robbing some of the program's most ruthless drug dealers. Omar's rigid moral code and his Western aesthetic attributes and characteristics actually come remarkably close to the image of American masculinity that was so prevalent in mainstream cultural and political arenas after

9/11. Omar's characterization in *The Wire* owes just as much to John Wayne and the classic Western protagonist, as the Bush Administration's characterization of the president did. However, Omar is a much more complex than some kind of postmodern Western hero, and his identity much more loaded: he is openly gay, sensitive and as openly emotional as he is tough (and openly heart-broken at the death of lover Brandon). He is pitiful towards the poor around him who are trapped in addictions and abject poverty, and he is also intellectual (alluding to Greek mythology or making philosophical comments on the relationship between his role in the drug war and the lawyers who protect it). As Kathleen LeBesco states, he is an "unexpected collision of identities":

> Openly gay in a hypermasculine black urban subculture, and somehow off the radar while embedded in a surveillance-saturated culture that disproportionally and systematically targets young black men.... Omar is a bundle of seeming contradictions [2009, 219].

Omar is essential to the way *The Wire* is able to move beyond the simple refutation of good and evil and open up a series of other binaries—binaries which in many ways defined the American national condition during the peak years of the War on Terror: liberal and conservative, victim and avenger, philosophical and pragmatic, isolationist and influential. When Omar appears in 2.10 wearing a t-shirt that reads "I am the American Dream," it is a very resonant moment in the series, as his complexities and conflictedness as a character match the conflictedness of American society at the time. Omar is not representing what has come to be called the "dark side of the American Dream," which would be an easy assumption to make considering the program's stated aim of uncovering a hidden America, but he *is* the American Dream, in its traumatized, corrupted and inherently conflicted form. Omar is the man of humble origins, seeking opportunity, taking risks and building his own fiercely independent and individual life, but he is deeply scarred and traumatized by the violence of his world and unable to escape the entanglements of corruption and retribution.

This is not to suggest that Omar's narrative alone amounts to national allegory. However, *The Wire*'s characterization of Omar does move beyond the simple refutation of heroes and villains. It comments on the simplicity of this trope, but it also offers an alternative: a conflicted and complex individual coping with trauma and the pressures of vengeance. Indeed, the fact that for much of the series Omar is dealing with loss of his boyfriend Brandon (Michael Kevin Darnall), or his advisor Butchie (S. Robert Morgan), makes the allegorical traction of his character even more powerful. Omar's original trauma over the murdered and tortured Brandon culminates in his decision to testify in court against the Barksdale organization, and specifically against Marquis "Bird" Hilton (Fredro Starr); his decision to give a perjurious testimony is uncharacteristic and possibly the one time when he breaks his code. Nevertheless, the interrogation scene in 2.06 where Omar verbally attacks the Barksdale defense lawyer Maurice Levy (Michael Kostroff) amounts to the series' definitive statement on the blurring of good and evil, and crucially, legitimate and illegitimate behavior. Levy, trying to discredit Omar as a witness states that he is "feeding off the violence and despair of the drug trade ... stealing from those who themselves are stealing the lifeblood from our city." When Levy emphatically describes Omar to the jury as "a parasite who leeches off the culture of drugs," Omar replies flatly, "Just like you," to audible gasps in the courtroom.

At this point in the series the line or "wire" that divides the "legitimate" and the "illegitimate" is most clearly scrutinized as Omar, the most heroic of *The Wire*'s criminals, is examined next to Levy, possibly the most villainous of its "legitimate" characters, who Vitti describes as a "Dickensian villain, a mercenary defense lawyer comfortable manipulating the law" (2009, 86). Simultaneously, though, this scene resonates acutely with the particular moment in American history during which it appeared, a period characterized by division and divisiveness, when the War in Iraq, which President Bush repeatedly cited as "the central front in the War on Terror," had begun in earnest dividing the nation (2003). Indeed, this episode originally aired in July 2003, six months after the largest coordinated anti-war protest in history took place in 600 cities around the world and just before campaigns would begin for the most closely contested presidential election in American history (Verhulst 2010, 1). While there is nothing in the plot, or surface story, in this scene connecting it to the War on Terror, the conflicted character of Omar represents a vital intradiegetic element of the allegory here. Not only, though, does it feature a deeply conflicted and traumatized protagonist challenging institutional authority and morality, and attacking the crimes committed by the "legitimate" (and the idea of legitimacy itself), but it captures so many of the binaries and divisions that defined the American national climate of the Bush era: black and white, politics and trauma, legitimate violence and illegitimate violence; even the fact that Levy is a Jewish lawyer, and Omar has an Arabic name evokes the tensions between Israel and Palestine and between American Jews and Muslims, a tension that has represented a significant dynamic during the War on Terror. Crucially, it resonates with a conflicted nation and explicitly problematizes the idea of legitimate and illegitimate interventions in the drug war. The "two worlds of globalization represented through risk practice in the war on terror" as described by Louise Amoore and Marieke de Goede, are crystalized in Omar and Levy: "one populated by legitimate and civilized groups whose normalized patterns of financial, leisure or business behaviour are to be secured; and another populated by illegitimate and uncivilized persons whose suspicious patterns of behaviour are to be targeted and apprehended" (2008, 13). Allegorically, the idea of questioning the line between legitimate and illegitimate interventions in the War on Terror, is rife with implication and addresses a definitive issue of the War on Terror.

This scene is the most flagrant occurrence of *The Wire*'s depiction of the American justice system, which as Lynne Vitti states, shows the "wearing away and degradation of justice in our oldest and most precious institutions against the backdrop of a seemingly perpetual war" (2009, 89). Vitti is of course referring to the War on Drugs but her comment is equally applicable to the War on Terror.

The Enemy Others

In *Endless War: Hidden Functions of the War on Terror* (2006), David Keen describes the characteristics of terrorism and terrorists that made (and make) them uncomfortable enemies:

> the terrorist is elusive and frequently escapes punishment. Highly mobile and un-uniformed, the terrorist often blends into the host society. He or she may draw sustenance from a criminal underworld that constantly adapts to surveillance and attempted suppression. Very frequently, the terrorist is elusive even in death ... [Keen 2006, 85].

Keen could of course, easily be describing the "enemies" of Baltimore's drug war as depicted in *The Wire* in this passage. The following concluding section considers the way the depiction of these enemies—as well as the ways they are perceived and policed—allegorizes the enemies of the War on Terror. The intradiegetic element of this strand of the allegory comes in the way policeman and politician characters repeatedly liken the urban crime centers of Baltimore to "Fallujah" or "Baghdad." One of many examples sees the (at this point in the series) mayoral candidate Tommy Carcetti (Aiden Gillen) describe a deprived Baltimore neighborhood as "fucking Fallujah" (4.01) and *The Wire* repeatedly "invites us to view the organized urban violence within Baltimore as a variety of the new low-intensity wars that have been spreading around the globe since the end of the Cold War, turning cities into a primary space of military operation" (Joseph 2013, 210).

While the series-long narrative of *The Wire* is multifaceted, and moves through various sectors of the city and various institutions and themes, there is no doubt that there is a wider shift in the third season on account of the decline of the Barksdale organization and the rise of the Marlo Stanfield group. As noted previously, many commentators have identified the fall of the Franklin Towers, which opens the third season, and which Bonjean has pointed out is so reminiscent of 9/11, as symbolically registering a before and after. Mark Chou argues that because of this, the scene directly creates what he describes as an "analogy" between the War on Drugs and the War on Terror:

> Though the terrorist element was absent from this scene, the crumbling infrastructure of the Barksdale drug empire was very much at its center—the war on drugs in this sense becoming an analogy for the war on terror. Indeed, both the war on drugs and the war on terror in reality are evoked by the falling towers [2011, par. 36].

What is particularly relevant in Chou's account, though, is his argument that the evocation of 9/11 and the War on Terror "makes viewers long for a lost past that was destroyed with the demise of the Barksdale empire and the rise to power of Marlo Stanfield, which is marked by the falling of the towers" (2011, para. 39). This sense of a clear before and after, engendered by an explicit allusion to 9/11, and loaded with the notion that the "after" is somehow more problematic or complicated than the "before" is also posited by Anderson, in his account of the tautologies of *The Wire*. Anderson identifies Marlo as a character who is resistant to the tautologies of the Barksdale empire and particularly Avon's repeated statement "the game is the game." One of Marlo's more memorable statements, from 4.04, "you want it to be one way, but it's the other way," is particularly emblematic of this distinction. Anderson points out that while Avon's "practice of speaking in authoritative-sounding tautologies amounts to a holding strategy to keep present conditions in place," Marlo "seeks to finish off what now looks like the obsolete romantic communalism of old-school gangsters like Avon and Prop Joe" (2012, 95).

However, while the new ruthlessness of the culture of the Marlo Stanfield organization, and the new practices Marlo employs, such as hiding bodies in the derelict terraced houses (or "vacants"), represent a new set of challenges for law enforcement officers, the allegorical implications of the power shift in the third season are much richer than simply a stable before and disorienting after, and this richness has been located in the Franklin Towers scene as well. Philip Joseph argues that

> most obviously, the scene breaks down any easy distinction between *The War on Drugs* and *The War on Terror*, pointing to the state's ongoing anxiety over the territorial status of American spaces ... in addition to binding together the *Wars on Drugs and Terror*, the scene of the Towers collapsing also conflates state and nonstate violence—and more specifically, the spectacles which have become so crucial to each.... The Franklin Terrace Towers fall at the hands of the Baltimore mayor and his entourage, while the Twin Towers crumbled from an airplane strike by al Qaeda [227].

For Joseph, then, the scene "binds" the two wars, and reinforces one of the key strands of the allegory, the blurring of the lines between legitimate and illegitimate, or good and evil. However, what we see in *The Wire*, over 60 episodes, is the slow and fraught decline of one major drugs organization, which is quickly replaced by another, and it is here where the most significant and resident allegorical function of the narrative is found. After 9/11, the War on Terror was focused first in Afghanistan, then Iraq, and then again in Afghanistan, and while there have been declared victories, such as President Bush announcing "mission accomplished" aboard an aircraft carrier in 2003, or the assassination of Osama bin Laden in 2011, there remain accusations that the threat of terrorism has actually only intensified and that many of the societal conditions that foster terrorism are largely unchanged. Whether this is or is not the case is not the subject of this essay, but the fact that *The Wire* concludes without any real "victories" and with Marlo returning to the streets with a renewed appetite for "the game" can be seen as a depiction of the war on terror as a misguided enterprise.

The clear didactic position of the series (which Simon has repeatedly emphasized in other arenas) that the War on Drugs is fundamentally misguided in its approach, and that deeply entrenched institutional and social problems mean that there will always be a "reason" for an enemy to exist, is allegorically transferred to the War on Terror through this larger narrative of one defined enemy giving way to another, while the underlying "issues" remain unchanged. However, the cyclical nature of the problem is present on a smaller scale as well. The idea that societal conditions mean there will always be willing "soldiers" on the enemy side was noted in a *Guardian* "The Wire Re-up" blog post from 2009: "For every drug dealer arrested on the corner or every Taliban fighter killed in Afghanistan, 20 more will step up to take their place unless the root causes of the problems are addressed.... As much as the show is a call for the authorities to revolutionise their approach to tackling the drug trade, it is also a plea for a radical rethink of American foreign policy" (*The Guardian*, 2009). This notion certainly resonates with much of the criticism of the War on Terror, such as the argument put forward by Philip H. Gordon in *Foreign Affairs*. Gordon argues, articulating a fairly widespread criticism, that "it is impossible to win a war without knowing what its goal is," and that victory in the War on Terror will not come "when Washington and its allies kill or capture all terrorists or potential terrorists," but only when "they come to find more promising paths to the dignity, respect, and the opportunities they crave" (2007, 54). Certainly, one of the most prominent themes in *The Wire* is the cyclical nature of "the game." As the series concludes, the initially loyal and disciplined teenager Michael (Tristan Wilds) becomes the new Omar when he comes to disavow any institutional or gang loyalties. Similarly, his thoughtful and sensitive friend Duquan "Dukie" Weems (Jermaine Crawford) finally gives in to the bullying, neglect and abuse he has suffered as we see him shooting up, effectively becoming the new Reginald "Bubbles" Cousins (Andre Royo). Nowhere is the depiction of brutal cycles more prevalent than with the "soldiers" or pawns of *The Wire* (if we recall D'Angelo's chess allegory). Indeed, the three characters involved in the chess scene from Season One, Wallace, D'Angelo and Bodie, are all eventually killed and replaced. Some of the more minor roles in the various corner operations of the program are shown to be even more interchangeable. As Tiffany Potter and Tobias Sirzyk argue in this volume, many of the "soldiers" in *The Wire*, can be seen as "accidental guerrillas" who change allegiances based on whichever "side can best increase access to the means of survival." However, while this is undoubtedly the case, the defining characteristic of the "pawns" of the program are their dispensability, as D'Angelo's chess allegory demonstrates. Closely related to the "pawns" of society are the program's most vulnerable characters, namely the addicts and corner boys. The failure on the part of the police to protect these characters is another important aspect in the depiction of cycles of systemic failure, and adds further weight to this strand of the allegory. This phenomenon is particularly prominent in the fourth season. In story arcs that run the length of the season, Herc fails to protect Bubbles from The Fiend (Armando Cadogan, Jr.), resulting ultimately in the tragic death of Sherrod (Rashid Orange), and Carver fails to protect the teenager Randy Wagstaff (Maestro Harrell) who "snitched," ultimately ruining his life as his house is fire-bombed and his foster mother hospitalized. In these stories of the Baltimore Police's failure to protect, there is a clear echo of the perceived failure of American and allied forces to capture "hearts and minds," and it is certainly the case that the rare depictions of "citizens" in *The Wire* reveal negative opinions and emotions relating to the Baltimore Police Department ranging from distrust and fear to outright hostility.

Despite this antipathy to the police exhibited by *The Wire*'s citizen characters, in several scenes in Season Four, when Carcetti is attending various public forums and meetings, the citizens also convey the sense that something has to be done about the city's drug problem. Similarly, the political backdrop of the series saw the Bush presidency and America's approach to the War on Terror come under increasing scrutiny as it progressed, while the threat of terrorism continued and continues to be a major national and international concern. So while, in both the realistic and allegorical narrative, there is a strong sense of distrust on the part of the "citizens," in regards to the ability of its institutions to adequately protect them, there is undoubtedly a desire for some kind of action.

One final aspect of *The Wire* is particularly evocative in terms of how we might change course in these wars. One of the key problems identified in the War on Terror is the focus on enemy nations (Afghanistan, Iraq) rather than underlying issues. Keen writes that attacks on "states are now particularly redundant and counterproductive. The growing importance of sub-national and transnational dynamics ... means resentments can't be sealed neatly within the black box of the nation state" (2006, 1). The enemy organizations of *The Wire*, the Barksdale and Marlo Stanfield groups, are shown to be parts of systems relating to both the neo-liberal city (in the way they are variously connected to business and politics) and transnational organized crime systems (as dramatized in the second season), and the failure of the police to make progress in their cases against them is often linked to the organizations links with other institutions. Simply put, arresting any of the named villains will not win the war, because they represent parts of systems that will be (and are shown to be) replaced. This allegorizes the problem that Keen discusses above, that is, the idea that targeting a specific state or even a specific terrorist organization does not necessarily address the "resentments" or adequately handle the "dynamics" that characterize enemies who operate within different structures—structures that are not defined by the borders of nations or the borders of legitimacy.

The Wire is unwavering in its critique of corrupt and interlocking institutions and if its depiction of the War on Drugs (and allegorically the War on Terror) has one definitive message, it is that reducing "enemies" to known quantities or types of conflict into manageable narratives with clear outcomes will not work in a system-based society. Furthermore, *The Wire*'s narrative of the War on Drugs is not simply allegorizing and therefore offering a coded criticism of the War on Terror, but unlocking clear narrative similarities that are mutually revealing and instructive.

Notes

1. See the essay in this collection entitled "Insurgency, Accidental Guerrillas and Gang Culture in *The Wire*" by Tiffany Potter and Tobias Sirzyk, for a full discussion of guerrilla combat in *The Wire*.

Works Cited

Alvarez, Rafael. 2010. *The Wire: Truth Be Told*. London: Canongate. Print.
Anderson, Paul Allen. 2012. "'The Game Is the Game': Tautology and Allegory in *The Wire*." *The Wire: Race, Class, and Genre*. Eds. Liam Kennedy and Stephen Shapiro. Ann Arbor: Michigan University Press. 84–109. Print.
Bonjean, Elizabeth. 2009. "After the Towers Fell: Bodie Broadus and the Space of Memory." *The Wire: Urban Decay and American Television*. Eds. Tiffany Potter and C.W. Marshall. London: Continuum. 162–174. Print.
Bush, George W. 2003. "A Central Front in the War on Terror." White House Archives. http://georgewbush-whitehouse.archives.gov/news/releases/2003/09/20030909.html.
Bush, George W. 2009. "Selected Speeches of George Bush." White House Archives. http://georgewbushwhitehouse.archives.gov/infocus/bushrecord/documents/Selected_Speeches_George_W_Bush.pdf.
Chou, Mark. 2011. "'We Like Them Bitches on the Chessboard': Tragedy, Politics and *The Wire*." *CTheory* 15.1. http://www.ctheory.net/articles.aspx?id=677.
Feste, Karen. 2011. *America Responds to Terrorism: Conflict Strategies of Clinton, Bush, and Obama*. London: Palgrave. Print.
Gordon, Philip H. 2007. "Can the War on Terror be Won? How to Fight the Right War." *Foreign Affairs* 86.6. http://www.foreignaffairs.com/articles/63009/philip-h-gordon/can-the-war-on-terror-be-won.
Johnson, Gary. 2004. "The Presence of Allegory: The Case of Philip Roth's American Pastoral." *Narrative* 12.3: 233–248. Print.
Joseph, Philip. 2013. "Soldiers in Baltimore: The Wire and the New Global Wars." *The New Centennial Review* 13.1: 209–240. Print.
Keen, David. 2006. *Endless War: Hidden Functions of The War on Terror*. London: Pluto Press. Print.
Kelleter, Frank. 2012. "*The Wire* and Its Readers." *The Wire: Race, Class, and Genre*. Eds. Liam Kennedy and Stephen Shapiro. Ann Arbor: Michigan University Press. 33–70. Print.
Kennedy, Liam, and Stephen Shapiro. 2012. *The Wire: Race, Class, and Genre*. Ann Arbor: Michigan University Press. Print.
Lodge, David. 1970. "Realism, Allegory and Symbolism: Some Speculation About the Novel." *New Blackfriars* 51.3: 361–373. Print.
McMillan, Alasdair. 2009. "Heroism, Institutions, and the Police Procedural." *The Wire: Urban Decay and American Television*. Eds. Tiffany Potter and C.W. Marshall. London: Continuum. 37–49. Print.
Potter, Tiffany, and C.W. Marshall. 2009. *The Wire: Urban Decay and American Television*. London: Continuum. Print.
Simon, David. 2010. "Introduction." Rafael Alvarez, *The Wire: Truth Be Told*. London: Canongate. Print
Verhulst, Joris. 2010. "The World Says No to War." *The World Says No to War: Demonstrations*

against the War on Iraq. Eds. Stefaan Walgrave and Dieter Rucht. Minneapolis: University of Minnesota Press. 1–10. Print.

Vitti, Lynne. 2009. "'I Got the Shotgun, You Got the Briefcase': Lawyering and Ethics." *The Wire: Urban Decay and American Television.* Eds. Tiffany Potter and C.W. Marshall. London: Continuum. 78–90. Print.

PART THREE

The Detail: Domestic Policy in Bush-Era America

Rethinking Space

Anca M. Pusca

Building on a series of critiques in international relations, sociology, geography and cultural studies that see much of our current use of the concept of space as static or "hardened" due to assumptions that space can and must be increasingly controlled, this chapter looks for alternative possibilities of understanding space as "fluid and dynamic," a space of interaction, of doing, of reflection. The HBO TV show *The Wire* is used as a key entry point for understanding how a "hardened" as opposed to a "fluid or dynamic" understanding of space makes a significant difference in how space is managed, understood and inhabited.

The show becomes a reflective representation of a highly contested space—in this case the city of Baltimore—in which the city's bureaucracy and its more vulnerable inhabitants come head to head in their different strategies to make the city work for them. As the city's infrastructure and its vulnerable communities crumble under increased pressures of racial segregation, a dying industrial economy, and the rise of a dangerous underground drug economy, "solutions" from above seek to aggressively control, change and, in many cases simply wipe out "troubled" spaces. *The Wire* zooms in on these "troubled" spaces only to find that among the ruins, despite the rising crime, drug addiction and violence, a community that cannot be so easily wiped out continues to exist.

Turning to, among others, the philosophy of Walter Benjamin, this essay seeks to understand how the process of change—such as the transition from industrialism to post-industrialism, as well as the radical transformations in techniques of representation—such as the emergence of film and surveillance technology, are radically reshaping spaces such as Baltimore. Using Benjamin's unique understanding of "space" as reflected in his unfinished Arcades Project, his distinct conceptualization of "violence" as directly connected to the "law," his reflections on new technologies of representation such as film and the critical role of the "optical unconscious," the essay's arguments unfold in three different directions:

Firstly, it examines how *The Wire* manages to directly link the "drug problem" to the city as a "hardened" space problem through its focus on Baltimore's failed urban fabric; secondly, it discusses how "fluid" spaces such as the corner, Hamsterdam, the Pit, and the High Rises become the last vestiges of resistance to the local bureaucracy's encroachment on the territory, lifestyle and very existence of West Baltimore and its inhabitants; and thirdly it argues that while increased surveillance continues to privilege the view of an elite that can only see certain spaces as "troubled," an alternative gaze is not only possible, but also directly fostered by the TV show itself. This is achieved by creating a collective of TV watchers that join the virtual collective of actors to form what Benjamin calls an optical unconscious which serves to create an entirely new field of vision.

Baltimore Spaces: The Wire *Through a Benjaminian Eye*

In preparing his manuscript on the Parisian Arcades, Walter Benjamin left behind a large trace of notes, thoughts and images that have since laid the foundation of an interesting methodology of space: one that combined thinking of modern space as city space—a playground for both individuals and collectives eager to consume the phantasmagoria of the early industrial city—with thinking of space as the ultimate way to access our consciousness as a collective. The city and its streets provided not just a place for the collective to "dream" of the future, but also opened up passages into the "underworld." For Benjamin, these passages were key elements of any city: they were the city's reflective spaces, passages that led to the possibility of a collective self-discovery or awakening. He found such passages in the Arcades of 19th century Paris. He compared the Arcades to

> places in ancient Greece where the way led down into the underworld. By day, the labyrinth of urban dwellings resembles consciousness; the arcades (which are galleries leading into the city's past) issue unremarked onto the streets [*Arcades* 875].

Later, in his essay on "The Work of Art in the Age of Its Technological Reproducibility," Benjamin assigns a similar critical function, that of collective self-discovery and awakening, to film:

The most important social function of film is to establish equilibrium between human beings and the apparatus. Film achieves this goal not only in terms of man's presentation of himself to the camera but also in terms of his representation of his environment by means of this apparatus ["The Work of Art" 38].

Film, for Benjamin, can thus perform a negative function when it serves to further indoctrinate the masses through illusionary displays of idealized collectives.[1] More importantly, however, it possesses a positive function when allowing collectives to identify themselves and become aware of their social positioning through film. In this respect, film acts as a moving mirror that allows individuals and collectives to come face to face with their self-alienation[2] (Benjamin, "The Work of Art" 32). In combining the power of critical reflective spaces with the power of film, one could thus uncover the ultimate self-discovery and awakening potential of film. This chapter seeks to argue that *The Wire* achieves just that through its exploration of particular key spaces within West Baltimore, as well as through its open engagement with the "apparatus," which in this case stands both for the immediate technology of "wire-taps" and the film camera, as well as for the larger control apparatus of the local police and the state.

If Benjamin captures 19th century Paris at a key point in its transformation from an early- to a late-industrial city, *The Wire* also captures 21st century Baltimore at a key transitional point: from a booming industrial port, to a declining post-industrial city. Like Paris, large parts of Baltimore lie in ruin, a living testimony of an aggressive interaction with space that sought to exploit the city's resources, such as its access to water through the port and the industries surrounding the port, or to use the city's architectural layout as a clear visual display of wealth along a series of class gradations: the white high class vs. the white middle class, the white immigrant lower-middle class vs. a rising African American upper-middle-class, the white working class vs. an African American lower-middle-class, and an African American lower class vs. everyone else.

Perhaps more so than any other American city, Baltimore's class divisions are deeply written into the city's architecture and neighborhoods, transforming the city into a spatial war front where control of territory is key to ensuring both physical survival as well as class advancement. Space thus becomes something that needs to be captured and exploited at any cost. As Gretchen Boger explains, Baltimore has always been a spatially unstable city marked by continuous tensions between a white, immigrant middle-class which "sought to guarantee themselves stability and reputation by claiming properties once belonging to more affluent whites who had left for the expanding suburbs"

(Boger 238), and an African American bourgeoisie which saw that "the question of neighbourhood was central to upward mobility" and fought for city spaces to remain "fluid" (Boger 239).

In addressing the history of Baltimore's residential segregation, Boger identifies West Baltimore, and the West Ordinances of 1910–13, as a key turning point in the legalization of segregation, a process that sought to "harden" city spaces by sealing off neighborhoods along both class and, more importantly, racial lines. Boger's historical analysis points out, however, the extent to which this process was driven not by a white majority push for segregation, but rather by a minority interest group that sought to protect its particular street from affluent African American encroachment. This minority group was the so-called Madison Avenue, McCulloh Street and Eutaw Place Improvement Association, representing white families inhabiting these respective areas of Baltimore, and their legal mission was largely aimed at keeping one particular affluent African American family, the McMechens, out of McCulloh Street (Boger 236–7).

This initial legalization of segregation through the three different versions of the West Ordinance, which originally "mandated that from the date of its passage, no white person would be permitted to move to a block the majority of whose occupants were black, and no black person would be permitted to move to a block where the majority of whose occupants were white" (Boger 237), led to what I call an increasing *legalization/hardening of space* and along with it an increasing *legalization of violence* within these spaces. The West Ordinance, although legally abolished in 1917, only seven years after its initial passing in 1910, set the tone for how the city would continue to seek to solve racial tensions: spatial segregation of "safe spaces" vs. "troubled spaces," with increasing monitorization of "trouble spaces" through an entire bureaucratic apparatus based on the local police, the local administration, schools and the local media.

Resisting this bureaucratic apparatus are the inhabitants of different "troubled spaces": mainly lower-class African Americans segregated in West and East Baltimore, upper-class African American drug lords that used the crumbling architecture of these troubled inner city spaces as a safety ground for their operations, and lower working class whites seeking to survive within the crumbling industrial infrastructure of the Baltimore port. *The Wire* captures both the increasing state monitorization of these troubled spaces as well as the local resistance to it beautifully, by interspersing the human and the spatial elements in a manner that best shows the city as living, breathing space, with inhabitants that deeply identify with the streets and houses they inhabit, the port they work in, and the corners where they sell and buy their "product." Despite being abused, destroyed or abandoned, the city remains very much loved, for these troubled spaces are not only home for someone, but perhaps the only home that they can ever envision.

By focusing on this conflicted attachment to the city, including a certain sense of guilt and responsibility on the side of the monitoring bureaucratic apparatus, *The Wire* acts as an important modern visual critique of violence, that to a large extent, I will argue, follows the rhetorical steps of Benjamin's earlier essay "Critique of Violence." While appearing as a police show that traces the "War on Drugs" in the context of Baltimore City, *The Wire* is first and foremost an important reflection on the nature of violence in the context of the "troubled" cities of today as connected to an important process of legalization and monitorization that increasingly turns city spaces into *hardened* spaces of control as opposed to *fluid/dynamic* spaces of free movement and interaction. This hardening of space is increasingly made possible through a sense of distancing from "troubled" spaces which are monitored from afar: the white city elite can thus treat West Baltimore as an area that can be monitored, mapped, divided and controlled from the safe distance of the suburb.

Drug violence thus appears not only as a direct result of a certain "drug culture," but much more so of a historical spatial violence that resulted in racial segregation, in limited access to the city's resources, and in a strong attachment to failing neighborhoods that provided a powerful source of identity yet a limited source of income. The remainder of this chapter will seek to track in more detail the particular visual methodologies used in *The Wire* in order to capture the violence of hardened spaces and the possibilities of dynamic/fluid spaces.

Performing Violence, Legality and Resistance

In his 1921 essay "Critique of Violence," Walter Benjamin put forward a controversial argument about the process of "legalization of violence" and the extent to which the law itself is deeply implicated not only in judging but also in instituting violence. In looking for a criterion by which to define violence, Benjamin found that both the legal and the judicial system regard violence as a means to an end under the premise that just ends can be attained by just means. The law then serves to assess the justness of means while the justice system serves to assess the justness of ends. In distinguishing between just ends and just means, the law distinguishes between legitimate and illegitimate violence, with the justice system behind it to punish illegitimate violence.

For Benjamin, the very possibility of such a distinction between legitimate and illegitimate violence is troublesome, for the effects of violence, whether legitimate or illegitimate, are inevitably harmful to someone. In seeking to understand how the law justifies legitimate violence through examples such as the army, the police, the death penalty, or legal strikes, Benjamin reveals power as the real criteria for violence: legitimate violence, for him, is nothing but the violence the state needs to employ in order to secure its continuing hold on power. The very process of legalization of violence—distinguishing between legitimate and illegitimate violence and sustaining a mechanism and rewards one and punishes the other—is then revealed to be the underlying mechanism of state power. Legitimate violence, according to Benjamin, can be seen to serve two main functions: a law-making function and a law-preserving function. Violence thus initially provides the means to establish state-law and later serves to preserve both that law and through it, the power of the state. The state thus strategically employs violence to presumably solve violence.

Benjamin argues that our acceptance of such violent states ultimately results from our acceptance of violence as a means to an end. The only way to escape the current cycle of legalized violence is, for Benjamin, to imagine a kind of violence that is not a means to an end and thus unmediated by law. He argues that non-violent resolution of conflict, unmediated by the law, is often present in relationships between private persons through courtesy, sympathy, peaceableness, trust and conference. Benjamin argues, in the case of the latter,

> not only is non-violent agreement possible, but also the exclusion of violence in principle is quite explicitly demonstrable by one significant factor: there is no sanction for lying.... This makes clear that there is a sphere of human agreement that is nonviolent to the extent that it is wholly inaccessible to violence: the proper sphere of "understanding," language ["Critique" 289].

This brief exposition of Benjamin's argument provides the background for my argument that *The Wire* follows Benjamin's thinking very closely. As a critique of the violence committed in the name of a War on Drugs, *The Wire* openly questions the efficacy of dealing with the drug problem in Baltimore through the legal/police system. While other alternatives exist—the education system, the information system (media), the local state apparatus that deals with questions of urban planning and subsidies, local charities and sports clubs—they are, in the case of Baltimore, closely implicated in one way or another with the legal system, thus failing to exist as real mechanisms of non-violent mediation. The constant threat of punishment fails to deter, but instead creates an environment where violence becomes a way of life that cannot be escaped, for no alternative can be imagined.

The main characters in *The Wire* appear trapped within the confines of Baltimore City, and sometimes the even narrower confines of West Baltimore, as if they couldn't survive anywhere else (Kinkle and Toscano). Raised with a certain understanding of "the rules of the game," the "pions" are taught to obey, and the "kings" are taught to hold on to power at any cost. Resisting the game is futile, playing the game is the only chance one has to stay alive. The very existence of the game, as *The Wire* seeks to show, relies upon a number of particular historical developments, some of which have also been tracked in this article, that saw Baltimore emerge as an increasingly segregated city: one that confined the poor African American population to the inner city while pushing the white elites to the suburbs; one that increasingly associated property values with racial stigma causing entire areas of the city to collapse; one that turned to drugs as one of the few viable economic activities that could turn a profit in an otherwise dead local economy; and one that resisted increasing police and state brutality in order to hold on to the failed spaces that continue to shape their identity.

The Wire very nicely captures the characters' attachment to the spaces they inhabit, despite their otherwise decrepit nature: the corners, Hamsterdam, the Pit, the High Rises, even the abandoned row houses, are the key performative spaces that guard not only a sense of identity but also the very last *raison d'etre* of a desperate community. By resisting the law and the police, these spaces are creating their own law. Drugs are the last resort for resisting an otherwise likely "extermination," for the city, following the national policy of "zero tolerance," is responding to its failure to manage the drug problem through its police force by increasing plans for demolitions that will ultimately raze West Baltimore to the ground in order to make room for safer, yet neutral and homogenized white neighborhoods.

The War on Drugs is largely fought spatially, in a manner that treats space as "planar," and thus as easily classifiable. This view of space has been strongly resisted by social theorists like Amin, who argue that

> the materiality of everyday life is constituted through a very large number of spaces—discursive, emotional, affiliational, physical, natural, organisational, technological, and institutional; ... the geography of these spaces is not reducible to planar (single or multi) or distance-based considerations; ... "space is also a doing, that ... does not pre-exist its doing; ... doing is the articulation of relational performances [Amin 389].

If space is a doing, a performance that relies on a constantly changing geography of relations, then space cannot ever be captured in a "still" nor can it be analyzed as "stable." Any attempt to enter a space in order to "analyse" it or "solve" it, inevitably affects its very dynamics, making thus a "clean" intervention from a distance impossible. The detectives in *The Wire* become increasingly frustrated with the limits of the legal mechanism under which they function, its narrow understanding of the drug war as ultimately a war of classifying, controlling and monitoring space, as well as its inability to see beyond the immediate violence of the drug trade. As they become increasingly acquainted with the intimacy of some of the spaces in which their targets exist, they slowly realize the futility of their exercise. Thus, when Detective James McNulty (Dominic West) enters Russell "Stringer" Bell's (Idris Elba) apartment and pulls out a copy of Adam Smith's *The Wealth of Nations*, he begins to wonder, "Who the -- were we chasing?"

By resisting the oversimplified categorization of space through which the legal/police mechanism seeks to address the "drug problem" in Baltimore, *The Wire* underlines, on the one hand the importance of paying attention to the way in which local identities are performed and defended through space, and, one the other, the extent to which these spaces are the last pockets of resistance to the increasingly violent encroachment of the state.

Looking for Fluidity in Baltimore's Hardened Architecture

In his script pitch for HBO, David Simon describes *The Wire* as "far more than a cop show" because it will deal with larger, universal questions concerning "the human condition, the nature of the American city and, indeed, the national culture" (Simon 2). This "national existentialism" emerges in the context of a dysfunctional city whose apparatus shows complete indifference to the deep relationship between the urban fabric of the city and drug culture and, as such, refuses to accept the permanent nature of urban drug culture. For Simon, the drug problem is not one that can be solved by the police, nor is it one likely to go away soon. If anything, drugs become a natural fixture of the post-industrial city whose spaces have been abused for decades in the name of solving social problems from racial tensions to health epidemics, from poverty to poor education.

The show is mainly set in what is perhaps the city's most abused space, West Baltimore, that saw at least two main waves of demolition, first in the 1950s, when the low rises (the Pit) and the high rises of West Baltimore were built, and second in the 1980s and 1990s when several of these high rises were also erased along with an increasing number of abandoned Victorian row houses. Despite the first wave of demolitions and the urban solution of subsidized housing in the form of low and high-rises proving not only unsuccessful but also clearly deeply damaging to the urban and social infrastructure of the city, creating empty lots that were perfect grounds for drug exchanges and pockets of urban poverty to support the drug trade, the second wave of demolitions continues nonetheless as neighborhood preservation and rehabilitation programs are seen as not being "cost-efficient."

The Wire inhabits precisely these spaces, showcasing how even the most collapsed architectures, the abandoned streets of rowhouses, the empty lots, the corners, the liquor stores, continue to play an important role in the local social fabric, acting as unlikely buffers to the economic collapse of the city: abandoned houses serve to shelter and hide the "human debris" that results from the drug trade: these include the drug-addicted homeless, the orphaned children of drug addicted parents, and the bodies of those unlucky enough to be find themselves victims of the drug trade. The empty lots and the corners serve as drug sale points, sustaining a largely African American population with little to no other source of income and opportunity to escape the drug culture. The liquor stores serve as some of the few viable local businesses, often implicated in the drug trade as money laundering operations. To declare a War on Drugs ultimately means to declare a war on such entire neighborhoods and the people inhabiting them. To the extent that this war is fought on both the police front and the urban planning front through aggressive "cleansing" policies that seek to "clear out" social problems by literally clearing out buildings and people, a successful war would seem to imply a complete eradication of places like West Baltimore and a "safe repopulation" that would turn these spaces into mainly white, middle-class neighborhoods.

As Max Page notes, the drug problem is to a large extent the result of a larger socio-economic problem of continued segregation and racial discrimination, as well as a failure to implement policies that would secure better access to jobs for African Americans, thus creating real economic alternatives to the drug trade (458). Unfortunately, too many solutions address the physical decline of the city as an architectural or design failure as opposed to a sociopolitical failure. While urban theorists like James Cohen rightly note that the city is struggling with one of the worst rates of population decline or "white flight," with rates as striking as 32 percent since 1950, as well as one of the worst numbers of abandoned houses, as high as 43,000 units, they continue to support the same type of urban renewal projects that serve to justify large demolition projects ultimately aimed at breaking-up and dispersing African American areas seen as "troubled communities" (Cohen 415). Page argues that the deceiving rhetoric behind these renewal projects serves to hide the segregationist logic that caused these problems in the first place which is one that associates "the rottenness of the house" to "that of the tenant" (457).

The failure to recognize Baltimore's row houses as "also impressive as urban ensembles, creating a fabric of blocks and stoops and corner stores that have come to define an ideal of urban planning" (460) is also a failure to recognize the human potential behind these structures. *The Wire* offers no easy solution to these problems, but does approach Baltimore's urban fabric, particularly its "troubled neighbourhoods" and their inhabitants, in an endearing manner. As Simon himself explains in his pitch, the show seeks to depict "a deep if peculiar affection for the city felt, though rarely expressed, by its residents" (Simon 5).

This affection for the city renders it human, despite all of its flaws. In *The Wire*, this affection also extends to many of the city's spaces: these include the rowhouses praised by people like Page as "ideals of urban planning" despite being abandoned, the high- and low-rises that are often seen by outsiders as failed social experiments, and the urban renewal projects that become the first legitimate investment opportunities for the Barksdale organization, suggesting a potential way out of the drug business. This affection, however, fails to include alienating spaces such as the inner harbor renewal areas or suburban and outer Baltimore, often seen as inaccessible spaces that might as well belong to a different country. *The Wire* thus clearly links the inhabitants of West Baltimore to the city that they inhabit, showing not only a sense of affection, but also a sense of (sometimes fatalistic) attachment that cannot be broken.

West Baltimore and its neighborhoods display a fluidity and dynamism of space that is rarely encountered in the other carefully manicured spaces of the city, such as the inner harbor. As authors like David Harvey and Nigel Thrift note, such manicured spaces suffer from a homogenization that threatens to render space socially and politically neutral, thus taking away all of its character, uniqueness and community emotional and political investment. Such spaces, they argue, are all too common in today's global cities, often designed to imitate similar ideals of wealth and prosperity that lack, however, any sense of personal touch beyond a carefully marketed celebration of difference through stereotypical cultural statements. Space, like time, in such instances, becomes less of a naturally occurring social construct, and more of a carefully designed state and market construct that serves to create urban ideals reflective of a particular sense of "ideal justice," often chosen to fit the demands of the market (Harvey).

This homogenization and neutralization of space is visually and architecturally reflected in "hardened" architectures and spaces that are completely alien to the humans inhabiting them. The logic of space, in such cases, is no longer a social one, but rather an economic one based on efficiency and cost-effectiveness ensured by repetition and what Thrift calls "series technologies" (Thrift). This, Harvey argues, is both a result of the global capitalist market, and also of a particular intellectual treatment of space within the social sciences that privileges time over space, treating space as a result of temporal progress along the lines of the enlightenment philosophy that continues to underlie most of the social sciences today. An alternative to this is an "aesthetic" treatment of space that focuses on the spatialization of time, namely "how spatial constructs are created and used as fixed markers of human memory and of social values in a world of rapid flux and change" (Harvey 429). Harvey clearly favors the latter, suggesting that the social sciences have largely failed to recognize space as an important construct outside of its function in supporting notions of "progress."

In light of this critique, *The Wire* does seem to provide a very effective "aesthetic" treatment of space, showing how a vulnerable population, such as the inner city African American population, has still managed to turn even the most hostile environments into a home to which they are emotionally, mentally and socially attached both as individuals as well as a community. They have done so in spite of increasing attempts by city governments and lobbying groups to simply assign dollar values to city spaces and architectures, first through the use and abuse of house valuation policies that automatically assigned better house prices to white neighborhoods while financially dooming even affluent black neighborhoods, and later through attempts to address a failing urban fabric through "cost-effective" solutions such as demolitions. Baltimore is indeed presented as a "world of rapid flux and change" in which entire communities and their memories are desperately fighting to survive by any means possible. The aesthetic treatment of space in *The Wire* occurs through both a conscious and unconscious visualization of space. The following section of this article explores how this visualization is very effectively split into at least two different kinds of gazes: the privileged gaze of the city elite, often a part of the state apparatus, as opposed to the non-privileged gaze of the inner city's inhabitants.

Privileged vs. Non-privileged Gazes in The Wire

The Wire, as the title itself suggests, starts from a very important premise: that the city is being watched, surveiled at all times. The space of the city thus comes into sight through a number of different gazes: on the one hand the gazes of its inhabitants, who are increasingly weary of being watched, and on the other hand, the gazes of those who watch them—from the police to the local courts and the local elites. The gaze is essential in this show, for even though the police cameras seem to be aiming in one direction, what emerges is a situation where everyone watches everyone: West Baltimore watches East Baltimore and vice versa, the police watch both and are in turn watched back. The show seems to purposefully resist a single comprehensive view: no one, not even the spectator, can see it all. The action is thus driven by a constant back and forth in which images, although realistic, fail to capture a clear message: the police are always unsure what and who exactly it is that they are looking at and vice versa.

The show's obsession with "hyper-reality," the style that Simon was very eager to adopt (Simon 2) seems to work, whether intentionally or not, in at least two ways: on the one hand, as intended, it depicts a real, precise geography and realistic events; on the other, it questions the usefulness of this very reality for images often become unintelligible. The wire, as the sound that accompanies the image, is meant to serve as a translator or interpreter of the otherwise unintelligible image. It serves to give clues on who it is that we are watching and what exactly it is that they are doing. Yet *The Wire*, just like the police photographs and film footage, remains cryptic: the translator requires yet another translation. As the police gather more and more information, they seem to be less able to draw the full picture. Every small victory and promise of a new conviction opens yet another thread of guilt to follow, ultimately implicating not just the small drug ring around the Barksdale family but rather the entire city, from the port workers, to the local political elite, the court house, and the higher echelons of the police. The more we see and hear, the less we seem to know.

As Simon himself argues, *The Wire* seeks to show that "knowledge is always a double edged sword" particularly in a world in which "thinking cops and thinking street players must make their way independent of simple explanations" (Simon 2). Knowledge, either as information gathered, or as attempts to classify reality, clearly fails in these regards. Linda Spiedel carefully notes the extent to which the show is sprinkled with maps, charts, numbers that seek, in one way or another, to classify the city, its streets, its gangs, its problems. They adorn the police office, the mayor's office, the union building, the campaign offices, the newsroom, and still, the city resists being "read" (Speidel). This attempt to "harden" city spaces by translating them into easy to read numbers appears to serve only one purpose: justify so-called "solutions" to the city problems and keep those who proposed them in power.

The "numbers game" can be easily manipulated to create a semblance of "success" and no politician seems able to resist this, as they are in turn carefully watched by those "higher up." Everyone understands the real purpose of getting the "numbers up" or "down" and are well aware of the futility of the endeavor on the ground. Despite this, changes in approach are difficult when results have to be presented in monthly and quarterly reports, when terms in office are defined by set periods of time and when elections are always just around the corner. Radley Balko, in an interview with David Simon, underlines the fact that any attempt to fight the War on Drugs through numbers will ultimately fail. As Balko points out, the futility of playing the numbers game is nicely captured by detective Burns in the show: "if you get on the wrong train, running down the aisle in the opposite direction really doesn't help" (Balko).

If numbers, information gathered and classifications do not work, this raises the question of what form a successful approach to the problems represented in the show would take. Interpretation seems to also be compromised by the apparent futility of looking, and all we are left with are glimpses, fragments of reality and speech that encapsulate not so much a problem or a solution, as a particular way of being. The show is ultimately summarized through a series of "tags" in the shape of memorable "quotes": "The king stays the king" says D'Angelo Barksdale (Larry Gilliard, 1.03) when comparing "the game" with chess. Tommy Carcetti (Aidan Gillen), mayor-to-be, muses before his electoral debate: "Tomorrow night, I will kick his ass. But the next morning, I still wake up white in a city that ain't" (4.02). Disillusioned former detective Roland "Prez" Pryzbylewski (Jim True-Frost), now a school teacher in an inner city school, remarks: "No one wins. One side just loses more slowly" (4.04). In a conversation between Malik "Poot" Carr (Tray Chaney) and Preston "Bodie" Broadus (J.D. Williams) on the killing of their friend Little Kevin, Bodie refers to a previous conversation they had about global warming: "Thought you said it was getting warmer," Poot answers: "The world goin' one way, people another" (4.10).[3]

Despite the overwhelming sense of futility one is left with at the end of the show, the viewing experience itself is not meant to be futile. If anything,

Simon, like any good social scientist, has a specific goal in mind: the show is meant to show to the American people "an America, at every level at war with itself" (Simon 3). Coming face to face with a reality that rings close to home is clearly rippling through. Real drug dealers and cops from around the U.S. are closely watching *The Wire*.

The show's realism seems to have persuaded some to a point where the actor Reginald Cousins, playing Bubbles (the addicted police informant on the show), is said to have been approached by a real addict after filming, who slipped him a packet of heroin saying that he needed the fix more. The show has also triggered a series of conversations between sociologist Sudhir Venkatesh and a real New York-based gang watching *The Wire*, tracked in a series of opinion pieces in the New York Times. The gang, however, seemed to think that the show made decisions such as killings, much more complicated than they were in real life. By creating a virtual space in which real-life people could recognize themselves, the show opened yet another "dynamic space" in which communication was made possible between vulnerable communities across and beyond the narrow space of the city of Baltimore.

Perhaps as Walter Benjamin predicted much earlier, when the technology of film had just appeared, the potential of technological reproduction as an alternative form of representation is not to be ignored. Like Simmons, Benjamin was intrigued by the ability of film to bring the masses face to face with themselves. In his Work of Art essay, he gives the example of early Russian film in which "actors are not actors [...] but people who portray themselves" ("The Work of Art" 34). The eye of the camera manages to capture something that the unmediated gaze cannot:

> Clearly, it is another nature which speaks to the camera as compared to the eye. ... It is through the camera that we first discover the optical unconscious, just as we discover the instinctual unconscious through psychoanalysis ("The Work of Art" 37).

The camera makes possible, according to Benjamin, the collective dream, the collective imagination that is created in a process of distraction: "reception in distraction—the sort of reception which is increasingly noticeable in all areas of art and is a symptom of profound changes in apperception—finds in film its true training ground" (Benjamin, "The Work of Art" 41). For him, it is in this collective distraction that the possibility to focus and the power for change lies. When film lacks intention (is not aestheticized) it becomes most powerful.

Benjamin's thoughts on the role of film are important here for a number of reasons: firstly, he privileges the gaze made possible by film only to the extent that it captures people looking at themselves, thus raising self-awareness and clearly implicating the viewer in a reality in which, although he is a part of, he might not feel responsible for; secondly, he privileges the possibilities embedded in the optical unconscious and the ability of film to release this unconscious by creating a virtual visual environment in which, for the first time, we are allowed to have a "collective dream" as opposed to an individual dream, thus implicating us into a reality collectively; thirdly, he privileges film as a representational form that can carry powerful messages in its non-intentionality, thus opening up the possibility of acquiring knowledge through a representational method that is not a means to an end. In film, the visual/the aesthetic, unlike text, becomes a privileged, non-intentional source of knowledge.

The privileged as opposed to the non-privileged status of the gaze in *The Wire* is thus not only acquired in light of a particular social positioning but also in light of its ability to capture and represent a reality that awakens and calls to action the collective watching. I have argued that *The Wire* offers unique insights into the nature of violence in post-industrial Baltimore in a number of ways: firstly, it opts to contextualize violence within the context of a failing spatial/architectural reality, thus embedding violence into urban politics; secondly, it offers a uniquely reflective juxtaposition of the privileged gaze of the bureaucratic apparatus and the city elite as opposed to the gaze of vulnerable communities; and thirdly it focuses on particular dynamic spaces of resistance in which not just the violence generated by drug gangs, but also, and perhaps more importantly, the violence generated by the War on Drugs is performed.

Conclusion

Nigel Thrift argues that an intellectual engagement with the performability of space has the potential to "change our practices in two vital ways: The first is by changing what we regard as method [...] The second [...] is by stressing that performance is itself a form of knowledge, an intelligence in-action" (Thrift 424–5). In this sense, *The Wire* presents itself as a very successful research project that engages the performability of space through the ultimate visual tool, film, and uses this performance not only for its entertainment value—the show is after all a cop show—but at the same time for its potential to "illuminate," and raise self-awareness.

This chapter has sought to trace the unique use of space in *The Wire* and its success in providing, firstly, a clear identification of the drug problem as ultimately a space problem through its focus on Baltimore's failed urban fabric; secondly, a subtle engagement with the limitations of surveillance and the possibilities that exist in the enlightened, privileged gaze of the film camera; and thirdly, a depiction of particular "performative" spaces—the corner, Hamsterdam, the Pit, the High Rises—as the last vestiges of resistance to the State's encroachment on the territory, lifestyle and very existence of West Baltimore and its inhabitants.

Notes

1. He speaks here mainly of a Fascist use of film.
2. Here Benjamin uses the concept of (self)-alienation in a Marxist way to mean a distancing from nature, each other, and our own humanity.
3. See also Paul Allen Anderson's argument that the tautologies uttered by a number of characters in the show suggest an abnegation of agency.

Works Cited

Amin, Ash. "Spatialities of Globalization." *Environment and Planning D: Society and Space* 34 (2002): 385–99. Print.

Anderson, Paul Allen. "'The Game Is the Game': Tautology and Allegory in *The Wire*". *Criticism* 52.3/4 (2010): 373–98. Print.

Balko, Radley. "'30 Years of Failure' a Conversation About the War on Drugs with Ed Burns, Co-Creator of the Wire," *Reason Online*. Web. June 28, 2009. http://www.reason.com/news/printer/126026.html.

Benjamin, Walter. *The Arcades Project*. Trans. Howard Eiland and Kevin McLaughlin, ed. Rolf Tiedemann. Cambridge: Belknap Press of Harvard University Press, 1999. Print.

———. "Critique of Violence." *Illuminations*. Ed. Hannah Arendt. New York: Schocken, 1968. Print.

———. "The Work of Art in the Age of Its Technological Reproducibility." *The Work of Art in the Age of Its Technological Reproducibility and Other Writings on Media*. Eds. Michael Jennings, Brigid Doherty and Thomas Levin. Cambridge: Belknap Press of Harvard University Press, 2008. Print.

Boger, Gretchen. "The Meaning of Neighborhood in the Modern City: Baltimore's Residential Segregation Ordinances, 1910 1913." *Journal of Urban History* 35.2 (2009): 236–58. Print.

Cohen, James. "Abandoned Housing: Exploring Lessons from Baltimore." *Housing Policy Debate* 12.3 (2001): 415–48. Print.

Harvey, David. "Between Space and Time: Reflections on the Geographical Imagination." *Annals of the Association of American Geographers* 80.3 (1990): 418–34. Print.

———. *Justice, Nature and the Geography of Difference*. Cambridge, MA: Blackwell, 1996. Print.

———. "Social Justice, Postmodernism and the City." *International Journal of Urban and Regional Research* 16 (1992): 588–601. Print.

Kinkle, Jeff, and Alberto Toscano. "Baltimore as World and Representation: Cognitive Mapping and Capitalism in the Wire." Presented at Senate House, March 27, 2009.

Page, Max. "Comment on James R. Cohen's 'Abandoned Housing: Exploring Lessons from Baltimore.'" *Housing Policy Debate* 12.3 (2001): 457–63. Print.

Simon, David, "The Wire: A Dramatic Series for HBO." 2000. Web. June 29, 2009. http://kottke.org.s3.amazonaws.com/the-wire/The_Wire_-_Bible.pdf.

Speidel, Linda, "'Thin Line 'Tween Heaven and Here' (Bubbles): Real and Imagined Space in the Wire'," *Dark Matter*, Web. June 28 2009 http://www.darkmatter101.org/site/2009/05/29/thin-line-tween-heaven-and-here-bubbles-real-and-imagined-space-in-the-wire/

Thrift, Nigel. "Dead Geographies—and How to Make Them Live." *Environment and Planning D: Society and Space* 18 (2000): 411–32. Print.

———. "Remembering the Technological Unconscious by Foregrounding Knowledges of Position." *Environment and Planning D: Society and Space* 22 (2004): 175–90. Print.

———. "Space." *Theory, Culture & Society* 23.2–3 (2006): 139–55. Print.

Watching, Policing
Surveillance and Complicity
Ivan Stacy

> "You show who gets paid, behind all the tragedy and fraud ... you show how the money routes itself, how we're all, all of us vested, all of us complicit...."—Lester Freamon (5.02)

Lester Freamon's (Clarke Peters) assertion that we are "all of us vested, all of us complicit" seems to implicate the whole of the series' sprawling cast in the corruption, crime and neglect represented in *The Wire*. Yet his accusatory comment remains strangely unelaborated: his interlocutor, Detective Leander Sydnor (Corey Parker Robinson), having stated that he prefers "street work," does not interrogate Freamon as to how it is that "all of us" collude in the dereliction and violence present in *The Wire*'s Baltimore. Sydnor's apathy towards Freamon's fiendishly complex investigation is symptomatic of the attitudes exhibited by many of *The Wire*'s protagonists. His unwillingness to question how his own actions may be implicated in, or contribute to, destructive criminal activity is one of many acts of turning away from an examination of the consequences of self-interest. This volume is born from the premise that Baltimore is a dark corner of America which disintegrates as attention is turned elsewhere. My chapter argues that, in *The Wire*, the complicity to which Freamon alludes is just such a turning away on the part of the show's protagonists. Specifically, these failures of responsibility stem from the protagonists' participation in institutions and systems—specifically the police force, schools, unions, and political organizations—whose values and structures of power appeal to their self-interest, but which also induce them to remain blind to the consequences of their actions.

A number of responses to *The Wire* have touched on the notion of complicity, but have done so mainly by debating the way in which the show's aesthetics either succeed or fail in drawing the viewer's attention to their own culpability in the events represented. Some, such as Erika Johnson-Lewis, have argued that the camera's appearance of detachment, "absolves the viewer of needing to think about his or her complicity within a larger social structure" (Johnson-Lewis 5; see also Brooks 71, 82). Others have argued that the self-reflexive elements in the show, particularly Season Five's examination of the press, prompt a form of critical viewing that absolves the series of this accusation (Love 501; La Berge 548; McNeilly 203). While these arguments contain some sharp readings of *The Wire*'s cinematography, they imply a relationship between observation and complicity without quite fully articulating it, largely because of the difficulty of accurately anticipating the viewer's response. In this chapter, the notion of complicity that I employ always involves agency beyond observation: it is in the way that observation is acted upon (or fails to be acted upon) that violence and neglect are allowed to flourish. For this reason, this essay eschews further discussion of the viewer's subject position in favor of a close examination of the actions of the protagonists of *The Wire*.

If complicity is a form of blindness (and I argue that this is the case in *The Wire*), ways of looking are central to this discussion. Observation, in the form of surveillance conducted by the detail, is of course the central thread which draws the diverse strands of *The Wire* together. However, the constraints upon and limits of surveillance are indicated by the complaint, repeated through the five seasons, that attention is being turned away from domestic issues, namely the narcotics trade, and towards global issues in the form of the threat of terrorism. There is, therefore, a certain irony in David Simon weighing into the debate on surveillance sparked by the recent revelations about the National Security Agency's (NSA) Prism program.[1] Simon provoked no small amount of consternation as a result of his partial defense of government surveillance. A detailed discussion of Simon's argument regarding its nature or legitimacy is outside the scope of this essay,[2] but pertinent to my discussion of complicity in *The Wire* is Simon's scorn towards what he regards as a double standard in many of the outraged responses to the revelations. "We asked for this," he asserts, noting that increased government powers of surveillance were granted with the passing of the Patriot Act, through democratically elected representatives, in the aftermath of 9/11. Simon's assertion raises the question of the extent of the general population's desire for, and complicity in, the mass surveillance carried out in the period contemporaneous with the production of *The Wire*.

In suggesting that citizens are somehow culpable in a pervasive system of surveillance, his arguments accord with what others were arguing prior to the Prism revelations. For example, Vincent P. Pecora, writing in the immediate aftermath of 9/11, suggests that the ubiquity of observation is part of a "culture of surveillance" which was in fact viewed as comforting by the majority of the population (347). Moreover, Pecora suggests that citizens in modern nation states are in fact producers of their own surveillance, acting as "participant-observers" in this process (353). What is most troubling about Percora's argument is the sense that pervasive observation is not simply a result of short-term concerns (the threat of terrorism being one example of such) but rather that it is a consequence of a "liberal democratic demand to make the socially hidden visible, to expose the secret workings of individual choice and group authority" (353): in other words, although some forms of surveillance appear be a sinister aspect of state power, these may in fact be an extension of processes which have their roots in liberal and egalitarian intentions. Moreover, citizens' participation in surveillance is often the result of self-interest rather than fear or coercion and, building on Pecora's observations in a perceptive essay, Joseph Christopher Schaub argues that *The Wire* shows those who carry out surveillance also tend to be obsessed with their own images. Citing the actions in Season Five of members of institutions indispensible to liberal democracy, namely Detective Jimmy McNulty (Dominic West), Mayor Thomas Carcetti (Aidan Gillen), and the unethical journalist Scott Templeton (Thomas McCarthy), Schaub suggests that the protagonists' (and viewers') desire to be seen propels them into a "narcissistic loop" (131).

Given the prevalence of observation in *The Wire*, suggestive of the culture of surveillance identified by Pecora, there seems to be a paradox in the fact that the detail—one of the few organizations in the series capable of effective and meaningful surveillance—survives none of the five seasons unscathed. In this regard, *The Wire* is largely about the difficulty of surveillance. This difficulty stems from a systemic, willed blindness to these impoverished areas of the city, a blindness which is illustrated in chilling fashion by Marlo Stanfield's (Jamie Hector) ability to hide a morgue of his victims in the city's vacant housing. In this chapter, I therefore attempt to reconcile the apparent contradiction between pervasive surveillance and the inability, or unwillingness, of the BPD and other institutions to observe and intervene effectively in the crime-ridden areas of the city. I argue that surveillance fails to fulfill the liberal democratic goal of making the socially hidden visible because it is inextricably connected to forms of measurement which perpetuate a de-valuation of the lives of those in those areas. In short, the systems of surveillance and measurement that attach value to life in the legitimate half of the show, and seek to preserve that value, are the same systems that render another part of the population unworthy of the same attention, and thus leave them to wither outside structures of observation and care.

In making this argument, I draw a crude distinction between the two halves of the show. The first is the "legitimate" half, which contains politicians, educators, and the police. The second is the "illegitimate" half, which contains those employed in the "game" of the Baltimore drugs trade and related criminal activity (as Michael Lister notes elsewhere in this volume, "citizens," that is, law-abiding citizens working outside the city's main institutions of power, are a "missing middle" in the show's representation of Baltimore). A brief survey of the deaths across the five seasons of *The Wire* should suffice as an indicator of the relative value of life in the two halves. Of the eighty-plus deaths, the vast majority are directly related to criminal activity in the illegitimate half's cast of characters. The four exceptions are Colonel Raymond Forester (Richard DeAngelis) and Detective Ray Cole (Robert F. Colesberry), both of whom die of natural causes, Officer Derrick Waggoner (unlisted actor), who is accidentally shot by Detective Raymond "Prez" Pryzbylewski (Jim True-Frost), and Steven L. Miles, the duck belonging to Chester "Ziggy" Sobotka (James Ransone), who dies of alcohol poisoning in the bar frequented by the Stevedores in Season Two.

There is, then, an extreme discrepancy between life expectancies in the two halves of Baltimore represented by the show. In the first part of the essay, I argue that this discrepancy is a result of the different forms of power exercised in the two halves, drawing upon Foucault's concepts of sovereign power and biopower. I identify parallels between a sovereign's control over the lives and deaths of their subjects and the power wielded by the heads of the drug organizations in Baltimore. I also suggest that the legitimate half of the show operates according to a contrasting, biopolitical, logic of power in which measurement and statistical approaches serve to optimize a state of life for the majority of the population, but necessarily excludes those who are considered to be detrimental to that process of optimization.

In the second part of the essay, I argue that the valuation of life which creates this discrepancy is the result of the prevalent forms of measurement employed in the legitimate half, and that these are inextricably connected to a pervasive culture of surveillance and observation. *The Wire* presents a number of images of detectives on rooftops with their cameras, and listening to telephone conversations through their wiretaps. These shots invite an understanding of surveillance as a discrete action that involves observer and observed, with agency possessed only by the former (and these images have their parallel in the notion, evoked by Prism, of secret agents monitoring the population unseen from behind their computer screens). However, the challenges faced by the detail show that surveillance, rather than being a discrete act involving only the detectives and their targets, takes place within a network of actors, and that connections and effective communication must be established and maintained between these actors in order for surveillance to have any impact. I therefore attempt to problematize the image of surveillance as a discrete act, carried out by an agent of the state or law enforcement agency, and to situate the actions of those doing the watching in *The Wire* within the larger context of their networks of alliances.

In making this argument, I draw upon Bruno Latour's notion of the actor-network, which he defines as "what is made to act by a large star-shaped web of mediators flowing in and out of it" and that which "exist[s] by its many ties" (*Social* 217). Latour argues that "the more attachments [an actor-network] has, the more it exists" (*Social* 217).[3] The implication for surveillance in *The Wire* is that, where networks are not successfully established and maintained, surveillance either does not take place or is not put to use effectively. To demonstrate this, I trace two networks, these being the BPD's successful case against the Barksdale organization in Season One, and the failed prosecution of Senator Clay Davis (Isiah Whitlock, Jr.) in Season Five.

In addition, I argue that the construction of the networks required to enable successful surveillance requires chains of translation to be built, along which information is transmitted. In elucidating his notion of "circulating reference," Latour argues that translation, as he defines it, involves an abstraction of data or information. This process of abstraction creates chains of translation whereby each stage is aligned with "the ones that precede and follow it, so that, beginning with the last stage, one will be able to *return* to the first" (*Pandora* 64). The transmission of information garnered through surveillance thus involves its translation into other forms, and hence relies upon modes of representation in order for it to be presented in ways that are acceptable to the next parties in the chain. Typically in *The Wire*, such translations involve data being translated into legal terms in anticipation of a criminal case being brought, or into rhetorical terms in order for it to serve the political interests of either the BPD or the incumbent political elite; it is often the disjunction between these two demands that causes networks of actors to collapse and which scuppers attempts at surveillance.

It is these forms of representation employed in the act of translation that create the apparent paradox of a society obsessed with surveillance and measurement which at the same time somehow blinds itself to a whole section of its population. As Latour notes, the word "oversight" captures the dual and paradoxical meaning of domination by sight "since it means at once looking at something from above and ignoring it" (*Pandora* 38). In their attempts to regulate and hence control the city, the BPD, at the behest of the mayor's office, uses forms of representation that capture statistically the situation of the city as a whole, but which do so reductively, and hence blind them to phenomena that are not registered or measured by those same forms.

In the third and final section of the essay, I argue that it is this type of oversight, created by the logic of biopower and the statistical representations that it demands, which allows certain sections of the population to be rendered invisible. Expanding the notion of surveillance beyond the BPD, I identify similar networks of observation as pervading and informing the operation of structures of power in all of the institutions represented in *The Wire*. The shocking discrepancy both in quality of life and life expectancy between the two halves of *The Wire* is a result of such biopolitical power at work: the statistical approaches to government, based on surveillance and observation, operate within the legitimate half of Baltimore to ensure that its participants are made to live in a certain way. However, the darker, flip side to the culture of surveillance is that the same structures which create a prevalence of observation are also those that render a section of the population invisible, or rather unworthy of observation. Out of sight, I argue, this section of the population is ignored, devalued, and let die.

Baltimore's Two Halves

In his lectures at the Collège de France in 1975–76 and 1977–8 (published in English as *Society Must be Defended* and *Security, Territory, Population* respectively),[4] Foucault defined biopower as the form of power which addresses "man-as-species."[5] In contrast with its precursor, disciplinary power,[6] in which "multiplicity can and must be dissolved into individual bodies that can be kept under surveillance, trained, used, and, if need be, punished," biopower addresses humanity as "a global mass that is affected by overall processes characteristic of birth, death, production, illness and so on" (*Society*

242–3). Also pertinent to this discussion is a central distinction between biopower and sovereign power (which predates disciplinary power), which is that within a system of sovereign power, the sovereign has "the right to take life or let live." Conversely, in a system governed according to the logic of biopower, the state operates on the principle that it has the right and power to "make live and let die" (*Society* 241): the population must buy into a particular way of life—a means of living considered to be optimal for the species as a whole—or otherwise be regarded as surplus to the requirements of that system. As a consequence, when compared to the tools employed by disciplinary power, these statistical approaches to governing the population as a whole rely upon more subtle and rational measures which appeal to self-interest rather than working on the basis of fear and threat. Such measures include insurance, savings and safety measures (*Society* 244). *The Wire* shows that it is in these measures' appeal to the self-interest of the members of that society that the notion of complicity, rather than oppression, as the force through which power functions, emerges.

One of the features of *The Wire*'s purported realism is that it begins to break down the clear division between drug traffickers and police, largely through the way that it shows the structures of the criminal and legal organizations to parallel each other. It is also true that those operating within the game are shown to be subject to similar forms of measurement and observation to their counterparts in the legitimate half of the show. However, the sanctions faced by those in the game for transgressing against their superiors are much more severe, with the forms of power exercised by the drug organizations bearing a much closer resemblance to sovereign power than they do to biopower, particularly in the way that the heads of the criminal organizations, often referred to as the "kings," have the ability to take life. Moreover, while Foucault notes that a feature of biopower is the retreat of death from public view, the exercise of sovereign power often requires death to be ceremonial and spectacular (*Society* 247). This is certainly true in the way that it is exercised by Avon Barksdale (Wood Harris), the head of the dominant drug organization in West Baltimore in Seasons One through Three. When Barksdale orders the murder of Omar Little's (Michael K. Williams) accomplice and boyfriend Brandon Wright (Michael Kevin Darnall), he states that he wants the body "on display" (1.04). Stanfield's organization later uses murder in the same way. Although Stanfield's enforcers, Felicia "Snoop" Pearson (played by the actor of the same name) and Chris Partlow (Gbenga Akinnagbe), succeed in hiding the murders from the police in the city's vacant housing, these deaths are common knowledge within the Westside. The circulation of this knowledge thus allow the murders committed by Partlow and Pearson to "send a message" from the organization to those over whom they hold power. The importance of the dissemination of the knowledge of murder is shown when Michael Lee (Tristan Wilds), while being inducted into the Stanfield organization, questions the logic of committing a murder on the basis of hearsay, and Partlow responds by informing him that it "doesn't matter if he said it or not. People think he said it. Can't let that shit go" (5.02).

The Wire depicts resistance to sovereign power within the illegitimate half as futile, with dissent against the drug kingpins resulting in death in most cases. As tensions mount between Barksdale and his second-in-command Russell "Stringer" Bell (Idris Elba), for example, the latter accuses the former of an over-willingness to "snatch a life" (3.08); the quarrel exemplifies the different approaches of the two men to the drug trade, and this split impels Barksdale to arrange Bell's murder. Similarly, when Preston "Bodie" Broadus (J. D. Williams), a model "soldier" for most of his career under Barksdale and later Stanfield, finally breaks ranks due to the latter's willingness to take life arbitrarily and unnecessarily ("this motherfucker's killing niggers just to do it [...] just 'cause he can," 4.13), the result is also that he is gunned down within days.

In contrast, those in positions of power in the legitimate half of the show act to preserve their own positions within structures of power by appealing to the self-interest of those around them. Ranking officers in the Baltimore Police Department repeatedly invoke "chain of command" to their subordinates. This is not the crude exercise of power as a means of individual self-preservation seen in the illegitimate half of the show; it is, rather, an attempt to preserve the integrity of the structures within which individuals feel their best interests lie. McNulty's repeated insistence on bucking the chain of command is an exception to the rule, but his character serves to bring into relief the self-interest of those around him: at one point he rails against what he perceives as the complicity between the members of the legal profession to protect each other from any threat to their positions, even at the expense of justice being served, stating that "everybody stays friends, everybody gets paid, and everybody's got a fucking future" (1.11).[7] McNulty is shown to be correct, at least with regard to the legitimate half of the show. Clarence Royce (Glynn Turman) and Carcetti, for example, are shown joking with each other even after a bitter campaign battle, and those who do find themselves pushed out of their positions, either due to incompetence or political maneuverings tend to be granted a "soft landing" in exchange for their silence.

This silence is part of an agreement, sometimes tacitly enacted and sometimes made explicit, to maintain the invisibility of aspects of society that could threaten a status quo that those in the legitimate half regard as being in their best interests. However, if biopower seeks to optimize life for a population as a whole, divisions within a population as stark as those present in *The Wire*'s Baltimore may seem not to fit this model. Foucault accounts for such divisions within a population through what he terms "racism." This is not the racism conventionally defined as predicated on color lines or "the traditional form of mutual contempt or hatred between races" (*Society* 258), but on the principle that those who do not participate in processes and structures designed to optimize the state of life of the population as a whole instead weaken it, and can therefore be allowed to "let die" outside those structures. "Letting die" in *The Wire* takes the form of a turning away from a section of the population to the extent that sovereign power is allowed to function in those parts of the city, exercised brutally by the heads of drug organizations, and barely impinged upon by the BPD.

Thus, while death is ever present in the illegitimate half of *The Wire*, these same deaths remain unseen, unacknowledged, or at best noted without being acted upon, by the legitimate half. This systemic blindness towards death in certain parts of Baltimore indicates that there is an unobtrusiveness to death that allows it to go unnoticed. In other words, there exists an asymmetry of visibility and vision between the legitimate and illegitimate halves of the city. This asymmetry occurs as a result of the forms of measurement, and related forms of representation, employed by and within the legitimate half of Baltimore: it is precisely the obsession with measurement with respect to one part of the population in turn allows another part to be ignored and let die; and it is this asymmetry of value and measurement that is the "racism" present in biopower. *The Wire* shows that, if something is deemed not to matter, that is, if its measurement does not impact on the perceived effectiveness of the systems and institutions in place (and the self-interested positions of those within the institutions), then those systems possess the capability (and more often than not, the willingness) to render that phenomenon invisible. In the sections that follow, I therefore discuss the way in which the forms of vision, measurement and representation employed in *The Wire* make certain phenomena visible while simultaneously overlooking others.

Translating the Street

David Simon's dismissal of the concerns surrounding the Prism program center on the argument that it would be counter-intuitive for law enforcement agencies to pretend that the data generated through increased internet use does not exist. The question, according to Simon, is not whether this data should be collected, but is whether the "government [is] accessing the data for the legitimate public safety needs of the society," or whether it is doing so "in ways that abuse individual liberties and violate personal privacy" ("We Are Shocked"). While it is not the aim of this chapter to engage in detail with numerous responses and objections to Simon's argument, one surprising aspect of the passage cited above is his evocation of "government." *The Wire*'s extensive and detailed depiction of Baltimore shows that there is no single, central body that can be identified as the source of surveillance. Where arguments and counter-arguments about surveillance might evoke a "government" and its shadowy agents, *The Wire* depicts government as a multiplicity of actors, working as often at cross-purposes as they do in accord with each others' aims. For example, Carcetti is required to fight for every square inch both within the Democratic Party and against other bodies of power. Moreover, the FBI, which perhaps exemplifies the kind of covert, technologically advanced surveillance feared by critics of Prism, is nevertheless circumscribed by national policy (shown to be the prioritization of counter-terrorism) as well its internal and external relationships, as exemplified by the leaking of the detail's information by agent Kristos Koutris (Tom Mardirosian) to the criminal organization headed by the protagonists collectively known as "the Greeks" in Season Two.

The Wire thus shows that surveillance is not simply a matter of the agents of government watching citizens in order to maintain a disciplined population. Surveillance is in fact bound up with a whole complex of other processes and values, to the extent that it cannot be taken as a separate or discrete tool of governmental power. Moreover, the political obstacles faced by the detail within the BPD show that effective surveillance requires the involvement of a network of actors in order to take place, and in order for observation to be translated into effective prosecutions. Yet the institutions' vested interests in keeping certain phenomena—particularly crime—hidden, mean that there is an ingrained, institutional resistance to the kind of surveillance work that makes too much visible. The fluctuating fortunes of the detail are a result of the way that its work expands the networks involved in surveillance beyond the players in the illegitimate half and begins to impinge on the legitimate half.

A reprise of the detail's surveillance of the Barksdale organization in Season One shows the way in which surveillance involves multiple actors. In the initial stages of their surveillance, the detectives working in the detail succeed in identifying numerous drug traffickers and enforcers, up to and including Stringer Bell, but are initially clueless as to the appearance of Barksdale himself. Lester Freamon's initiative enables him to locate the first visual likeness of Barksdale on an old boxing poster (1.04); and it is only through another series of chance encounters that Detectives Thomas "Herc" Hauk (Domenick Lombardozzi) and Ellis Carver (Seth Gilliam) are able to set eyes upon Barksdale at the Eastside-Westside basketball game (1.09). Moreover, in the process of building up a picture of the structure of the criminal organization, the detail requires repeated help of Detective Kima Greggs' (Sonja Sohn) confidential informant (C.I.), Reginald "Bubs" Cousins (Andre Royo). Bubs performs his "hat trick," whereby he poses as a street salesman, perching a red hat on the heads of any dealers of note as the police take photographs from their hidden positions (generally on rooftops), and later identifying these individuals from the photos taken.

The detail's reliance upon Bubs, Freamon's footslog across Baltimore to pull an old poster, and Herc and Carver's fortuitous opportunity to watch Barksdale may all seem to suggest that Schaub is correct in his assertion that *The Wire* privileges the low-tech gaze (126), as part of a broader argument that the show highlights the limitations of high-tech surveillance. This view seems to be supported by McNulty's wistful recollection of a former C.I. who "saw the street like we wish we could" (1.05). However, Bubs' role could more accurately be described as one of translation because, while his information is essential to the detail, his gaze in isolation would be as useless as the detectives' photographs without his ability to correlate dealers' faces and names. Bubs acting on his own is nothing more an addict with his finger on the pulse of the Westside drug trade, and the police acting on their own flounder haplessly in alien territory (a point made by Herc, Carver and Prez's ill-advised foray into the high-rises in 1.02). It is only when they act together, translating their information into terms meaningful to the other party, that Bubs' information allows the detail to align textual information (names, nicknames and associated identifying details, such as dates of birth) with the visual data collected by their photographic surveillance. This is the first link in a chain of information, because the identities established at this stage are then linked to the aural data collected by wiretapping telephones and cloning pagers; and it is only at this point that the detail's surveillance is able to produce the evidence needed for a criminal case.

In elaborating his notion of "circulating reference," Latour argues that reference relies "not so much on resemblance as on a regulated series of transformations, transmutations, and translations" and that it is "a way of keeping something *constant* through a series of transformations" (*Pandora* 58). The surveillance conducted by the detail is a series of actions in which data is gathered, aligned with other data, and translated into meaningful terms for the next party in the chain. When seen as such, it becomes increasingly difficult to identify the end points of such chains of translation. As a result, the notion of surveillance as a discrete act—whether enabled by technology or the natural or low-tech gaze—becomes problematic.

Again, the surveillance of the Barksdale organization in Season One illustrates the need for surveillance to take place within a network of alliances because, even before Bubs enables the alignment of visual and aural data described above, significant efforts are required just to initiate the process. The BPD initially has no interest in setting up a sustained surveillance operation, and it is only when McNulty, irked by D'Angelo Barksdale's (Larry Gilliard) acquittal in a murder trial, steps outside his chain of command to first approach Judge Daniel Phelan (Peter Gerety), and then attempts to make the case a federal concern, that such an operation is conceived. However, McNulty's efforts are unsuccessful, and only result in his receiving a dressing down from Major Bill Rawls (John Doman), who prefers to keep his homicide detectives working murders in strict rotation in order to address the need to meet statistical targets, while the FBI are unwilling to assign resources to drugs targets, this now (post–9/11) being the "wrong war" (1.01). The murder of another witness, William Gant (1.01), creates the political will to target the Barksdale organization, and even at this point Lieutenant Cedric Daniels (Lance Reddick), heading the investigation, is willing to follow Deputy Commissioner Ervin Burrell's (Frankie Faison) orders to keep the investigation quick and simple. It is only through the continual prodding of McNulty and Freamon, and with the sometimes serendipitous shedding of the less able members of the detail, that Daniels' charges emerge as a unit with the will and capabilities to put together the sophisticated surveillance operation that Season One describes.

The evolution of the detail in Season One shows that any act of surveillance is unlikely to take place without the requisite interest in the information that such surveillance may produce. Burrell and Rawls are concerned only with the immediately visible statistics upon which they are judged, primarily the homicide clearance rate, and as such they hold a vested interest in the crime associated with the Barksdale organization remaining invisible. It is only because McNulty and Freamon are able to forge a network of alliances with those working within the legal and political institutions, often by challenging or stepping outside of the chain of command, that the pressure on Burrell and Rawls to present visible evidence of an investigation into the Westside drug trade outweighs their desire to keep this crime hidden.

Surveillance thus begins with a demand for meaningful, visible results from those capable of exerting pressure on others working within the same institutional framework. The demand for results initiates a chain of surveillance in which these demands are passed from Phelan downwards through Burrell, Rawls, Daniels to McNulty and the other detectives who, with the help of Bubs, conduct the street-level surveillance of the Barksdale dealers. Bubs' translation of street names and faces into terms acceptable for legal casework is the first act of a reverse process whereby information is passed back along the chain, translated at each link into the type of information acceptable to the next party.[8] Once bound in such a chain, the protagonists in the legitimate half of *The Wire* watch each other, demanding visible and measurable data of other parties and themselves passing on (or tactically withholding) their own information within these chains of translation.

Season One thus shows the detail overcoming institutional inertia, born from vested interests in keeping certain data invisible, in order to construct a chain of translation whereby their surveillance of the Westside drugs trade is successfully translated into information that is used to prosecute members of the Barksdale organization. The contrast between this case and the failure to prosecute Clay Davis in Season Five is revealing because it shows how acts of translation may fail. The surveillance required to prosecute Davis, primarily conducted by Freamon, is more patient and more detailed than the case assembled against the Barksdales, and more remarkable in that it succeeds in forging a network of alliances sufficient to challenge an established institutional figure. Freamon's interest in Davis, and his inclination to "follow the money," begins in Season One, when Greggs and Carver catch Davis's driver leaving the Westside towers with $20,000 in cash (1.08). However, the detail is again confronted with institutional vested interests. Greggs initially puts the surveillance and arrest of Davis's driver in legal terms ("you were observed in one of the city's designated drug-free anti-loitering zones, where a drug suspect leaned into your vehicle and handed you something") as does Daniels, who informs Burrell that "we pulled this off the wire ... it's drug money in that car" (1.08). However, Daniels does not fully grasp the political implications of the seizure, specifically the way in which Burrell's alliance with Davis is born from his self-interested concern for the department. This alliance outweighs Burrell's desire for a successful resolution of the Barksdale case and, informing Daniels that "you shit all over yourself [...] all over this department," he instructs him to return the money (1.08).

As the political implications of the rapidly sprawling Barksdale case begin to dawn on Daniels, he correctly reasons that if "you follow the drugs, you get a drug case; you start following the money, you don't know where you're going" (1.08). In other words, following the money creates a chain of surveillance that is unpredictable and, by making visible that which would be better kept hidden, may implicate those with whom the BPD feel it politic to keep as allies. However, despite the resistance which results from these political concerns, Freamon continues to pursue the money trail over the five seasons of *The Wire*. While Davis appears in Seasons Two and Three, mainly in conjunction with Bell's attempts to break into the real estate market, it is not until 4.01 that Freamon, seeking to take advantage of the upcoming Democratic primary, issues subpoenas in an attempt to trace leads from the Barksdale investigation. However, this action once again results in the detail—now the Major Crimes unit—being effectively disbanded, and it is not until 4.11 that Freamon finds himself in a position to examine the returned subpoenas. Freamon succeeds in arriving at this position by overcoming institutional inertia: he does so by circumventing an inattentive lieutenant to issue subpoenas, and by aligning his own interests with the desire of Rupert Bond (Dion Graham), the new State's Attorney in the Carcetti administration, to make a name for himself.

When Davis's trial takes place in 5.07, Freamon finally has the opportunity to present in a court of law a narrative of the chains of translation that he has been assembling, tracing the routes by which drug money is siphoned into Davis's accounts, where it is fraudulently assigned to not-for-profit organizations. However, the case fails because even then, the alliances on the prosecuting side are shown to be inadequate with Bond's ambition leading him to attempt to prosecute the case himself, rather than allowing it to be pursued federally. Secondly, and more importantly, Freamon's painstakingly assembled evidence fails in its translation. It is translated into legal terms by Bond and Pearlman for the benefit of a court of law. Unfortunately for the prosecution, Davis and his attorney Billy Murphy (played by the Baltimore defense attorney of the same name) ambush them with a defense based on portraying Davis as a Robin Hood figure, a champion and ally of the people, translating the evidence into an emotive rhetoric to which the jury responds. Standing on the courthouse steps following Davis's acquittal, a shell-shocked Bond asks Pearlman, "What the fuck just happened?" to which she replies, "Whatever it was, they don't teach it in law school" (5.07). What they fail to realize is that Murphy and Davis have succeeded in translating the evidence into terms meaningful to a jury which believes that Davis's activities work in their own interests more than a legal system which is shown to have repeatedly failed them.

The Barksdale and Davis cases show that networks of alliances are required in order to initiate and conduct surveillance, whether this takes place through street-level observation or through the acquisition of information buried in a paper trail. Moreover, for surveillance to be sustained and successful, the information that it gathers must be regarded as valuable enough to outweigh other considerations, specifically the potential for damage to other alliances. Surveillance is not, therefore, a single, discrete act carried out by a representative of the state or member of a law enforcement agency observing a target. It is in fact a chain of actions which can be seen in terms of the translation of data along that chain, to an end point at which evidence is presented in a manner, language and form that can be received and interpreted by its intended audience. Moreover, for surveillance to take place, and particularly for the kind of sustained surveillance carried out by the detail, those carrying out the physical act of surveillance must do so within a network of alliances.

Because individual acts of surveillance must always be oriented towards other parties in that network, the way in which the data collected by surveillance is represented, the way in which it allows itself to be measured, is a crucial factor in the success or otherwise of the operation. As I show in the following section, while these forms of representation may ostensibly appear to conform to the liberal-democratic aims of making social phenomena visible, the pressures exerted by the anticipation of measurement and judgment in fact create forms of representation that render aspects of life in Baltimore invisible.

Overlooking Baltimore

In the section above, I have attempted to complicate the notion of surveillance, describing the multiple actors and stages required for meaningful data to be gathered and put to use. While these observations apply to the actions of the police throughout the five seasons of *The Wire*, they are also of import to the wider argument that I am making in this chapter in that all protagonists in the legitimate half are at once observed and observing. In this section, I show how the forms of representation required by these processes of observation are a type of oversight that at once captures some phenomena while remaining blind to others. It is in this blindness, I argue, that the members of all the institutions represented in *The Wire* are complicit with the "letting die" of the illegitimate half of the city.

Chains of translation are not only present in the BPD, and exist in (and between) all of the other institutions represented across the five seasons, these being, primarily, schools, trade unions, the political system, and the press. In particular, Season Four draws a number of parallels between the police and the school system. In the same way as the police, those involved in the school system feel themselves under pressure to deliver the statistics demanded by their political and professional superiors. This pressure produces the same results, with Prez, now teaching at Edward Tilghman middle school, making a direct comparison between the two organizations when he complains of being asked to "juke the stats" in 4.09 (reinforcing the implication made through the juxtaposition of police- and teacher-training scenes in 4.01). The need for statistical results is passed down the chain in the form of standardized testing, which in turn encourages standardized teaching, even though the educators working directly with the children are well aware that such teaching is ineffectual.[9] For example, Prez's use of gambling to successfully teach mathematics to his class is contrasted with scenes in which he attempts to teach language arts tests questions, based on Greek classics, to his visibly bored students. Despite his misgivings, as a newly appointed teacher Prez feels compelled to teach in a way that he knows to be ineffective due to the presence of observation. The only strategy he therefore feels able to use is to hide his "real" teaching, and to teach in the terms required when observed: in 4.10, he is shown teaching test questions in the presence of the watching superintendent, and immediately reverting to his preferred style once she has left.

For actors possessing stronger alliances both within and outside the system, alternative strategies exist. For example, armed with a grant and a University of Maryland sanctioned mandate "not only to rethink the way we utilize institutions, but to help us start getting past having to rely on jail and drug rehab," the academic David Parenti (Dan DeLuca) is able to intervene in the educational system. However, in the same way that the detail requires Bubs' translations of the street in order to operate effectively, Parenti requires a partner who is able to mediate between his goals and the subjects of his research. Colvin's work of translation proves to be invaluable for Parenti, who initially intends to conduct his research on a sample of eighteen to twenty-one year olds. Colvin's experience on the streets tells him that this is too late for any meaningful intervention, and that Parenti's research would be wasted as a result. Colvin therefore engineers a situation in which Parenti is verbally and physically threatened by a representative of his intended target group. Visibly shaken as a result of this encounter, the academic admits that this age range "might already be too seasoned" (4.03), and Colvin thus succeeds in persuading him to conduct his research on younger, school-aged children. Even at this stage, the success of the research is not guaranteed, and it requires the skill of the group's teacher, Miss Duquette (Stacie Davis), and Colvin's interventions in the classroom, in which he repeatedly uses behavior on the street as a starting point for discussion, to translate education into terms that are relevant to the "corner kids," and thus to persuade them to buy into the project.

Parenti's project is shown to be a success in pedagogical terms, with the problem students participating in trust games, taking turns in group discussions, and cooperating to write down what they regard as the "rules" of the street. Yet where the project fails is in forging a chain of translation that allows these results to be transmitted in the reverse direction to those funding and sanctioning it. In a similar fashion to the Clay Davis case, their results are never translated into terms acceptable to their superiors. When given a short meeting with Carcetti's Chief of Staff, Michael Steintorf (Neal Huff), the two are unable to present their findings either in the statistical or rhetorical terms required by the politicians. Their failure to represent their work in statistical terms meaningful to the Carcetti administration results from the special class not having studied the test curriculum. Moreover, the two are unable to find a term with sufficient rhetorical force to throw off the stigmatic label of "tracking," described by Parenti as the "grouping of children based on expected performance" (5.04). Likewise, the term "corner kids," coined early in the project to refer to those pupils identified as the most disruptive to their classes, is never revised into a register acceptable to the project's stakeholders. A stumbling Colvin is thus unable to articulate the project in terms strong enough to challenge the memorable but simplistic rhetoric created by the politicians in order to sell their educational policy to voters. As a result, Steintorf dismisses their plea by declaring that "these would be the children left behind" (4.13).

The school system is therefore representative of the way in which *The Wire* shows all institutional systems to rely upon observable data. While observation is oriented towards its target, the forms of representation in which the data gathered is made visible are oriented in the reverse direction, generally back upwards in the chain of command. Acting as mediating links in these chains of translation, the vast majority of the protagonists are both observed and observing. While being observed constrains action, the requirement to act as observers also, and perhaps to a greater extent, forces the protagonists into alignment with the norms that they are supposed to police.

The desire to present the results of observation in visible and easily measureable form tends to result in the use of reductive statistical approaches. The BPD's COMSTAT meetings, present from Season Three onwards, are symptomatic of this tendency, showing how an obsession with statistical targets leads to quick-fix strategies and low quality arrests. The patient, intelligent work done by the detail is placed in opposition to these methods, as is Colvin's renegade "free zone" initiative. It is suggested that changing the statistically-obsessed mentality of the police department will lead to better policing: following Carcetti's election, he promises the rapidly rising Daniels that this will be the case henceforth, yet the new administration soon gives way to old tendencies under pressure to deliver his election promise of a reduction in crime.

The reason for Carcetti's backsliding is suggested in Foucault's analysis of the growth of governmentality, in which he argues that a statistical approach is not simply one mode of policing that could be replaced with another, better, approach. Instead, he argues that, within a biopolitical system, "police makes statistics necessary, but police also makes statistics possible ... police and statistics mutually condition each other." This is because "statistics is the state's knowledge of the state" and the police, being the product and tool of this biopolitical mentality of government, are intrinsically connected to the attempts to control the population as a whole (*Security* 315). If this is the case, Daniels' attempt to change the statistical mentality of the police department as a precondition for "fixing" it is doomed to failure. *The Wire*'s pessimistic conclusion, with Daniels stepping down in order to leave the Commissioner's post empty for the cynical and petulant, but politically astute, Stanislaus Valchek (Al Brown) suggests that the statistical approaches used by the Baltimore police are, at the very least, embedded in the mentalities of the political structures and that for any change to take place this must occur in a wider arena than the police department.

At one COMSTAT meeting, Rawls (now Deputy Commissioner of Operations) wryly comments that "crime is down and no one wants to take any credit" (3.08). His amusement stems from a rare reversal: instead of his subordinates using the system to make their own successes visible to others (a practice which he encourages and in which he unabashedly participates), a statistical improvement goes unclaimed. Unbeknown to Rawls, the reason for this improvement is Colvin's unsanctioned "free zone" experiment, which he must keep hidden from his superiors. The irony present in this scene captures the paradox created by statistical approaches, in that an apparently rational approach creates in the police, and in all of the institutions represented, the inverse of the intended result. These unintended consequences stem from the protagonists' awareness of their being observed, and their desperation to be measured favorably by their statistics. This desire often results in them abandoning or forgetting the original rationale of their role as police officers, educators, journalists or politicians, and in producing results in forms that hide phenomena—be these crime, underperforming school children, or failing policies—whose visibility would undermine the position of those measuring them.

Each of the institutions present in the show is an integral part of liberal democracy: the BPD exists to police laws created under a democratic constitution; the politicians govern according to that constitution; the teachers educate their children to be participant-citizens in a liberal democracy; and the press acts as check on any excesses. Pecora argues that surveillance and observation are intended to serve this system, stemming from the belief that such observation will make the hidden visible and hence result in an accountable and hence just society (353). Yet *The Wire* shows that the observation always produces oversight: the need to capture a global picture of the population inevitably leads to reductive forms of representation which omit certain aspects of the picture. Where self-interest drives the production of these representations, the resulting omissions, as *The Wire* shows, result in the ghetto being made invisible. For this reason, when Freamon, having discovered Marlo's morgue concealed in the city's vacant housing, faces stern resistance to having the bodies acknowledged as murders. This resistance stands in direct opposition to the principles of visibility and accountability, and it is only Carcetti's recent election, which allows him to avoid blame for the statistical rise in murder that acknowledging the bodies will produce, that results in the investigation being permitted.[10] More often, the sometimes-willful—and always self-interested—creation of blind spots allows these failures to be hidden, places the population in these areas outside the measurement of value, and hence lets life die.

Conclusion: Complicit Positions

The notion of surveillance executed by an observing camera, itself unobserved, is suggested by the images of detectives crouched on rooftops often shown in *The Wire*; the image of NSA agents at their computers evoked by Prism also conforms to this model. Yet this is precisely the model of surveillance that I am attempting to complicate in this chapter. I have argued that any act of surveillance, if it is to be effective, that is, if it is to be translated into meaningful action, is only one act in a chain of translation; furthermore, the observing party must also be part of, or form, a network of alliances in order for surveillance to be able to be placed in such a chain. Effective surveillance therefore necessarily involves and compels action. For these reasons, surveillance is one aspect of a pervasive system of measurement and value in which numerous actors are implicated, and to which they contribute.

Because surveillance always involves alliances and impels action, it produces a society of "participant observers." This prevalence of surveillance means that, where inaction is possible, it is generally presented in *The Wire* as an active (and often negligent) choice which contributes to the "letting die" of a section of the population. More often, the protagonists' complicity in this network of observation and measurement results from their being impelled to act on their observations and in anticipation of or response to others' observation of them. It is thus the protagonists' desire to progress and thrive within a way of life considered to be desirable, rather than coercion or fear produced by centralized surveillance conducted by the federal government, that exerts the greatest pressure on the protagonists. These same pressures produce blind spots in their overview of Baltimore which place sections of the population outside these systems of measurement and observation and hence allow a brutal and deadly form of sovereign power to thrive in this separate sphere.

The debate continues as to whether the surveillance carried out by the NSA is cause for concern or paranoia, or is, as Simon has argued, no different qualitatively from the legitimate surveillance carried out by law enforcement agents on a local level. Speculation will continue as to the extent of the threat to liberal democracy posed by this form of surveillance, and as to the probability of it resulting in the kind of totalitarian state that is at least, for now, and in the experience of most of *The Wire*'s audience, the preserve of dystopian fictions. However, as to the question of whether, as Simon states, we "asked for this," what *The Wire* shows is that surveillance is already here, more pervasive and more subtle, perhaps, than the modes present in the popular imagination, but already in existence prior to the Prism program as an inherent and insidious part of liberal democratic society: it is complex of observation in which all those who work for the institutions of the liberal democratic state are complicit in perpetuating forms of measurement and related values that render a section of the population invisible, ignorable, and hence killable.

Notes

1. The National Security Agency's (NSA) Prism program provides its agents with direct access to data held by internet service providers and social media sites. The information was initially reported by *The Guardian* and *New York Times* newspapers in early June 2013; Edward Snowden revealed himself to be the source of these leaks several days later (Greenwald, MacAskill and Poitras, "Edward Snowden").
2. Simon's essential argument is that there is no qualitative difference between what the NSA is doing, and has been doing, through the Prism program, and the methods used by law enforcement agencies across the country. He contends, with one or two caveats, that the difference is simply quantitative ("We Are Shocked").
3. Frank Kelleter also uses Latour's actor-network theory in his examination of *The Wire*, but does so in order to identify how the series defines itself through the creation of a specific type of audience (34). My own chapter, as stated above, restricts its argument to a discussion of the protagonists' actions and alliances.
4. These two sets of lectures can be seen as consecutive, given that Foucault took a sabbatical in 1977. François Ewald and Alessandro Fontana, Foreword to *Security*, 10.
5. Foucault favored the term "security" over "biopower" in the second set of lectures; however, "biopower" has generally been adopted as the label for these concepts, so I retain it here.
6. Disciplinary power is often employed in debates about surveillance due to Foucault's use of panopticism to illustrate its workings (*Discipline and Punish* 195–228). While the notion of a central power being able to exercise control over a population through surveillance, and through the population's awareness of their being surveiled, is pertinent to my discussion up to a point. However, as my discussion of networks of surveillance in the second half of this essay indicates, I see coercion being more decentralized than in the panoptic model of power.
7. This is not to say that McNulty is free from self-interest: he is an egotist whose motivation is a drive to prove his individual brilliance as a detective rather than climbing the career ladder.
8. See Andrew Moore's discussion of bureaucracy in this volume, and particularly his use of Hannah Arendt's diagnosis of the way that bureaucracies "demand an account" of their participants.
9. See Laura Bolf-Beliveau and Ralph Beliveau in this volume for a more detailed critique of standardized testing.
10. The lack of priority given to the dead and missing in the poorer sections of the city is revealed when Freamon leafs through a thick file of missing persons reports, and is told that, for the last five years, only one detective has been assigned to these cases.

Works Cited

Brooks, Ryan. "The Narrative Production of 'Real Police.'" Marshall and Potter 71–84.
Foucault, Michel. *Discipline and Punish: The Birth of the Prison*. Trans. Alan Sheridan. New York: Vintage, 1995.
_____. *Security, Territory, Population: Lectures at the Collège de France 1977–78*. Ed. Michel Senellart. Trans. Graham Burchell. Basingstoke: Palgrave Macmillan, 2007. Print.
_____. *Society Must Be Defended: Lectures at the Collège de France 1975–76*. Ed. Mauro Bertani and Alessandro Fontana. Trans. David Macey. New York: Picador, 2003. Print.
Greenwald, Glenn, Ewan MacAskill, and Laura Poitras. "Edward Snowden: The Whistleblower behind the NSA Surveillance Revelations." *The Guardian*. 10 June 2013. Web. 26 November 2013.

Johnson-Lewis, Erika. "The More Things Change, the More They Stay the Same: Serial Narrative on *The Wire*." *Darkmatter* 4 (2009). Web. 26 November 2013.
Kelleter, Frank. "The Wire and Its Readers." *The Wire: Race, Class, and Genre*. Ed. Liam Kennedy and Stephen Shapiro. Ann Harbor: Michigan University Press, 2012. 33–70. Print.
La Berge, Leigh Claire. "Capitalist Realism and Serial Form: the Fifth Season of *The Wire*." *Criticism* 52.3/4 (2010): 547–67. Print.
Latour, Bruno. *Pandora's Hope: Essays on the Reality of Science Studies*. Cambridge: Harvard University Press, 1999. Print.
_____. *Reassembling the Social: An Introduction to Actor-Network Theory*. Oxford: Oxford University Press, 2005. Print.
Love, Chris. "Greek Gods in Baltimore: Greek Tragedy and *The Wire*." *Criticism* 52.3/4 (2010): 487–507. Print.
McNeilly, Kevin. "Dislocating America: Agnieszka Holland Directs 'Moral Midgetry.'" Marshall and Potter 203–16.
Pecora, Vincent P. "The Culture of Surveillance." *Qualitative Sociology* 25.3 (2002): 345–58. Print.
Potter, Tiffany, and C.W. Marshall, eds. *The Wire: Urban Decay and American Television*. New York: Continuum, 2009. Print.
Schaub, Joseph Christopher, "*The Wire*: Big Brother Is Not Watching You in Body-more, Murdaland." *Journal of Popular Film and Television* 38.3 (2010): 122–32. Print.
Simon, David. "We Are Shocked, Shocked." *The Audacity of Despair: Collected Prose, Links and Occasional Venting from David Simon*. 7 June 2013. Web. 26 November 2013.

A Dystopian Fable About America's Urban Poor

Peter Dreier and John Atlas

No television show about urban life has received as much praise as *The Wire*, a dramatic series about Baltimore that was broadcast on HBO for five years, ending in 2008. The entire show is now available in a five-CD set.

Although not a major commercial success with viewers, it was a huge hit with critics who applauded its gritty depiction of urban life.[1] The show won praise from reviewers across the political spectrum—from the *New York Times* to the *Wall Street Journal*, from the liberal *American Prospect* to the libertarian *Reason* magazine. Jack Dunphy, a columnist for the right-wing magazine *National Review*, wrote that *The Wire* is "still the best show on television." *Slate*'s Jacob Weisberg called it "the best TV show ever broadcast in America." Novelist Stephen King, writing in *Entertainment Weekly*, called the show "a staggering achievement." *The Wire* has been the subject of many university courses, using the show as a "text" to depict the social reality of inner city life in America.[2]

Yes, *The Wire* is an absorbing, compelling drama about a slice of life in America's urban ghettoes. But it is not a very accurate portrayal of urban poverty in general or even poverty in Baltimore. Those who depend on *The Wire* as a lens through which to understand the realities of class, race, and urban life in America get a distorted and misleading picture. It portrays the urban poor as helpless victims with no capacity to mobilize and organize on their own behalf. It depicts everyone in the city—the poor, educators, police, politicians, union members, and journalists, among them—as caught in a web of corruption, incompetence, or indifference.

In some ways, *The Wire* was a sociological treasure chest. The main focus of the show was life on the mean streets of Baltimore's inner city, especially its African American neighborhoods, and particularly the world of the gangs that controlled the city's drug trade. But in each season, the show focused on a different aspect of life in Baltimore—the police, the waterfront docks, City Hall, the schools, and the daily newspaper. The show juggled over 65 vivid characters. The large ensemble cast (with mostly African American actors) included police, teachers, reporters, drug dealers, dockworkers, politicians, and other characters in the real dramas of a major American city. Each year of the show, at least 25 of the characters had important parts. The writers wove these settings and characters into the show throughout its five year run. As a result, viewers got a sense of how people were shaped by the larger system—their relationships with each other and with the web of institutions.

This wasn't just a formulaic cops-robbers-and-lawyers show (like *Law and Order*). Some critics compared *The Wire* to a great literary novel. Unpredictable plot twists, deft foreshadowing, and complex characters justify that judgment. Like most great stories, the main characters were morally ambiguous, but so finely etched that we cared about them. Even the gangsters were complex personalities, not the stereotypes typical of TV crime dramas. We ended up taking sides in gangland battles, rooting for Omar, Proposition Joe, and Bodie, and wanting Marlo annihilated. Unlike other TV crime shows, *The Wire* allowed viewers to see the characters and situations from multiple perspectives, not just through the point-of-view of the police and prosecutors.

David Simon, the show's creator and chief writer, is a former *Baltimore Sun* reporter; the other major co-writer, Ed Burns, is a former Baltimore police officer and school teacher. Before writing *The Wire*, Simon wrote two books about Baltimore – *Homicide: A Year on the Killing Streets* (the basis for the excellent NBC television series, *Homicide*, which he served as a writer), and (with Burns) *The Corner: A Year in the Life of an Inner-City Neighborhood* (which Simon adapted into an HBO mini-series, *The Corner*). Both books are full of sociological insights about urban life.

The writers paid attention to detail. The workplaces, neighborhoods, language and events portrayed in *The Wire* had the kind of verisimilitude that justifies the torrent of praise. The show really captured Baltimore's nuances, flavor, language, and culture. Police detectives drank "Natty Boh" – National Bohemian, a beer originally brewed in Baltimore. And the dialogue rang true. Snoop, second in command to drug thug Marlo, explained to a hesitant gang member how she'll retaliate if he doesn't cooperate: "We will be brief with all you motherfuckers—I think you know." Another drug kingpin, Avon, locked in jail and eager for stories in the street, asked Marlo: "What about you? How you been?" Marlo shrugs: "You know. The game is the game."

But in most ways, *The Wire* could have been about any older American city, facing the realities of the 1990s and 2000s—the loss of blue-collar union jobs, a shrinking tax base, racial segregation and the concentration of poverty, street gangs and the drug trade, and troubled schools.[3]

The show's two creators had a political agenda. They wanted *The Wire* not only to examine the realities of urban life, but also to provoke moral outrage. In interviews during and after the show's five-year run, they explained that they considered *The Wire* to be a form of muckraking reporting. Simon said he considered himself a "gadfly" and called the show "a political tract masquerading as a cop show" and a "critique of what ... has gone wrong in America."[4] They didn't simply want to entertain. They wanted to expose injustice. They wanted to get people upset—perhaps upset enough to actually *do* something about the conditions portrayed in the show.

But if that was their goal, they failed. They failed not because the show wasn't upsetting, but because it portrayed urban life as hopeless. They portrayed the characters in the show as victims of a "system" beyond reform.

The show's writers may have thought that they were presenting a radical critique of American society and its neglect of its poor, African Americans, and cities. But there's nothing radical about a show that depicts nearly every character—clergy and cops, teachers and principals, reporters and editors, union members and leaders, politicians and city employees, social workers and everyday people—as corrupt, cynical, or well-intentioned but ineffective.

In an interview, Simon observed, "*The Wire* is dissent." But when asked, "Do you think change is possible?" Simon answered, "No, I don't. Not within the current political structure."[5]

This view is reflected in the show. All writers make choices about what to include and what to exclude. This is called "artistic license." But those choices have consequences. *The Wire* was the opposite of radical; it was hopeless and nihilistic. The city portrayed in *The Wire* is a dystopian nightmare, a web of oppression and social pathology that is impossible to escape. *The Wire*'s unrelenting bleak portrayal missed what's hopeful, or at least possible, in Baltimore and, indeed, in other major American cities.

The Wire was broadcast from 2002 through 2008 – the era of President George W. Bush, who was in office from 2001 to 2008. During that period, America faced the biggest concentration of income and wealth since 1928. A growing number of Americans—not only the poor but also the middle class—found that their jobs, their health insurance, their pensions, even their homes were increasingly at risk (Hacker, *The Great Risk Shift*). The cost of housing, food, health care, gas, and college tuition rose faster than incomes. During Bush's presidency, the number of Americans in poverty increased dramatically—from 32.9 million (11.7 percent of the population) in 2001 to 37.3 million (12.5 percent) in 2007 – many of them among the growing army of the "working poor."

These conditions *should* provoke outrage. But simply being aware of these outrageous conditions doesn't guarantee that middle-class Americans, faced with their own economic insecurities, will identify with and make common cause with the poor. For that to occur, they need to believe three things:

First, that the plight of the poor is the result of political and social forces, not self-inflicted by the poor themselves; *second*, that lifting up the poor will not come at the expense of middle-income Americans; and *third*, that the problems of the urban poor *can* be solved.

In other words, they need some sense that all, or most, Americans share a common fate—a view that economist Jared Bernstein (*All Together Now*) calls "we're in this together," in contrast to the conservative view that "you're on your own." They also need some sense of hope. Hope springs from a combination of political leadership and grassroots activism.

Each of these three conditions took root in the first decade of the 21st century. Polls showed that more and more Americans wanted the government to address the issues of poverty, housing, health care, and the environment. Even before the nation's economy took a sharp nosedive in late 2008, a growing number of Americans, including those in the middle class, believed that the widening gap between the rich and everyone else was a serious problem that government should deal with.

Since Congress enacted welfare reform in 1996, putting time limits on receiving federal welfare assistance and pushing more and more low-income people into the workforce, Americans have changed their views about the poor. They now increasingly view poverty through the prism of work and working conditions. They view people who remain in poverty, despite working, the "deserving" poor. As a result, polls reveal that a vast majority of Americans wanted to raise the federal minimum wage so that it is above the poverty level. The popularity of Barbara Ehrenreich's best-selling 2001 book, *Nickel and Dimed*, the challenges to Wal-Mart (the world's largest employer, with a large low-wage workforce), and the remarkable success of the "living wage" movement in about 200 cities all reflect an upsurge of concern about poverty. Polls also show that support for labor unions has reached its highest level in more than three decades.

What does this have to do with *The Wire*? Three things.

First, to the extent that *The Wire* helped raise awareness of these problems—and the systemic nature of the urban crisis—it deserves all the praise it has received. No other major industrial nation has allowed the level of sheer destitution that we have in the United States. We accept as "normal" levels of poverty, inequality, hunger, crime, homelessness, and inadequate and unequal school funding that would cause national alarm in Canada, Western Europe, or Australia. *The Wire* brilliantly portrayed these realities, putting a human face on the "urban crisis."

Second, *The Wire* showed how people cope with "the system" and the overwhelming obstacles they face in just trying to get by or do their jobs. It showed how even people with good intentions and some idealism face enormous hurdles. By exploring the dysfunction of many key urban institutions—including politics, the schools, the criminal justice system, and the media—*The Wire* revealed how urban politics is often a struggle over crumbs, whether the issue is funding for schools, police, housing subsidies, or drug-rehab programs.

But *third*—and most important—*The Wire* failed to offer viewers any understanding that the problems facing cities and the urban poor are *solvable*.

To bring about the change that the show's writers hoped for, people need to feel not only that things *should* be better but that they *can* be better. *The Wire* offered viewers little reason for hope that the lives of the people depicted in it could be improved not only by individual initiative but also (and primarily) by collective action and changes in public policy. It offered viewers no hint that in Baltimore there was a small but growing movement to mobilize urban residents and their allies to address these problems—a movement that exists in every major city in the country and that has borne fruit in many ways.

The Wire's portrayal of Baltimore buttresses the myth that the poor, especially the black poor and the black working class, are helpless victims, unable to engage in collective efforts to bring about change. In other words, *The Wire* reinforced the notion that the status quo cannot be changed.[6]

Ironically, *The Wire*'s last season ends with a critique of the press for failing to tell the true story of the inner-city. David Simon criticized the *Baltimore Sun* for its inadequate reporting about poverty and its decisions to drop its poverty beat in the early 1990s (Lanahan "Secrets of the City"). Simon was determined to show the real inner-city, warts and all, but ends up showing only the warts.

The Wire was populated by low-income African Americans and a handful of working class and middle-class people whose jobs—police, teacher, social worker, government bureaucrat, reporter, minister—involve relating to the poor as "problems" or "clients" rather than as fellow citizens.

The show virtually ignored Baltimore's black working class. Although the show portrayed African Americans in a wide range of occupations (police administrators and cops, principals and teachers, union leaders and dockworkers, social workers and clergy, editors and reporters), almost all of the African Americans living in Baltimore's ghetto were depicted as dangerous criminals, drug addicts, welfare recipients—an unemployed underclass—culturally damaged, a class of people whose behavior and values separate them from respectable society.

Much of the Baltimore we see in *The Wire* focused on the residents of the low-income black neighborhoods. In 2006, blacks comprised 65 percent of the city's population. Among them, 23 percent were poor.[7] True, many were jobless. Baltimore has been hemorrhaging jobs for decades, an issue that *The Wire* addressed in its second season, when it looked at the decline of the city's port. As a result, finding a job has become a problem, especially for African Americans. The black unemployment rate in Baltimore in 2006 was 13.7 percent, more than double the white rate of 5.7 percent. In 2006, 42,300 black Baltimoreans were jobless. That's a big number, but that means that 86.3 percent of Baltimore's black adults in the labor force *were* working.

Virtually absent from *The Wire* were the working poor—those who earn their poverty in low-wage jobs. Among the 180,000 Baltimore residents who worked full-time, 38 percent earned less than $30,000. Among the 105,266 African Americans in Baltimore working full-time, almost half (46 percent) earned below $30,000.

Indeed, the role of Baltimore's business elite and major private sector employers—who have played an influential part in shaping Baltimore's economic development and its low-wage economy, especially among blacks, is completely absent from *The Wire*.[8] Likewise, *The Wire* revealed the symptoms of Baltimore's racial segregation, where whites and blacks live almost entirely in neighborhoods with people of the same race as well as the same economic class. But the show provided viewers with no understanding that this segregation was not an accident, but was perpetrated by banks involved in the practice of mortgage lending discrimination, called "redlining."[9] During the period depicted in *The Wire*, Baltimore's black neighborhoods were victimized by a wave of "predatory" lending by banks, discussed briefly below.[10]

The show offered a few small rays of hope by portraying some characters as people who were able to maintain their dignity and pride amid enormous turmoil. One such character was Reginald "Bubbles" Cousins (Andre Royo), a recovering heroin addict and homeless person who displays an incredible will to live and extraordinary survival skills. *Slate* magazine's Jacob Weisberg ("*The Wire* on Fire") lauded his aspect of the show. *The Wire*, he wrote, "is filled with characters who should quit but don't, not only the boys themselves but teachers, cops, ex-cops, and ex-cons.... This refusal to give up in the face of defeat is the reality of ghetto life as well. Feel me: It's what *The Wire* is all about."

The few heroes depicted in *The Wire* were individualist renegades and gadflies. These include cops like James McNulty (Dominic West) and Lester Freamon (Clarke Peters) and the stick-up artist Omar Little (Michael K. Williams), as well as social worker Walon (a Narcotics Anonymous sponsor played by the singer Steve Earle), the Deacon (an influential West side clergyman played by Melvin Williams), and Dennis "Cutty" Wise (Chad Coleman) (whose boxing program may stop a teenager from succumbing to life of drugs).

Unlike unions and community organizing groups, the few do-gooders portrayed in *The Wire* didn't seek to empower people as a collective force. They tried to help individuals, one at a time, rather than try to reform the institutions that fail to address their needs. One person alone, no matter how well-intentioned, can't save a school system, create jobs, or make a neighborhood safer.

But Baltimore *was* (and *is*) filled with labor and community activists who were doing just that—mobilizing people to reform *institutions*, to change the *system*, to change the relationships of *power* in the city. Those people were *completely absent* from the show over its entire five-year and 60-episode run.

Baltimore's recent history is filled with examples of effective grassroots organizing that Simon and Burns could have used to portray a different slice of the city's sociological and political realities.

For example, in 1994, a community group known as BUILD (Baltimoreans United in Leadership Development) led a campaign that mobilized ordinary people to fight for higher wages for the working poor.[11] One of those people was Valerie Bell. She lived in a small row house in Baltimore. With just a high school degree, she secured a job with a private, non-union custodial firm that contracted with the city to scrub floors and take out the garbage at Southern High School. Baltimore was trying to cut costs by outsourcing jobs to private firms. Bell earned $4.25 an hour with no health benefits. Like so many others who earned a minimum wage each month, Bell coped with how to pay the electricity bill, groceries, and the rent.

BUILD put together a coalition of churches and labor unions, and lobbied the city to pass a "living wage" law that would increase wages above federal poverty line. The law applied to employees who worked for private firms that had contracts with the city. It affected 1,500 workers, hired by private bus, security, and janitorial companies. The ordinance forced wages up from $4.25 to $8.80 an hour over three years, and then increased each year to account for inflation.

At some risk to herself, Bell organized other custodians to join the living wage campaign. When the company discovered Bell's activities, it fired her. Undeterred, Bell stayed active with BUILD and helped gather petition signatures and organize demonstrations. BUILD recruited academics who produced studies showing that it made no sense for the city government to save money in the short term by underpaying workers, who then had to resort to a variety of government-supported homeless shelters and soup kitchens to supplement their low wages. Working with BUILD, Bell and others put so much pressure on the city, they convinced then–Mayor Kurt Schmoke to support them. As a result of this grassroots organizing effort, Baltimore passed the nation's first living-wage ordinance. By the time *The Wire* aired, the rate was $9.62 an hour. In 2007, community and labor activists led a successful campaign to get the state of Maryland to enact a state living wage law—the first state in the country to do so (Green, "Living Wage Becomes Md. Law").

Economists estimate that the Baltimore living wage law puts millions of dollars into the pockets of the city's working poor each year, and has had a ripple effect pushing up wages in other low-paid jobs in the city. Following Baltimore's lead, there are now similar laws in about 200 cities across the country. The political momentum created by these local living wage victories changed the political climate at the national level; in May 2007, President George W. Bush reluctantly signed a bill increasing the minimum wage from $5.15 to $7.25 over two years.

For 30 years, BUILD—which is part of the Industrial Areas Foundation network founded by organizer Saul Alinsky and which has affiliates in many cities—has been dedicated to transforming Baltimore's struggling inner-city neighborhoods. BUILD has not only won the nation's first living wage campaign, it also has built hundreds of affordable housing units called Nehemiah Homes (named after the Biblical prophet who rebuilt Jerusalem).

BUILD also created a network of after-school youth programs called Child First. That program began in 1996 with city and private money, and provides free after-school care for over 1,000 children every year at the city public schools. Child First is an academic enrichment program. The program involves parents, staff, administrators, church members, and other community members to help students, a real "it takes a village" approach. Child First trains parents to take part in their kids' education by volunteering at schools and coming together to discuss how they can improve the school system. Volunteers tutor students in math and English, help them with study skills, and nurture their artistic talents.

During the 2007 election, BUILD signed up 10,000 voters as part of its "Save Our Youth" campaign. Every candidate for City Council and Mayor, including Mayor Sheila Dixon, committed to the agenda, which included doubling the number of summer jobs for young people and funding neighborhood recreation centers.

In December 2007, after several years of working with Dixon (as a City Council member and then as Mayor) to renew the run down section of Baltimore, known as Oliver—where much of *The Wire* is filmed—BUILD persuaded the city to transfer 155 abandoned properties to the community group, which will either rehab the homes or tear them down and build new ones, then sell them to working-class homebuyers.

"BUILD is making steady progress in eliminating blight throughout the Oliver neighborhood, where 44 percent of properties are vacant," said Bishop Douglas Miles, 59, pastor of Koinonia Baptist Church.

A native Baltimorean, Bishop Miles, BUILD's co-chair, grew up in public housing projects. He's been involved with BUILD for 30 years. Under his leadership, Koinonia Baptist Church initiated a number of innovative ministries including an after-school program called Project Safe Haven, a juvenile alternative sentencing program that has saved many teenagers from the fate of a life in and out of jail.

Bishop Miles, who watched every episode of *The Wire*, was outraged at the way the church community was portrayed. "*The Wire* ignores all the good work the faith community had done," he complained.

BUILD isn't the only group in Baltimore engaged in successful grassroots organizing.

The fourth year of *The Wire* focused on Baltimore's school crisis through the lives of several young boys barely coping with problems at home and lured by the illegal drug business. At one point in the show (4.13, "Final Grades"), the boyish but cynical Mayor Thomas "Tommy" Carcetti lobbies Maryland's governor to help bail out the city's bankrupt public school system.

Missing from the storyline is what actually occurred in 2004 when two groups—ACORN and the Algebra Project—mobilized parents, students and teacher to pressure then–Mayor Martin O'Malley (now Maryland's governor) to ask for state funds to avoid massive lay-offs and school closings (Vozzella,

"Allies, Foes"; Bowie, "Trustee Suggested"; Gehring, "Velvet Glove, Steel Hand," "Studies, Sit-Ins" and "Blacks Support for ACORN Grows.").

ACORN, a community organizing group, built a coalition that included public employee unions and the Algebra Project (a group founded by civil rights icon Bob Moses to organize young people around school issues). The community and union activists hit the streets and filed lawsuits to get more money pumped into the school system.

In November 2003, ACORN members rallied at City Hall to deliver Maryland ACORN's second annual "Turkey of the Year Award" to O'Malley for his plan to balance the school district's budget at the expense of Baltimore students' education, in part by laying off a thousand school employees. The next month, ACORN organized a confrontation at a board of education meeting. With hundreds of ACORN members attending, and one member shouting through a bullhorn, ACORN took over the meeting before police hauled them out of the room.

The protests were part of a months-long campaign of agitation that forced O'Malley to come up with the money and avoid unnecessary lay-offs and a state take-over.

"The system is in meltdown," Mitch Klein, an ACORN organizer at the time, told us. "Cutting funds is like the Baghdad version of putting back together the Baltimore city public schools."

School reform is only one of several issues that Baltimore ACORN—an affiliate of a national organization with chapters in over 100 cities—addressed.[12] Its young organizers have identified and trained tenant leaders to wage a campaign to clean up hundreds of lead-contaminated rental units. ACORN's tenants organized a rent strike to pressure slumlords to remove lead hazards in thousands of apartments. ACORN's members also closed corner stores dealing drugs, improved the city's housing code enforcement program, and pressured the police department to assign more foot patrols to the low-income Cherry Hill section of Baltimore.

Banks have persistently redlined its minority neighborhoods or engaged in abusive, discriminatory predatory lending practices, leading to a wave of widespread foreclosures during the first decade of the 21st century. Lobbied by ACORN and other community groups, Mayor Dixon and the City Council sued Wells Fargo Bank in January 2008 for targeting risky sub-prime loans in the city's black neighborhoods that led to a wave of foreclosures that reduced city tax revenues and increased its costs of dealing with abandoned properties.[13] It was the first lawsuit filed by a municipality seeking to recover costs of foreclosure caused by racially discriminatory lending practices.

"Some things I can't accomplish by myself," said Sonja Merchant-Jones, a former public housing resident who was active in Baltimore ACORN, "but together we've been able to confront elected officials, banks, and the utility companies, and get them to meet with us, negotiate with us, and change things. But I'm disappointed that I never see things like this on *The Wire*."

Robert Mathews is a 64-year-old janitor in an 11-story office building in downtown Baltimore. He rents a small house in Montebello, one of Baltimore's most troubled neighborhoods, with his wife and two grown sons. The former Merchant Marine has been a deacon in his church for many years and a mentor for many of the church's youth. He takes them on trips and counsels them when they appear to be heading in the wrong direction. For almost three decades, Mathews has also been a union activist, utilizing the same skills to counsel, mentor, and organize his fellow low-wage janitors across the city.

After 30 years cleaning office buildings, he was making $9.10 an hour.

In December 2007, Mathews helped lead a campaign of thousands of janitors in Baltimore, Philadelphia, and Washington, D.C., to win a better contract, among them 700 cleaners, most of them African American, at over 40 Baltimore buildings, including the high-rise Candler, Legg Mason, and Bank of America buildings downtown.

After months of protesting, picketing, threatening to strike, and negotiating, the janitors –part of the Service Employees International Union's Justice for Janitors campaign—won a 28 percent pay increase.[14] The janitors also won up to two weeks vacation and employer-paid family prescription drug coverage. The agreement added dental and vision benefits to the employer-paid health plan.

Mathews, who remembers when Baltimore's schools, movie theaters, and restaurants were segregated, participated in civil rights protests in the 1960s. "To make change, you have to take a stand," he told us.

Mathews only occasionally watched *The Wire*. He was offended by its bad language, but also by its unrealistic depiction of the Baltimore he's lived in his entire life. "It's more negative than positive," he said. "The people on the show don't have anything to live for. The young people have no vision. If you want change, you have to believe things can change."

These real-life organizing campaigns by BUILD, ACORN, and Justice for Janitors were reported in the *Baltimore Sun* and by local TV and radio stations. Yet David Simon, the show's creator, found no room to tell any of these stories in the 60 episodes of *The Wire* over its five-year run.

Rob English, a 38-year-old organizer for BUILD, was hardly a romantic radical. He served for four years as a platoon leader in Somalia.

Referring to *The Wire*, he said: "The show does an excellent job of telling one side of the story. But it's missing all the pastors, parents and teachers, principles, young people who are doing amazing work, radically trying to change and improve Baltimore."

People like Valerie Bell, Bishop Miles, Sonja Merchant-Jones, and Robert Matthews are committed activists who have persisted in the organizing through victories and disappointments. They never succumb to cynicism or corruption. The people organized by BUILD, ACORN, SEIU, the Algebra Project, and other community, labor, and environmental justice groups maintain a sense of hope and possibility in the face of difficult odds. And, slowly and steadily, their organizations have won significant victories that improve the lives of Baltimore's poor and working class residents.

These community activists are not super-heroes or naive idealists. They are ordinary people who sometimes manage to do extraordinary things. What distinguishes them is their patience, political savvy, street smarts, empathy, faith, and people skills required to build strong organizations that can mount grassroots organizing campaigns. They harness what organizers call "cold anger" and turn it into outrage against injustice rather than indiscriminate rage.

They do not expect to turn Baltimore upside down. Rather, they mobilize people to win small, concrete victories that improve people's living and working conditions, and whet their appetites for further battles. They challenge the city's political and business establishment and seek to get Baltimore's power players and institutions—employers, landlords, politicians, police chiefs, school superintendents, and others—to the bargaining table, where they can negotiate on a somewhat level playing field. They don't always win, but by their persistence and their ability to recruit people to join them, they have to be taken seriously by the city's powerbrokers. They recognize that organizing people in their communities and workplaces is a precondition for mobilizing people from across the country into a broader movement for social justice. They know that there are limits to what can be accomplished in one city— that many of the problems facing America's cities can only be solved with changes in federal policy.[15]

Those who lead union- and community-organizing fights have the same foibles and human weaknesses we witnessed in the characters in *The Wire*. But incorporating their stories in the series would have shown a different aspect of Baltimore, one in which the poor and their allies seek *change, not charity*, and learn how to marshal their collective power.

Unfortunately, community activists and leaders like these didn't exist in the Baltimore depicted in *The Wire*. Without them, and the organizations they belong to, we were left with a view of Baltimore's poor as people sentenced for life to an unchanging prison of social pathology. This, in fact, was how *The Wire* views the poor.

It is probably no accident that *The Wire* ended its five-year run just as the Bush era was ending. The zeitgeist of the Bush era was a culture of fend-for-yourself cynicism, with no agenda to address the needs of cities like Baltimore.

In May 2008, Simon and Burns received an award from the Liberty Hill Foundation, a Los Angeles organization that provides funding for cutting-edge grassroots community, environmental, and labor organizing. In accepting the award, they offered congratulations to the activist groups whose leaders were represented in the audience.

Simon said, "*The Wire* spoke to a world in which human beings—individuals—matter less, a world in which every day, the triumph of capital results in the diminution of human labor and human value. Is that world an accurate depiction of America? I hope not. But we live in interesting times, and perhaps the only thing that is left to us as individuals is the power to hope, and to commit that hope to action."

In that statement, Simon reflected a new spirit of possibility that is a precondition to transforming the country. Unfortunately, that attitude was not evident in *The Wire*.

Simon told *Slate* magazine that, "thematically, [*The Wire* is] about the very simple idea that, in this Postmodern world of ours, human beings—all of us—are worth less. We're worth less every day, despite the fact that some of us are achieving more and more. It's the triumph of capitalism." (O'Rourke 2006).[16]

He added, "It's the triumph of capitalism over human value. This country has embraced the idea that this is a viable domestic policy. It is. It's viable for the few."

But Simon's world view—at least as it revealed in *The Wire* – is hardly radical. He generally views the poor as helpless victims rather than as people with the capacity to act on their own behalf to bring about change. He may think he's the crusading journalist exposing injustice, but, based on the show, he's really a cynic who takes pity on the poor but can't imagine a world where things could be different.

Notes

1. Unlike several other critically-acclaimed HBO series, such as *The Sopranos,* HBO did not re-broadcast *The Wire* in later years; nor did another television network do so.

2. Among the colleges and universities that have offered courses devoted to analysis of *The Wire* are Middlebury College, University of Wisconsin, Harvard University, American

University, Boston University, Johns Hopkins University, St. Joseph's University, Loyola University, Georgetown University, Catholic University, University of Virginia, University of California–Berkeley, Gettysburg College, and University of Houston. The courses were taught in departments of sociology, religious studies, urban studies, media studies, journalism, public health, American studies, law, philosophy, and others. See Wilson and Chadda (2010) and Lageson, Green, and Erensu (2011).

3. See Wilson, *When Work Disappears* and *More Than Just* Race; Rae, *City*; Dreier, Mollenkopf, and Swanstrom, *Place Matters*; Ranney, *Global Decisions, Local Collisions*; and Greenhouse *The Big Squeeze*.

4. "*The Wire*'s David Simon," KQED's Forum, December 4, 2008 http://huffduffer.com/Clampants/1278.

5. Meghan O'Rourke, "Behind *The Wire*: David Simon on where the show goes next," *Slate*, December 1, 2006, http://www.slate.com/id/2154694. In a 2006 speech, Simon said, "I am wholly pessimistic about American society. I believe *The Wire* is a show about the end of the American Empire. We are going to live that event. How we end up and survive, and on what terms, is going to be the open question." http://immasmartypants.blogspot.com/2007/12/on-behalf-of-human-dignity.html.

6. This is typical of how the media in general report on urban affairs. See Drier, "How the Media Compound Urban Problems."

7. In 2006, 19.5 percent of Baltimore's residents—and 27.5 percent of its children under 18—were poor, according to the U.S. Census.

8. See Levine, "Third-World City in the First World" and "Downtown Redevelopment"; and Davis and Brocht, *Subsidizing the Low-Road*.

9. Baltimore's racial segregation, and the role of banks in perpetuating it, is discussed in Pietila, *Not in My Neighborhood*.

10. See Relman (2013).

11. For more about BUILD, see Orr, "Baltimoreans United in Leadership Development."

12. Baltimore ACORN was part of the national organization that began in 1970 in Arkansas and won many victories in cities around the country—as well as in states and at the federal level—until its demise in 2010 as a result of a campaign led by business groups, right-wing media, and Republican politicians. For an overview of ACORN's rise and fall, see John Atlas, *Seeds of Change* and Dreier and Martin, "How ACORN Was Framed."

13. Morgenson, "Baltimore Is Suing."

14. For more about the Justice for Janitors campaign, see Erickson, et al. "Justice for Janitors."

15. The show left it to the viewers to put the problems of Baltimore in a wider context. Although the United States has many serious problems that are disproportionately located in cities, these are national problems. Local governmental policies are not their cause. Even the most well-managed local governments, on their own, don't have the resources to significantly address them. A good example is the current mortgage meltdown. Baltimore sued Wells Fargo for its predatory lending practices. But the problem extends far beyond Baltimore. It was caused by the failure of the federal government to regulate the financial services industry. Only the federal government can address the issue of regulating banking practices. Likewise, only the federal government has the resources to provide adequate funding for housing, public schools, health care, child care, and environmental cleanup; and address the shortage of decent jobs that is ultimately at the root of Baltimore's crisis, from the docks to the ghetto to the inner suburbs. See Dreier, Mollenkopf, and Swanstrom, *Place Matters*.

16. See also Bowden, "The Angriest Man in Television."

Works Cited

Atlas, John. *Seeds of Change: The Story of ACORN*. Nashville: Vanderbilt University Press, 2010. Print.

Bernstein, Jared. *All Together Now: Common Sense for a Fair Economy.* San Francisco: Berrett-Koehler, 2006. Print.
"Blacks Support for ACORN Grows." *Sun Reporter,* January 8, 2004. Print.
Bowden, Mark. "The Angriest Man in Television." *The Atlantic,* January/February 2008. http://www.theatlantic.com/doc/200801/bowden-wire .
Bowie, Liz. "Trustee suggested for city schools: Grasmick bombshell comes at funding hearing." *Baltimore Sun.* August 5, 2004. Print.
Davis, Kate, and Chauna Brocht with Phil Mattera and Greg LeRoy. *Subsidizing the Low-Road: Economic Development in Baltimore.* Washington, D.C.: Good Jobs First, 2002. Print.
Dreier, Peter. "How the Media Compound Urban Problems." *Journal of Urban Affairs,* 27, no. 2, (2005): 193–201. Print.
Dreier, Peter, and Christopher Martin. "How ACORN Was Framed: Political Controversy and Media Agenda-Setting." *Perspectives on Politics.* 8, no. 3 (September 2010). Print.
Dreier, Peter, John Mollenkopf, and Todd Swanstrom. *Place Matters: Metropolitics for the 21st Century,* 2d ed. Lawrence: University Press of Kansas, 2004. Print.
Dunphy, Jack. "*The Wire* Returns." *National Review,* January 11, 2008. Print.
Erickson, Christopher, Catherine Fisk, Daniel J. B. Mitchell, Ruth Milkman, and Kent Wong. "Justice for Janitors in Los Angeles and Beyond: A New Form of Unionism in the Twenty-First Century?" *The Changing Role of Unions: New Forms of Representation.* Ed. Phanindra V. Wunnava. Armonk, NY: M.E. Sharpe, 2004. Print.
Gehring, John. "Studies, Sit-Ins Earn ACORN's Activists Voice in Education." *Education Week.* February 18, 2004. Print.
_____. "Velvet Glove, Steel Hand." *Education Week,* January 14, 2004. Print.
Green, Andrew. "Living Wage Becomes Md. Law." *Baltimore Sun,* May 9, 2007. Print.
Greenhouse, Steve. *The Big Squeeze: Tough Times for the American Worker.* New York: Alfred A. Knopf, 2008. Print.
Hacker, Jacob S. *The Great Risk Shift.* New York: Oxford University Press, 2006. Print.
King, Stephen. "Setting Off a 'Wire' Alarm." *Entertainment Weekly.* February 1, 2007. Print.
Lageon, Sarah, Kyle Green, and Sinan Erensu. "*The Wire* Goes to College." *Contexts,* August 2011. Print.
Lahanan, Lawrence. "Secrets of the City: What *The Wire* Reveals About Urban Journalism." *Columbia Journalism Review,* January/February 2008. Print.
Levine, Marc. "Downtown Redevelopment as an Urban Growth Strategy: A Critical Appraisal of the Baltimore Renaissance." *Journal of Urban Affairs.* 9, no. 2 (February 1987). Print.
_____. "'Third-World City in the First World': Social Exclusion, Racial Inequality, and Sustainable Development in Baltimore, Maryland." *The Social Sustainability of Cities: Diversity and the Management of Change.* Eds. Mario Polèse and Richard Stren. Toronto: University of Toronto Press, 2000. Print.
Morgenson, Gretchen. "Baltimore is Suing Bank Over Foreclosure Crisis." *New York Times,* January 8, 2008. Print.
O'Rourke, Meghan. "Behind *The Wire*: David Simon on where the show goes next." *Slate.* December 1, 2006. http://www.slate.com/id/2154694. Print.
Orr, Marion. "Baltimoreans United in Leadership Development: Exploring the Role of Governing Nonprofits. " *Nonprofits in Urban America.* Eds. Richard C. Hula and Cynthia Jackson-Elmoore. Westport, CT: Quorum, 2000, pp. 151–167. Print.
Rae, Douglas W. *City: Urbanism and Its End.* New Haven: Yale University Press, 1993.
Pietila, Antero. *Not in My Neighborhood: How Bigotry Shaped a Great American City.* Chicago: Ivan R. Dee, 2010. Print.
Ranney, David. *Global Decisions, Local Collisions: Urban Life in the New World Order.* Philadelphia: Temple University Press, 2003. Print.
Relman, John. "Finding a Home for the Occupy Movement: Lessons from the Baltimore and

Memphis Wells Fargo Litigation." *From Foreclosure to Fair Lending: Advocacy, Organizing, Occupy, and the Pursuit of Equitable Credit.* Eds. Chester Hartman and Gregory Squires. Oakland, CA: New Village Press, 2013. Print.

Talbot, Margaret. "Stealing Life: The Crusader Behind *The Wire.*" *The New Yorker*, October 22, 2007. Print.

Vozzella, Laura. "Allies, foes of mayor swap sides over loan: O'Malley's schools plan praised by labor, activists; business leaders worry." *Baltimore Sun.* March 15, 2004. Print.

Weisberg, Jacob. "*The Wire* on Fire: Analyzing the Best Show on Television." *Slate.* September 13, 2006. http://www.slate.com/id/2149566 .

Wilson, William Julius. *More Than Just Race: Being Black and Poor in the Inner City.* New York: W.W. Norton, 2009. Print.

_____. *When Work Disappears: The New World of the Urban Poor.* New York: Alfred A. Knopf, 1996.

_____, and Anmol Chadda. "Why We're Teaching 'The Wire' at Harvard." *Washington Post*, September 12, 2010. Print.

"*The Wire*'s David Simon." KQED's Forum, December 4, 2008. http://huffduffer.com/Clampants/1278 .

Post–9/11 Educational Reform and the Epistemology of Ignorance
A Critique of No Child Left Behind

Laura Bolf-Beliveau and Ralph Beliveau

When the first plane hit the World Trade Center, United States President George W. Bush was visiting a second grade classroom at Emma E. Booker Elementary School in Sarasota, Florida. He was there to speak about literacy, and teacher Sandra Kay Daniels was demonstrating the school's reading program. A sign behind Bush's head states, "Reading makes a country great." The footage of the President being interrupted and apprised of the situation is now an iconic, stunning moment in U.S. history. Bush stayed in the room for the reading of "The Pet Goat," but he was clearly upset and, as Daniels reminisced, "He left the room, mentally he was gone" ("Florida Students"). As soon as the lesson was over, he rushed next door for a briefing. The teacher was left to explain to her students that something terrible had happened.

This crystalizing moment has been discussed in terms of Bush's reaction, or as some have critiqued, his inaction. Rarely has the focus been on Bush's purpose in the classroom that day: he was there to experience the direct instruction method of teaching reading. Direct Instruction (DI) is a model of teaching "that emphasizes well-developed and carefully planned lessons designed around small learning increments and clearly defined and prescribed teaching tasks. It is based on the theory that clear instruction eliminating misinterpretations can greatly improve and accelerate learning" ("What Is Directed Instruction"). Analysis of raw footage of Bush's visit shows how DI is implemented. Teacher Daniels, at one point, says to the class, "Get ready to use these words the fast way" (Radosh n. pag.). This phonetic-based way of teaching is scripted; teachers must read the script without deviating from it in order to facilitate students' learning. DI has claimed that the method consistently shows to improve achievement, especially achievement with "disadvantaged children" (Radosh n. pag.).

In 2001 George Bush had introduced No Child Left Behind (NCLB) legislation, which "mandated that only 'scientifically based' education programs be eligible for federal funding" (Radosh n. pag.). With a plethora of "scientific" backing behind it, DI, and its publisher, McGraw-Hill, were supposedly a way for schools to use products that would, it seemed, guarantee success in this new set of school mandates. "The Pet Goat" became more than the book the president was reading when the 9/11 attacks happened; this book became symbolic of a major educational movement in the United States, and the effects of NCLB are vividly explored in the fourth season of David Simon's *The Wire*. One way to better understand *The Wire*'s critique of the educational system is through the application of Charles Mills' theory on the epistemology of ignorance. In brief, this argues that in "the case of racial oppression, a lack of knowledge or an unlearning of something ... is actively produced for purposes of domination and exploitation" (Sullivan and Tuana 1). Other educational theorists like Paulo Freire and Michael Apple also demonstrate the ways in which control over official knowledge is more about imposing power rather than expanding the possibilities of empowerment. For the purposes of this analysis, the post 9/11 reform movement, No Child Left Behind, serves as the oppressive neoliberal agent that deforms, rather than informs, educational practices in *The Wire*.

NCLB was passed into law on January 8, 2002, and made sweeping changes to the United States public education system. Billed as a bi-partisan effort between Republicans and Democrats, the purpose of the law was "to ensure that all children have fair, equal, and significant opportunity to obtain a high-quality education" (U.S. Department of Education). This goal would be actualized by various means, some of which focused on "meeting the educational needs of low-achieving children in our Nation's highest-poverty schools" (U.S. Department of Education). Likewise, the achievement gap between high and low performing students, especially "the achievement gaps between minority and nonminority students," and also that faced by those labeled "disadvantaged," would be narrowed through NCLB's increased accountability for schools and required reports of adequate yearly progress. These would be measured primarily through additional standardized tests. NCLB also focused on highly qualified teachers and the use of choice and charter schools to provide alternatives for students whose local schools were not succeeding (U.S. Department of Education). In short, this act required states to develop assessments in basic skills to administer to all students in particular grades. Primary and secondary schools now faced lengthy tests to demonstrate competency in math and reading (Ravitch 28).

Early critics of NCLB were accused of perpetuating the "'soft bigotry of low expectations'" and were labeled as "'apologists for a failed system'" (Houston 744). NCLB was itself criticized for many reasons, including the notion that schools were broken; the belief that test scores effectively assessed learning; the idea that impoverished schools and students would be helped by testing alone; the belief motivation is less important than fear and coercion; accountability systems not being clear and understandable to all stakeholders; the belief that those at the federal level know more than those in the schools; and the ability of the new law to automatically raise America's international competiveness (Houston 745–748).

The effects of NCLB were more than merely troublesome. Worried by the 2014 deadline by which time all students had to be proficient in math and reading, the focus of classrooms became test preparation. As Diane Ravitch, a one-time supporter of NCLB suggested, the negative effects were worse for students whose native languages were not English and for students who were homeless or were lacking "any societal advantage" (27). The goal of complete proficiency of all students meant the risk of school privatization. Many schools in major U.S. cities were closed because they could not meet the demands of NCLB. Another negative impact of NCLB was the reduction of time spent on any subject beside math and reading (Ravitch 27–29). The obsession with test scores meant that much classroom time was focused on drill and practice. This was especially true in urban schools (Ravitch 29). Ravitch suggested that NCLB's goal of shaming schools would lead to higher test scores caused by "lazy" teachers and principals (29).

The historical perspectives and criticism of No Child Left Behind above have close parallels with Season Four of *The Wire*. As a newly trained middle school teacher, Roland "Prez" Pryzbylewski (Jim True-Frost) works with multiple students, but the focus is on four West Baltimore boys: Duquan "Dukie" Weems (Jermaine Crawford), Namond Brice (Julito McCullum), Michael Lee (Tristan Wilds), and Randy Wagstaff (Maestro Harrell). Prez is quickly schooled on the NCLB's systematic approach to math. Although not as scripted as "The Pet Goat," Prez's required approach to math, contrasted to the real-life applications that meet with success, show the serious limitations and implications of NCLB. Later in Season Four, a different approach to education comes in the form of a grant-funded alternative program. Howard "Bunny" Colvin (Robert Wisdom), a former police officer and controversial character earlier in the series, is hired by a professor, Dr. David Parenti (Dan DeLuca). They work with the middle school administration to identify ten eighth grade students who are "corner" kids. One of the students selected is Namond, a focal character of the season. These are the students who often disrupt class and will, it is assumed, be part of the drug trade. The philosophy of this nontraditional classroom is socialization, and, more importantly, the opportunity for these students to see beyond the corner. Our focus will be on these two educational settings.

Others have addressed the series' commentary on NCLB. For example, Johnette Ruffner-Ceaser studied the cultural messages the show conveyed about African American male students under the reign of NCLB, and the author finds that many institutions, like educational reform, "struggle with identifying appropriate methods to address the needs of African American male students" (n. pag.). Chris Love also studied different elements of *The Wire* and NCLB; specifically, the ways in which the series parallels Greek tragedy. In this analysis, Love found that the middle school in Season Four was "sabotaged by the No Child Left Behind Acts" (488). Another scholar, Erin Buzuvis, focused on education in general and uses philosopher and social critic Ivan Illich as entrance into Prez's class and the school-within-a-school program run, in part, by former police officer Bunny Colvin. Illich's *Deschooling Society*, Buzuvis found, shows how institutional mandates like NCLB's required standardized tests end up as a series of statistics "and other false indicators of success" that promoted the myth of progress (379). Finally, our previous work examining the educational system in Season Four concluded that critical consciousness was reached via institutional systems not mandated by governmental acts. For example, Namond's success in the specialized school funded by a grant and Michael's success in gaming the game of the street are antithetical to NCLB but show, nonetheless, a complexity beyond statistics (Beliveau and Bolf-Beliveau 103).

Although others have examined the intersection between NCLB and *The Wire*'s fourth season, our analysis in this chapter is unique given its use of Charles Mills' theoretical frame, the epistemology of ignorance. Described in more depth below, Mills' analysis of knowing and unknowing, studied within the contexts of power, is, we argue, an appropriate and powerful way to see the effects of NCLB on the imaginary students in *The Wire* and the real outcomes experienced by millions of students in the United States in a post–9/11 society. Critical pedagogy scholar Henry Giroux states this about No Child Left Behind:

> [I]t imposes a model on education that is fabulous for measuring the heights of trees, but has almost nothing to do with raising the most fundamental questions that drive education: Why are we there? What is knowledge for? How does it relate to a democratic public life? What does it mean in terms of providing the conditions for forms of individual and social agency? How does it address questions of injustice? How does it make us better citizens? How does it close the gap between the poor and the rich? How does it prepare us for a global democracy? [9].

This chapter argues, like Giroux and others, that NCLB proved disastrous for education in the United States. If we explore Season Four through the lens of the epistemology of ignorance, it becomes clear that David Simon's *The Wire* clearly agreed with the skeptics of NCLB; however, this season went farther. It proved, as Simon himself said, that "there exists a deep and abiding faith in the capacity of individuals. They are, in small and credible ways, a humanist celebration in which hope, though unspoken, is clearly implied" (34).

It is no small irony that the best way to argue about *The Wire*'s take on NCLB is through a consideration of the epistemology of ignorance. It is also no small irony that the contradiction at the center of this notion reflects with chilling clarity the relationship between authentic learning and the practices of NCLB. The epistemology of ignorance is an idea credited to Charles Mills, whose work in moral philosophy generated ideas about identity and knowledge that are clearly connected to the struggles of an underfunded educational system that is systematically and intentionally undermined to the detriment of the notion of a thriving public made up of a well-educated citizenry. In his 1997 book *The Racial Contract*, Mills first proposed the notion of epistemologies of ignorance. These are ways of knowing (and of "unknowing") grouped around notions of knowledge and power that use gaps in knowledge to intentionally create obfuscation. As Mills discusses, epistemologies of ignorance are a central product of attempts to repress a realization of race (or class, or gender, etc.) to a point of re-estrangement, a position that refuses to recognize the world that was created to establish that position and its accompanying power. Mills argues that dominant white culture represses its own dominance, and then maintains a calculated blindness to its own source of privilege.

Mills offers several examples to illustrate the operation of this willful unknowing. One example is non-recognition, a position that either does not recognize the characteristics of identity that have led to a particular position of disempowerment and marginalization, or does not recognize the individual in that position at all. Citing examples from Ralph Ellison and James Baldwin, Mills identifies descriptions where the appearance of Black Americans is rendered invisible. As Ellison wrote in *Invisible Man*, they "refuse to see me" (qtd. in Mills 96–97).

Mills describes these conditions as elements of a racial contract, a set of formal and informal agreements agreement between members of a subset of individuals who, in racial terms, are designated "white," to categorize the remaining subset of human beings as "non-white" and of a different and inferior moral status (Mills 11), into experiencing an inferior and subordinate civil standing. This makes the subordinate group the objects rather than the subjects of these agreements. Consequently the racial contract

> requires its own peculiar moral and empirical epistemology, its norms and procedures for determining what counts as moral and factual knowledge of the world.... The requirements of "objective cognition, factual and moral, in a racial polity are in a sense more demanding in that officially sanctioned reality is divergent from actual reality.... Thus in effect, on matters related to race, the Racial Contract prescribes for its signatories an inverted epistemology, an epistemology of ignorance, a particular pattern of localized and global cognitive dysfunctions ... producing the ironic outcome that whites will in general be unable to understand the world they themselves have made [Mills 17–18].

The racial contract includes an epistemological contact, an epistemology of ignorance, and "Recognition [as] a form of agreement" (Mills 96–98). By the terms of the racial contract, whites have agreed not to recognize African Americans as equal persons. Thus the white pedestrian that bumps into Ellison's black narrator at the start is a representative figure, somebody lost in a dream: "But didn't *he* control that dream world—which, alas, is only too real!—and didn't *he* rule me out of it? And if he had yelled for a policeman, wouldn't *I* have been taken for the offending one? Yes, yes, yes! ... Evasion and self deception thus become the epistemic norm" (Mills 97).

This contract is grounded, Mills argues, in a "cognitive model that precludes self-transparency and genuine understanding of social realities ... an invented delusional world, a racial fantasyland, a 'consensual hallucination,' to quote William Gibson's famous characterization of cyberspace, though this particular hallucination is located in real space" (18). Mills goes onto discuss how the value of contemporary American civilization required a conceptual erasure of the civilizations that had come before, as surely as the descendants were "erased" themselves. For those who are descendants of the perpetrators of the erasure, a choice must be made between honoring the achievements of history and acknowledging that the achievements were accompanied by horrendous actions.

In Mills' work, the epistemology of ignorance is grounded in self-deception. This idea becomes salient to questions of pedagogy when the central contract that suppresses the knowledge of this history is reconstructed for use in educational institutions. In addition to this contractual practice of ignorance, however, lies the possibility of turning this ignorance against itself. For example, Sullivan and Tuana describe different variations on the epistemology of ignorance in the introduction to their essay collection on Mills' theory. They describe not only the powerful tool of ignorance in the mind of the dominant cultural group, but also outline the ways in which ignorance can be used strategically by the victimized group as a survival strategy (2). The idea of the "Master's Tools," for example, which Audre Lorde (1984) argued could never be used to dismantle the master's house, suggests the need to opportunistically become ignorant of the tools and their use.

Much of the power of this epistemology comes through its ability not just to define the conditions of history, but also to define the limits and characteristics of identity. The racial contract allows for the definition of the objects—the non-whites—by the dominant group. Even under circumstances where the moral and social contacts elevate self-determination, identity characteristics related to race are still subject to the racial contract. This does, however, allow for the expression of a strategic response from those subordinated by this contract. They can reverse the terms and refuse the dominant identity, strategically achieved through reflecting the conditions of ignorance on their own terms. Freedom arises from resisting the definition of self from outside, specifically from the dominant group. Strategically, this move to assert a definition of self through the use of the same epistemology of ignorance tools serves two functions. As already suggested, it allows individuals who have been defined by a system that does not want to see them to return to visibility, to become an identifiable object. But more importantly, this objectification sheds light on the way ignorance has been deployed, and through that assertion reconstructs the objectified into subjects.

From this larger context on the epistemologies of ignorance, we have used four specific elements to gauge *The Wire*'s criticism of No Child Left Behind. First, the manifestations of ignorance come from sources of power in the show. Second, there are ways in which pedagogy is transformed to reinforce ignorance. Closely connected to this second element is the third:

instances where efforts to reverse ignorance or bring obscured knowledge to light are eliminated. Finally, the inversion of the epistemology of ignorance, coming from the marginalized, often uses the frame of ignorance for its own benefit under the reassertion of its identity. Although Mills' critique was originally used to describe the invisibility of non-whites, through the effects of hegemony, the reinforcement of ignorance can come from non-white sources of power. Our analysis of Season Four, then, considers the ways in which two educational settings, Prez's 8th grade math classroom and Bunny Colvin's work with the grant-funded school-within-a-school program, provide insight into the perils of NCLB.

Throughout Season Four, ignorance is manifested through the power of standardized testing and the fear of failing scores. In 4.04, "Refugees," Bunny Colvin is taking a tour of Edward Tilghman Middle School, and he overhears an unnamed, faceless teacher returning tests who tells his students:

> What do you think this 20 stands for? No, it's not the number of days you've been suspended. It's not the number of years you'll spend in prison if you don't shape up. It's 50 percent below average. It's 30 percent below failure even. But, really, it stands for the amount of interest you're taking in your own future [4.04]

From this point until the annual standardized tests are administered near the end of the season, the show makes the pressure of testing evident on school personnel and students. In 4.08, "Corner Boys," Prez tries to discuss the situation with his support team of veteran teachers, they assure him that this is normal, and as one tells him, "That test in April is the difference between the state taking over the school or not." Prez responds, "Maybe the state should." She counters, "You don't teach math, you teach the test ... [it] is about the leave-no-child-behind stuff getting spoon-fed" (4.08).

In an episode aptly titled "Know Your Place" (4.09), Assistant Principal Marcia Donnelly (Tootsie Duvall), preparing her staff for the tests, tells them that they must rise above the twenty-second percentile. In fact, an increase of ten points is required of all middle schools in Baltimore. When her staff protests at this request and complain that this is teaching to the test, she responds, "This year, the preferred term is 'curricular alignment'" (4.09). Administrators from the district office begin to observe Prez and other teachers to make sure they are all doing test preparation. When the actual test window opens, there are scenes of students taking the tests. Many are disengaged and disinterested. Although Donnelly has professed that teaching to the test means teaching real skills, the camera's gaze makes it evident that very few skills are being used during hours of testing.

These manifestations of ignorance coming from sources of power do more than just test students. They also affect the ways in which pedagogy is transformed to reinforce ignorance. During Prez's story arc as a novice, alternatively certified math teacher, he comes to better understand what teaching practices are effective with his students. After struggling with teaching word problems, he discovers that his students love playing cards, and that their favorite form of gambling is dice. After explaining that dice is about odds and probability, he uses dice and cooperative learning to engage the students. He tells another teacher who observes the engagement of his class, "Trick them into thinking they aren't learning, and they do." Earlier in this episode, "Unto Others" (4.07), he finds newer textbooks sitting in storage. He also finds an unused computer. These discoveries mark Prez's move from novice to effective practitioner, but these gains are short-lived, for he is soon told that all teachers will teach test preparation in language arts. He works on the board with the students giving them directions like, "Take your time but do it fast" (4.07), a comment reminiscent of the teacher trying to impress President Bush on 9/11. As he continues with test preparation, students are confused when the practice tests use different nouns. He assures them to follow the same steps, but one student yells at him and leaves the room.

Colvin's work with the University of Maryland at first seems to rise above these manifestations of ignorance: there are no textbooks, no talk of tests, and teaching practices are experimental and unique. At first this seems like an opportunity to reverse ignorance and identify language not usually part of the traditional school setting. We see Colvin, Dr. Parenti, and doctoral student Ms. Duquette (Stacie Davis) asking students to name their world, insisting that they write about where they see themselves in ten years. This specialized program creates a dualism between writing for tests and writing for one's own knowledge of self. This program is trying to reestablish understanding that had been taken away from the institution. At the end of "Corner Boys," Colvin, Parenti, and Duquette are excited about what is transpiring. This conversation ensues:

> COLVIN: Yeah, when they talk about what they know, they talk from here, and they stay on point. Shit, they have been even taking turns in there."
> PARENTI: Question is: Can we get them in that kind of mindset on stuff they don't know? Can we have them learn on faith alone?"
> DUQUETTE: In all honesty, this is uncharted territory [4.08].

It therefore seems that this alternative program has the potential to stop the cycle of ignorance. However, institutional forces more concerned with lawsuits and test scores eliminate any such reversal of ignorance. Episode 4.10, "Misgivings," shows the power of hegemony in the shape of concerned district administrations more worried about potential embarrassment from this program. Ms. Shepherdson (Sheila Cutchlow) from Baltimore schools' central office adamantly believes Colvin's students should take the test. Colvin tells her that giving them a test won't matter "because they're not learning for our world, they're learning for theirs." Yet when Shepherdson insists that they be students, Colvin responds:

> But it's not about you or us, or the tests or the system. It's what they expect of themselves. I mean, every single one of them know they headed back to the corners. Their brothers and sisters—shit, their parents, they came through these same classrooms, didn't they? We pretended to teach them, they pretended to learn, and where—where'd they end up? Same damn corners. I mean, they're not fools, these kids. They don't know our world, but they know their own. I mean, Jesus, they—they see right through us [4.10].

This passionate speech demonstrates the hope for an inversion of the epistemology of ignorance. The marginalized could potentially use the frame of ignorance for its own benefit; it could help to reassert identity. These corner kids know who they are better than the well-intentioned and not so well-intentioned adults charged with their care and education. Colvin continues to press his case, all the way to the mayor's office. There he is told, in 4.13, "Final Grades," that he needs to be teaching test curriculum, otherwise "These would be the children left behind, so to speak." Colvin retorts, "Yeah, but as it is, you know, we're leaving them all behind anyway. We just don't want to admit it" (4.13). It is clear that the mayor's office has no interest in a grant-funded, specialized program built to empower student voices and identity. Bunny concludes, "I'm a liability in there, man. Seems like every time I open my mouth in this town, I'm telling people something they don't want to know" (4.13).

The epistemology of ignorance is evident in these classrooms because teaching is realigned to underscore specific priorities that happen to be alien to the experiences of the students. In both the traditional classroom and the experimental environment, the attempts to keep learning and socialization connected show the greatest connection to the students and the greatest hope for a positive outcome. Efforts to describe the learning as skills-based, especially those skills that are specifically directed toward test preparation, are the same ideas that are at the furthest remove from the lives of the students. In both Prez's class and in the alternative program, the breakthroughs and successes come when a connection is made between the lives of the students and the possibilities for learning that build on the knowledge they bring into the school with them from the corners.

Other theorists have offered perspectives that speak to this same parallel. Paulo Freire, for example, contrasts the idea of the "banking model" with authentic learning. In the banking model, students are empty containers and teaching involves depositing knowledge into them:

> Education thus becomes an act of depositing, in which the students are the depositories and the teacher is the depositor. Instead of communicating, the teacher issues communiqués and makes deposits which the students patiently receive, memorize, and repeat. This is the "banking" concept of education, in which the scope of action allowed to the students extends only as far as receiving, filing, and storing the deposits. They do, it is true, have the opportunity to become collectors or cataloguers of the things they store. But in the last analysis, it is the people themselves who are filed away through the lack of creativity, transformation, and knowledge in this (at best) misguided system. For apart from inquiry, apart from the praxis, individuals cannot be truly human [72].

The knowledge that is being left out through this approach includes all of the student's characteristics, values, and ideas. The knowledge that is included is the same regardless of the individual, thus producing the template of knowledge that is objective, and tests that can measure the extent to which the students have taken this knowledge in and can spit it back out.

Central to the operation of the epistemology of ignorance is the suppression of the idea that a system is being created and valued that creates the very conditions of failure that the schools system seems to produce. As the individual efforts of Prez—his version of Freire's idea of "problem posing education" – are turned back into test preparation, and as the experimental classroom is defunded, the kinds of knowledge that offered glimpses of hope return to obscurity. It is not that a system has been created that is alienating to the individual students that walk through the door of the school; it is that these students make themselves alien to this institution by their failure to consume and spit back the verifiable knowledge that is offered.

In addition to Freire's insight on problem posing education, Michael Apple's term, "official knowledge," further conceptualizes the epistemology of ignorance:

> The politics of official knowledge are the politics of accords or compromises. They are usually not impositions, but signify how dominant groups try to create situations where the compromises that are formed favor them [*Official Knowledge*, 10].

Apple describes two ways investigators have investigated school knowledge: one called the achievement model, the other the socialization approach. The achievement model focuses on knowledge that is never made problematic; its status as "official knowledge" is grounded in how its neutral character makes it easy to measure, compare, test, and eventually use as a motivational tool. We see this in the way that raising test scores at first becomes a driving goal, and later becomes a source of corruption as the measures are adjusted and redefined to give the impression of improvement without actually accomplishing anything; what Prez correctly identifies as "juking the stats."

The second way of approaching school knowledge, the socialization approach, focuses on what Apple suggests, "might be called 'moral knowledge.' It establishes as given *the* set of societal values and inquiries into how the school as an agent of society socializes students into its 'shared' set of normative rules and dispositions" (*Ideology and Curriculum* 30). Apple's critique shows how the socialization model reinforces the values of a culture that have been inscribed and perpetuated by larger social institutions. The approach does not contend with the economic and political contexts from where these values arise, nor does it investigate how this set of values becomes *the* set of values. The suppression of the context where these values are produced gives them additional power, since their lack of contexts implies that they are universal, perhaps even eternal. The epistemology of ignorance critique, then, offers an opportunity to investigate what happens when the creators of this set of powerful social values neglect to identify how they were created, when, and most importantly for whose benefit.

Mills, Freire, and Apple all provide useful frames that help illuminate David Simon's critique of No Child Left Behind. Season Four's focus on inner city public schools and the problems of standardized testing do more than just criticize this post-9/11 educational shift in the United States. Simon once asked of No Child Left Behind, "When reform itself becomes the lie, what then?" (qtd. in Grant 24). His answer lies in the study of Prez's and Colvin's work at Edward Tilghman Middle School. The lie, in essence, promotes an institutional ignorance that works against emancipatory education. Houston, Ravitch, and Giroux, along with scores of other critics, were right to speak so adamantly against George W. Bush's educational changes. "The Pet Goat" was more than a choice of reading instruction; it symbolized the sacrifice of genuine education.

Works Cited

Apple, Michael. *Ideology and Curriculum*, 2d ed. New York: Routledge, 1990. Print.

———. *Official Knowledge: Democratic Education in a Conservative Age*. New York: Routledge, 2000. Print.

Bailey, Alison. "Strategic Ignorance." *Race and Epistemologies of Ignorance*. Ed. Shannon Sullivan and Nancy Tuana. Albany: State University of New York Press, 2007. 77–94. Print.

Beliveau, Ralph, and Laura Bolf-Beliveau. "Posing Problems and Picking Fights: Critical Pedagogy and the Corner Boys." *The Wire: Urban Decay and American Television*. Eds. Tiffany Potter and C.W. Marshall. New York: Continuum, 2009. 91–103. Print.

Buzuvis, Erin E. "Illich, Education, and *The Wire*." *Western New England Law Review* 34.363 (2012): 363–380. Print.

"Florida Students Witnessed the Moment Bushed Learned of 9/11 Terror Attacks." *Nightline*. abcnews.gowww. 8 Sept. 2011. Web. 13 Sept. 2013.

Freire, Paulo. *Pedagogy of the Oppressed*, 30th anniv. ed. Trans. Myra Bergman Ramos. New York: Continuum, 1993. Print.

Giroux, Henry. "Culture, Politics, & Pedagogy: A Conversation with Henry Giroux." Transcript. Media Education Foundation. 2006. 1–24. PDF file.

Grant, Nick. "Schools of Little Thought: Why Change Management Hasn't Worked." *Improving Schools* 12.1 (2009): 19–32. Print.

Houston, Paul D. "The Seven Deadly Sins of No Child Left Behind." *Phi Delta Kappan*, 88.10 (2007): 744–748. Print.

Lorde, Audre. *Sister Outsider: Essays and Speeches*. Berkeley, CA: Crossing Press, 1984. Print.

Love, Chris. "Greek Gods in Baltimore: Greek Tragedy and *The Wire*." *Criticism* 52.3–4 (2010): 487–507. Print.

Lugones, Maria. *Pilgrimages/Peregrinajes: Theorizing Coalition Against Multiple Oppressions*. New York: Rowman and Littlefield, 2003. Print.

Mills, Charles. *The Racial Contract*. Ithaca: Cornell University Press, 1997. Print.

Radosh, Daniel. "The Goat Approach." *The New Yorker*. Newyorkerwww. 26 July 2004. Web. 13 Sept. 2013.

Ravitch, Diane. "Stop the Madness." *Education Review* 23.1 (2010): 27–34. Print.

Ruffner-Ceaser, Johnette Yvonne. "Imagery Matters: Exploring the Representation(s) of African American Male Students in Season Four of 'The Wire.'" Diss., University of Maryland, College Park. *DAI* 73.12 (2013). Print.

Simon, David. "Introduction." *The Wire: Truth Be Told*. Rafael Alvarez. New York: Pocket, 2004. 2–34. Print.

Sullivan, Shannon, and Nancy Tuana, eds. *Race and Epistemologies of Ignorance*. Albany: State University of New York Press, 2007. Print.

U.S. Department of Education. "No Child Left Behind." *Ed.gov*. n. d. Web. 15 Sept. 2013.

"What Is Direct Instruction (DI)?" National Institute for Direct Instruction. n. d. Web. 13 Sept. 2013.

About the Contributors

Robert **Andersson** is an associate professor in criminology at the Institute of Police Education, Linnæus University, Sweden. He has published extensively on Swedish crime policy. His latest publication is on the history and knowledge production of Swedish criminology.

John **Atlas** is vice president of Pandora Education Films and the president and founder of the National Housing Institute, which publishes *Shelterforce*. His books include *Seeds of Change*: *The Story of Acorn, America's Most Controversial Anti-Poverty Community Group* (2010) and *Saving Affordable Housing* (1977). He is an alumnus of Boston University Law School, George Washington Law Center and Columbia University.

Ralph **Beliveau** is an associate professor in the Gaylord College of Journalism and Mass Communication and affiliate faculty in Film and Media Studies and Women and Gender Studies at the University of Oklahoma. His scholarship has concerned horror media, *The Wire*, African American biographical documentaries, Richard Matheson, Alex Cox, documentary, rhetoric, and critical media literacy.

Laura **Bolf-Beliveau** is an associate professor in the English department at the University of Central Oklahoma. She coordinates the English education program and works with preservice teachers and student teachers. Her research interests include feminist poststructural theory, young adult literature, and social justice pedagogy.

Jørgen **Bruhn** is a professor of comparative literature at Linnæus University, Sweden. His most recent books are *Lovely Violence: The Critical Romances of Chrétien de Troyes* (2010) and *Adaptation Studies: New Challenges, New Directions* (edited with Gjelsvik and Hanssen, 2013). With Anne Gjelsvik he has published articles on *The Wire* in Scandinavian and anglophone journals and books.

Peter **Dreier** is the Dr. E.P. Clapp Distinguished Professor of Politics and chair of the Urban & Environmental Policy Department at Occidental College. He writes regularly for the *Los Angeles Times, The Nation, American Prospect, Dissent, New Labor Forum*, and *Huffington Post*, and occasionally for the *New York Times* and *Washington Post*.

Anne **Gjelsvik** is a professor of film studies at Norwegian University of Science and Technology. She has worked on popular cinema and television, film violence and ethics, and the representation of gender in the media. Among her recent publications are the co-edited anthologies *Eastwood's Iwo Jima* (with Schubart, 2013) and *Adaptation Studies* (with Bruhn and Hanssen, 2013).

Mike **Gow** is a global postdoctoral fellow at NYU Shanghai. His research aims to forge understanding of China's rise as an ideational power, with his doctoral project focusing on the role of higher education in the economic, political, social and cultural transformation of China in the late 20th and 21st century. His research draws on several social science disciplines and the theories of Antonio Gramsci and Pierre Bourdieu.

Niall **Heffernan** is a PhD candidate at University College Cork in the School of English. His doctoral thesis, "The Postnuclear Technical Imperative: *Dr. Strangelove, End Zone, Crash* and *The Wire*," investigates what those works reveal about the effects the Cold War and its technology have had on the organization of the contemporary Western world.

Arin **Keeble** is the author of several refereed articles on the literary and cultural representation of 9/11 and Hurricane Katrina in journals such as *Modern Language Review, European Journal of American Cultures, Journal of Comparative American Studies* and *Reconstruction*. He is also the author of *The 9/11 Novel: Trauma, Politics and Identity* (2014). He teaches at Newcastle University and works for the UK charity Changing Lives, which works with the socially disadvantaged.

Michael **Lister** is a reader in politics at Oxford Brookes University. He is the co-author of *Citizenship in Contemporary Europe* (with Pia, 2008) and co-editor of *Critical Perspectives on Counter Terrorism* (with Jarvis, 2014) and *The State: Theories and Issues* (with Hay and Marsh, 2005).

Andrew **Moore** is an assistant professor in the Great Books Program at St. Thomas University in Fredericton, New Brunswick, Canada. His research is interdisciplinary, focusing on different kinds of engagements between narrative and political theory. He has published work on a diverse range of subjects including Shakespeare, political theory, social media, and television.

Tiffany **Potter** teaches English at the University of British Columbia and publishes on popular culture and eighteenth-century literature. With C.W. Marshall, she has written several articles on *The Wire* and co-edited *The Wire: Urban Decay and American Television* (2009), as well as the PCAA award-winning *Cylons in America: Critical Studies in Battlestar Galactica* (2008). Her most recent book is *Women, Popular Culture and the Eighteenth Century* (2012).

Anca M. **Pusca** is a senior lecturer in international studies at Goldsmiths, University of London. Her research focuses on the relationship between aesthetics and politics, particularly in the context of post-communist transitions. She has published in *International Studies Perspectives*, the *Cambridge Review of International Affairs*, the *Journal of International Research and Development* and *Space and Culture*.

Tobias **Sirzyk** received a bachelor of arts degree in political science from the University of British Columbia. He is particularly interested in analyzing patterns of violence within the ongoing Israeli-Palestinian conflict.

Ivan **Stacy** is a senior lecturer in English at Royal Thimphu College in Bhutan, where he teaches American, folk, and twentieth-century literature. His Ph.D. from Newcastle University examined complicity in the novels of W. G. Sebald and Kazuo Ishiguro. He specializes in contemporary fiction, and his research interests include complicity and the ethics of witnessing and testimony.

J.D. **Taylor** is the author of *Negative Capitalism: Cynicism in the Neoliberal Era* (2013) and numerous articles on critical theory and contemporary politics. He is a doctoral research student at the University of Roehampton, where his research interrogates the problem of collective desire in the theory of Spinoza and Gilles Deleuze.

Index

ACORN (community organization) 200–3, 205n12
activism 11, 195, 198–9, 201–4
Afghanistan, war in *see* WAR in Afghanistan
AIDS *see* HIV / AIDS
Akinnagbe, Gbenga 63, 176
allegory 7, 136, 137, 138, 146, 149–150
al Qaeda 18, 39, 49, 116, 148
Alvarez, Rafael 23, 41, 43, 57, 61, 69, 74, 88, 143
the American Dream 50, 51, 61, 65–66, 145
American Exceptionalism 7, 41
Arendt, Hannah 14–17, 20, 23–26

Bailey, John 7
Baker, Tyrell 122
Bakhtin, M.M. 82, 86–89
Baltimore 9–11, 14, 20, 23–4, 31–2, 35, 38, 41, 43–4, 46, 49–51, 55, 58, 75, 83, 86, 97, 100–2, 108–9, 115, 120, 122, 126, 129–30, 134, 136–7, 139, 142–3, 146, 148, 153–68, 170, 173, 175, 178–80, 184, 189, 192–4, 196–8, 200–4, 205n15, 215, 217; East 124, 156;
West 21, 34, 36, 41–2, 52, 56, 58, 60–1, 62–5, 69, 73, 78, 93, 95, 101, 103, 114, 120, 122–9, 154–64, 168, 176, 210; ghettos 4, 143, 197; port 51, 55, 60, 64–5, 70, 86, 136, 155–7, 164, 193, 197; postindustrial 96; schools *see* education
Baltimore Police Department 38, 43, 51–3, 56–60, 119, 125–6, 135, 149–50, 172, 174–5, 177–9, 181, 183, 185, 187–8, 193
Baltimore Sun 42–46, 58, 102, 105, 130
Barksdale, Avon 4, 41, 59, 63–5, 71, 97–8, 106, 110, 114, 118–9, 123, 139, 147, 176, 194
Barksdale, Brianna 119, 125
Barksdale, D'Angelo 54–5, 58–9, 61, 63, 69, 115, 118–22, 129, 133–4, 137, 149, 165, 181
Barnett, Lloyd 108

Barrett, Marlyne 130
Bauer, Chris 53, 70
Bell, Russell "Stringer" 22–3, 39, 41, 53, 57, 60, 63–5, 70–1, 93, 97, 110, 119–20, 121, 131, 133, 140, 160, 177, 180
Benjamin, Walter 153, 154, 166
bin Laden, Osama 49
biopower 11, 187
Bird (character) *see* Hilton, Marqsuis "Bird"
Bodie *see* Broadus, Preston "Boadie"
Bond, Rupert 183
Bourdieu, Pierre 50–52, 62
Brice, De'Londa 125, 127–8
Brice, Namond 53, 115, 123, 125–30, 210–1
Brice, Roland "Wee-Bey" 54, 123
Broadus, Preston "Bodie" 21, 23, 46, 58–9, 63, 69, 115, 120–4, 128–9, 137, 149, 165, 177, 193
Broom, Maria 71
Brother Mouzone 23, 63
Brown, Al 53, 130, 187
Brown, Shamyl 119
Bubbles *see* Cousins, Reginald "Bubbles"
Bubs *see* Cousins, Reginald "Bubbles"
Bug (character) *see* Manigault, Aaron "Bug"
BUILD (community organization) 198–200, 202–3, 205n11
Bunk *see* Moreland, William "Bunk"
bureaucracy 13, 15, 25, 72; *see also* statistics
Burns, Ed 14, 24, 65, 77–8, 136, 143, 193, 198, 204
Burrell, Ervin 35–6, 55–6, 97, 108–9, 112, 130, 181–2
Busch, Benjamin 58, 106
Bush, George W. 3, 13, 16, 18–19, 25, 35, 49, 135, 140, 142, 208
Bush Doctrine 5–7
Butchie 144

Cadogan, Armando, Jr. 149
Campbell, Nerese 64, 130

Index

Carcetti, Tommy 42, 53, 71, 77, 89, 92–3, 97, 104–5, 109, 112, 130, 146, 150, 165, 172, 177, 179, 183, 186–8, 200
Carr, Malik "Poot" 21, 23, 58–9, 120–2, 165
Carver, Ellis 37, 58, 87, 102–6, 129, 134–5, 149, 180, 182
Chaney, Tray 21, 58, 120, 165
Chew, Robert F. 76, 124
Christianity 19, 46, 55
CIA 3
citizenship 5, 7, 9, 13, 15, 22, 67–8, 72–9, 83, 100, 130, 133, 137, 139, 142–3, 149–50, 172–3, 179, 188, 197, 212
Cold War 8, 33–35, 44, 46
Cole, Ray 173
Coleman, Chad 26, 103, 123, 198
Colesberry, Robert F. 173
Colicchio, Anthony 58, 106, 110
Colvin, Howard "Bunny" 3–4, 9, 22, 26, 36–7, 53, 55–9, 63, 65, 70, 81, 85–92, 95–112, 120, 126–9, 139, 185–7, 211, 215–9
cop show see police, TV shows
The Corner (book) 77, 193
The Corner (TV series) 93n3, 120, 193
Corners 10, 14, 23, 37, 56, 59–60, 64, 87, 92, 97, 101–3, 106–7, 109, 111, 115, 120–1, 124, 127–9, 139, 148–9, 157, 160–2, 168, 201, 211, 217; corner boys 10, 14, 28n16, 54–5, 59, 63, 101, 115, 128, 149, 215; "Corner Boys" (episode) 215–6; "corner kids" 3, 186, 211, 217
Costabile, David 45
Cousins, Reginald "Bubbles" 26, 29n20, 39, 53, 57, 62, 72, 88, 90–2, 94n5, 104, 149, 166, 180, 198
Crawford, Jermaine 56, 120, 149, 210
CSI 84, 86
Cutchlow, Sheila 217
Cutty see Wise, Dennis "Cutty"

Daniels, Cedric 57, 98, 102, 130, 142, 181–3, 187
Daniels, Marla 71, 75, 78
Davis, Clay 70–1, 97, 122, 174, 182–4, 186
Davis, Stacie 186, 216
the Deacon (character) 89, 92, 99, 104, 111, 198
DeAngelis, Richard 173
decriminalisation of drugs see drugs, legalization of
DeLuca, Dan 4, 56, 120, 185, 211
democracy 8, 14–22, 27n2, 28n15, 29n19, 41, 46, 74, 137, 171–3, 188–9, 212
Democratic Party 71, 179, 183, 210
Department of Homeland Security 25
DiBiago, Bruce 64
Dingwall, Thuliso 125
docks see Baltimore, port
Doman, John 24, 36, 55, 71, 99, 181

Donette 119
Donnelly, Marcia 215
Dozerman, Kenneth 58
drugs 14, 32, 36, 41, 46, 52, 55, 58, 63 , 71, 77, 82–3, 87–8, 90–2, 96–103, 105–7, 109–10, 123–4, 126, 128, 133–6, 145, 147, 159, 173, 181–3, 198, 201; legalization 82, 89, 91, 95–6, 102–4, 107, 111–2; see also "Hamsterdam"; war on see War on Drugs
Dukie see Weems, Duquan 'Dukie'
Duquette, Miss 186, 216
Duvall, Tootsie 215

Earle, Steve 198
East Side see Baltimore, East
education 6, 10–11, 22, 26, 28n15, 35, 43, 47n11, 50–3, 56, 59, 62, 68, 73, 86, 93n1, 99, 112, 115, 120, 123, 125–6, 129–30, 156, 158, 160, 165, 170, 173, 185–6, 188, 192–4, 196, 198–203, 205n15, 208–12, 214–5, 217–9
Elba, Idris 22, 39, 53, 70, 97, 119, 133, 160, 177
employment 24, 42, 52, 61, 70, 72–3, 76, 92, 99–100, 103, 118, 120, 136, 173, 194–5, 197, 199, 200–3; see also unemployment

Faison, Frankie 36, 55, 97, 130, 181
Fat Face Rick see Hendrix, Ricardo
FBI 3
the Fiend (character) 149
Fitzhugh, Terrance 133, 140
Fitzpatrick, Leo 88, 111
Forester, Raymond 173
Foucault, Michel 38, 173, 175–176
Freamon, Lester 28n17, 42–5, 57, 60, 107, 170, 180–3, 188, 190n10
Freed, Sam 45
freedom 14–26, 28n11, 74, 101, 140, 214
Fruit (character) 62
Fukuyama, Francis 14–15, 22, 34

Game Theory 9, 31, 33–34, 40, 45, 73
Gant, William 119, 122, 181
Gerety, Peter 181
ghetto 4, 64, 103, 143, 188, 192, 197–8, 205n15; see also Baltimore, ghetto
Gillen, Aiden 43, 53, 71, 89, 97, 130, 146, 165, 172
Gilliam, Seth 37, 58, 87, 126, 134, 180
Gilliard, Larry, Jr. 69, 115, 133, 165, 181
Glover, Anwan 4, 106, 139
Graham, Dion 183
Gramsci, Antonio 50–51, 61, 62
Greenwald, Glenn 190n1
Greggs, Shakima 57, 90, 134–5, 180, 182
Guttierez, Alma 43

"Hamsterdam" 36, 77, 83, 85–92, 95, 97, 101–108, 110–112, 159; see also drugs, legalization

Index

Harrell, Maestro 56, 76, 122, 149, 210
Harris, Wood 4, 41, 71, 97, 114, 139, 176
Hauk, Thomas "Herc" 58, 87, 103, 105–6, 134–5, 149, 180
Haynes, Gus 44–5, 56
HBO 81, 105, 153, 160, 192–193
Hector, Jamie 41, 56, 97, 114, 172
Hegel, G.W.F. 14–15, 22
Hendrix, Ricardo 64
Herc *see* Hauk, Thomas "Herc"
Hilton, Marquis "Bird" 131n2, 145
HIV/AIDS 88, 104, 129
Hobbes, Thomas 100, 105
Huff, Neal 186
Hull, Larry 119
Hurricane Katrina 3, 5–6, 139
Hussein, Saddam 18, 21
Hyatt, Michael 119

incarceration 82, 83; *see also* jail
Iraq, war in *see* War in Iraq
Islam 39, 145

jail 63, 83, 103, 112n1, 119, 185, 194, 200, 215; *see also* incarceration
Johnson, Clark 44, 56
Johnson, Hassan 123
Jordan, Michael B. 58, 119, 137
Katrina, Hurricane *see* Hurricane Katrina
Kenard 125
Klebanow, Thomas 45
Kostroff, Michael 23, 45, 64, 69, 145
Koutris, Kristos 179

Landsman, Jay (actor) 102
Landsman, Jay (character) 3, 71
Lee, Michael 56–7, 63, 115, 120, 122–3, 125–9, 149, 177, 210–1
legalization of drugs *see* drugs, legalization of
Levy, Maury 23, 45, 65, 69, 145–6
Little, Omar 23, 25, 29, 39, 53, 57, 60, 62, 69, 71–3, 89, 118, 131, 137, 142–6, 149, 176, 193, 198
Little Kevin 121–2, 165
Locust Point *see* Baltimore, port
Lombardozzi, Domenick 58, 87, 103, 134, 180
Lost 7
Lovejoy, Deirdre 23, 53

Manifest Destiny 46
Manigault, Aaron "Bug" 119, 123, 125, 129
Mardirosian, Tom 179
Marx, Karl 13
McCarthy, Thomas 43, 56, 172
McCree, Sandi 125
McCullum, Julito 53, 115, 210,
McNulty, Jimmy 23–6, 43–6, 53–8, 63, 71–6, 98, 107, 109, 119, 121–2, 133, 140, 142, 160, 172, 177, 180–2, 190, 198

Mello, Dennis 102, 110, 112
Miles, Steven L. 173
Moreland, William "Bunk" 39, 43, 72, 119, 143
Morgan, Robert S. 144
Mouzone *see* Brother Mouzone
Murphy, Billy (actor) 183
Murphy, Billy (character) 183

National Security Agency 5, 171
National Security Strategy 2002 13, 20–21, 134
neoliberalism 31, 40–41
9/11 3, 5–7, 11, 13, 16, 19–20, 25, 49, 98, 106, 112, 115, 134–135, 141, 144, 148, 172, 181, 208, 212, 219
No Child Left Behind Act 11, 35, 209–220

Olear, Doug 133
Orange, Rashid 149
Otto, Rick 58

Parenti, David 4, 56, 120, 185–6, 211, 216
Paress, Michelle 43
Partlow, Chris 63, 176–7
Patriot Act 5, 49, 171
Pearlman, Rhonda 23, 53, 57, 183
Pearson, Felicia "Snoop" 124, 127–8, 136, 176–7, 193
Peters, Clarke 42, 57, 107, 170, 198
Phelan, Daniel 57, 181–2
Pierce, Wendell 39, 72, 119, 143
police 3, 10, 14, 24–6, 33–42, 49–50, 54, 57–8, 60–1, 63, 68–76, 82–3, 85–92, 94, 96, 100–2, 105–12, 121–30, 136–7, 142, 146, 149–50, 155–6, 158–61, 164–6, 170, 173, 176, 180, 184–8, 192–3, 194, 196–8, 201, 203, 211, 213; COMSTAT meetings 55, 99, 104, 108–9, 187; TV shows 5–6, 53, 58, 67, 81, 86, 157, 160, 167, 194; *see also* Baltimore Police Department
Poot *see* Carr, Malik "Poot"
Port *see* Baltimore, port
postindustrial 38, 41, 46, 96; *see also* Baltimore, postindustrial
postmodernism 39–40, 69, 106, 109, 144, 204
Potts, Michael 23
the press 51, 110, 171, 185, 188, 196
Prezbylewski, Roland "Prez" 71, 105, 126, 165, 173, 180, 184, 210–1, 215–9
Prism Program 171–2, 174, 178–9, 188–9, 190n1–2
prison *see* jail
procedural, police *see* police, TV shows
Proposition Joe *see* Stewart, "Proposition" Joe

Ransone, James 55, 173
Rawls, William 24, 28, 35–6, 55–6, 71, 74–5, 99, 102, 106, 108–10, 181–2, 187

Reagan, Ronald 50, 84
Reddick, Lance 98, 130, 142, 181
Republican Party 205*n*12, 209
republicanism 65, 74
Royce, Clarence 20–1, 71, 97, 106, 112, 130, 177
Royo, Andre 26, 39, 53, 72, 88, 104, 149, 180, 198
Rumsfeld, Donald 5

Salconi, Michael 134
Santangelo, Michael 134
school *see* education
Schreiber, Pablo 56
Second World War *see* World War II
Shepherdson, Ms. 217
Sherrod 149
Simon, David 5–6, 9, 14–6, 21, 23–7, 28*n*17–8, 39, 42, 44, 48*n*15, 50, 52–3, 56–8, 61, 65, 67–9, 74–8, 81–3, 93*n*3, 95, 97, 102, 104–5, 107–8, 111, 120, 134, 136, 139–41, 143, 148, 160, 162, 164–6, 171, 178–9, 189, 190*n*2, 193–4, 196, 199, 202, 204, 205*n*5, 209, 212, 219
Slim Charles 4, 106, 139
Snoop *see* Pearson, Felicia "Snoop"
Sobotka, Chester "Ziggy" 55, 57, 173
Sobotka, Frank 53, 55, 61–2, 64, 70
Sobotka, Nick 55
Sohn, Sonja 90, 134, 180
Spinoza, Benedictus de 10, 96, 100–2, 107, 111–2
Stanfield, Marlo 10, 41–3, 45, 56, 62–5, 89, 97, 106, 110, 114–6, 118–30, 135, 139, 147–8, 150, 172, 176–7, 188, 193–4
Starr, Fredro 145
statistics 33, 35–40, 42, 46, 60, 71, 78, 86, 99, 102, 109, 130, 181, 185, 187–8, 211, 219; *see also* bureaucracy
Stenitorf, Michael 186
Stewart, "Proposition" Joe 60, 63–5, 76, 124, 147, 193
Stringer *see* Bell, Russell "Stringer"
surveillance 5, 10–11, 39, 144, 146, 153–4, 168, 171–5, 179–84, 188–9, 190*n*6

Taylor, Marvin 108
television 4, 6–7, 49, 53, 81, 86, 89, 106, 133, 135, 137, 154, 192–3, 202; *see also* police; TV shows
Templeton, Scott 43–5, 56, 65, 172
Terror, War on *see* War on Terror
terrorism 4–7, 13, 49, 102, 133–5, 140–1, 146–50, 171–2; *see also* War on Terror

Thatcher, Margaret 50
Tocqueville, Alexis de 14–17, 22
torture 6
True-Frost, Jim 71, 105, 165, 173
Turman, Glynn 20, 71, 97, 130, 177
24 7–8
Tyson, Darnell 59

unemployment 96, 103, 197

Valchek, Stanislaus 53, 55, 130, 187
Vietnam War 34–37
violence 3, 10, 25–6, 31, 33, 36–7, 41, 45–6, 47*n*1, 56–7, 88, 90, 92, 95–7, 99–106, 111, 114–5, 117–25, 133, 144–6, 148, 153–4, 156–60, 167, 170–1

Waggoner, Derrick 173
Wagstaff, Randy 56, 63, 76, 122, 125, 128–9, 149, 210
Walker, Eddie 63
Wallace 58–9, 119, 121–2, 137, 149
Walon 198
war in Afghanistan 3, 39, 46, 146–148
war in Iraq 3, 19–21, 36, 39, 46, 49, 116, 146
War on Drugs 3, 5, 8–9, 20, 25, 31, 34, 36–38, 40, 42, 46, 49, 75, 81–85, 87, 88, 92, 95, 98, 105–107, 114–115, 133–151, 157, 161, 165
War on Terror 3, 5–9, 39, 133–151
Wee-Bey *see* Brice, Roland "Wee-Bey"
Weeks, Johnny 88, 90–1, 111
Weems, Duquan "Dukie" 56–7, 63, 120, 128–9, 149, 210
West, Dominic 23, 43, 53, 71, 98, 119, 133, 160, 172, 198
West Side *see* Baltimore, West
The West Wing 6–7
Whiting, James: 45
Whitlock, Isiah, Jr. 70, 97, 122, 174
Wilds, Tristan 56, 115, 149, 177, 210
Williams, Delaney 3, 71
Williams, J.D. 21, 46, 115, 137, 165
Williams, Melvin 99, 198
Williams, Michael K. 23, 53, 69, 89, 176, 198
Wisdom, Robert 3, 22, 36, 53, 70, 85, 95, 120, 126, 139, 211
Wise, Dennis "Cutty" 26, 103, 123, 198
World War II 19, 20, 117
Wright, Brandon 7, 63, 131, 144–5, 176

zero-tolerance 9, 58, 82–3, 85, 159
Ziggy *see* Sobotka, Chester "Ziggy"

www.ingramcontent.com/pod-product-compliance
Ingram Content Group UK Ltd.
Pitfield, Milton Keynes, MK11 3LW, UK
UKHW041947140426
5217IPUK00014B/691